Group Work Practice to Advance Social Competence

Group Work Practice to Advance Social Competence

A SPECIALIZED METHODOLOGY FOR SOCIAL WORK

NORMA C. LANG

Columbia University Press   New York

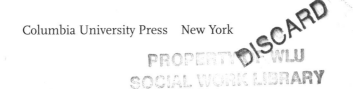

Columbia University Press
Publishers Since 1893
New York Chichester, West Sussex
Copyright © 2010 Columbia University Press
All rights reserved

Library of Congress Cataloging-in-Publication Data
Lang, Norma C.
Group work practice to advance social competence: a specialized methodology
for social work / Norma C. Lang.
p. cm.
Includes bibliographical references and index.
ISBN 978-0-231-15136-8 (cloth: alk. paper)—ISBN 978-0-231-15137-5 (pbk.: alk. paper)—
ISBN 978-0-231-52239-7 (e-book)
1. Social service—Methodology.   2. Social group work.   3. Social groups.
I. Title.

HV40.L286   2010
361.4—dc22   2010009013

Casebound editions of Columbia University Press books
are printed on permanent and durable acid-free paper.
Printed in the United States of America

c 10 9 8 7 6 5 4 3 2 1
p 10 9 8 7 6 5 4 3 2 1

References to Internet Web sites (URLs) were accurate at the time of writing.
Neither the author nor Columbia University Press is responsible for Web sites
that may have expired or changed since the book was prepared.

The text is dedicated to
Dr. Catherine Papell
quintessential practitioner, scholar, mentor,
guardian, and champion of the practice of
social work with groups

Contents

Contents

PART 3 A SPECIALIZED PRACTICE METHODOLOGY
FOR SOCIALLY UNSKILLED POPULATIONS

Preface

It is hoped that making the Specialized Methodology visible will encourage practitioners to undertake practice with other socially disabled populations, and that this text will provide practice guidelines for proceeding with populations whose greatest need is for help in becoming socially able, socially functional.

As this is a first articulation of this special practice with persons who need group belonging the most, it is hoped that practitioners will test out this methodology with other socially unskilled populations and make their own contributions to the verification and extension of this practice theory.

Acknowledgments

I acknowledge with thanks the kind permission of University of Chicago Press to reprint a modified version of "A Broad Range Model of Practice in the Social Work Group," originally published in *The Social Service Review* 46, no. 1 (March 1972): 76–89; Haworth Press for permission to reprint "Concurrent Interventions in Multiple Domains: The Essence of Social Work with Groups," originally published in *Social Work with Groups* 27, no. 1 (2004): 35–51; and Practitioners Press for permission to publish materials originally published as "Some Defining Characteristics of the Social Work Group: Unique Social Form," in S. Abels and P. Abels, eds., *Proceedings, 1979 Symposium* (1981), 18–50.

Many people have participated in the development of this text. Special thanks are extended to Catherine Papell, Ralph Garber, Ben-Zion Shapiro, Elizabeth Lewis, and Nancy Sullivan for reading the first draft and providing valuable commentary and suggestions for improving it.

I wish to thank the two reviewers who read the prospectus for this book for Columbia University Press, and who provided both affirmation of the need for such a text and an important cautionary linguistic note regarding terminology employed as the central concept.

A special thanks also to Dale Lewis, who has typed and retyped, always with pleasantness and cheerfulness, various drafts of the book, and to Arielle Dylan for help in proofreading.

Lauren Dockett, senior executive editor for Columbia University Press, has been a caring and supportive editor and a great pleasure to work with. Many thanks to Anita O'Brien for fine-tuning the manuscript

Deep thanks and appreciation to many colleagues who, over time, have cheered me on in the undertaking of this book: Betty Hartford, Ruth Middleman, Katy Papell, Betty Lewis, Joanne Sulman, Ralph Garber, Ben-Zion Shapiro, and many students and colleagues; and special thanks to Nancy Sullivan, who has been sounding board, cheerleader, and treasured colleague in the preparation of the final draft.

A special acknowledgment to Betty Lewis and Te Roth for providing a quiet corner in our once jointly rented and now their home on Cape Cod, where many of my writings had their beginning, on a tiny TV table at dawn, overlooking the Great Salt Marsh, the barrier beach, and the Atlantic Ocean.

Finally, a special remembrance of Albert Alissi, who looked forward so much to seeing this text in print.

Group Work Practice to Advance Social Competence

Introduction

Whatever else can be said about the human condition, the irreducible state of human life is membership. . . . The [task] of social work practice is to render professional aid in the management of membership.

—Hans Falck, 1988

Belonging in small social groups is the means through which human beings experience personal growth, social development, and socialization and sustain relevance to and influence on the society in which they live, throughout their lives. When the social skills for participating in group life are not developed and available, people who most need the socializing, sustaining effects of group belonging are unable to access and benefit from membership in successive small groups.

In recent decades, social work practice has moved increasingly into settings serving socially less able populations. Many practitioners struggle with the dilemmas faced in practice with socially disabled populations. A methodology for working with them needs to be made visible and accessible. The Mainstream practice theory of social work with groups contains a methodological gap for practice with populations whose lack of social competence impedes their capacity to form groups and therefore to benefit from the social influences inherent in group belonging (Papell and Rothman 1966). The requirement is for a practice methodology that focuses precisely on the social interactional dilemmas of socially unskilled populations and works with these to enable access to, entry into, and benefits of group life for persons who need it most and who have the greatest difficulty in constructing social relationships.

This book describes a specialized methodology designed for use with populations who lack social competence sufficient for constructing and using group. The methodology is shaped by two major sources: the Broad Range Model of practice in the social work group (Lang 1972) and the Mainstream Model of practice with groups—the dominant, enduring practice modality unique to the profession of social work (Papell and Rothman 1966).

The Broad Range Model

The Broad Range Model provides an analytic framework within which a practice can be located, based on the functioning capabilities of individuals and the characteristics of the social form generated by the adequacy of their social functioning. The model identifies essential elements of the social work practice technology across a continuum of individual and group functioning. The framework offers a means to classify, characterize, and describe in detail specific practices with groups in relation to the social functioning capacities of the participants and the associated tasks of the social worker.

The Specialized Methodology presented in this text elaborates the elements in the Broad Range Model in the particular instance that the social disablement of participants achieves only an allonomous (worker-directed) group form and requires major help from the social worker to overcome social deficits that limit the group experience.

The Mainstream Model

The Mainstream Model was forged in the early practice of social group work, evolving with socially able populations in community agencies and enduring through time. It is notable for its adaptability as a group work practice to group purposes and populations, and for its potency as a helping modality. It encompasses a range of purposes, from social growth and development of members in group to social action as group in the impinging environment. A small component of the Mainstream methodology is concerned with assisting less able group members to find their place in the life of the group and to achieve functional participation.

The Mainstream Model contains the view of an integral, balanced relationship between the content and process of the group experience, recognizing their mutual interaction and influence, progressing as "two movements in process together," each driving the other in development and elaboration of the group experience. The social worker treats content and process as of equal importance, tracking and comprehending how they are interrelated and how they drive the group experience, and recognizing where professional influence can be added.

The practice is characterized by its focus on working with social interaction, activities, group processes, and elements of group life to achieve group experiences functional for the participant members and for the environing community. It is this interventive pattern that the Specialized Methodology incorporates from the Mainstream Model.

The Specialized Methodology

The methodology presented in this book is identified as a Specialized Methodology precisely designed to meet the special needs of socially unskilled populations. The methodology is a paradigm shift (Kuhn 1970; Axelrod 1979) from the Mainstream Model, adapted for particular populations. It evolved in practice experience, in response to the special needs, anomalous functioning, and social dilemmas of socially unskilled persons and has been conceptualized from that practice.

The nature of the paradigm shift springs from the lack of applicability of a practice theory founded on the presumption that socially competent skills are in place and in use. The anomaly of socially unskilled functioning of would-be group members and the misfit between theory and practice provided the thrust to develop a new practice paradigm applicable to populations lacking social competence. The paradigm shift retains some elements of the original Mainstream methodology but is combined with new elements essential to practice with socially unskilled persons; hence it classifies as a paradigm shift rather than a full new paradigm.

The Specialized Methodology elevates work with individuals, acknowledged in the Mainstream Model, to a major, central component, a necessity of the practice. It provides for a pregroup experience in a presocial period and focuses on remedial provisions to prepare for and facilitate social functioning. It deals with dysfunctional individual behaviors that interfere with social interaction and assists social interaction to become functional. It provides a route for evolving toward adequate social functioning and makes visible a presocial process that proceeds in an order different from the typical social processes of the socially competent in their progression to group forming and functioning.

In effect, the typical processes of interacting, building relational ties, identifying common purpose, evolving the structures and processes of group functioning, selecting content forms appropriate to the group purpose, and undertaking the productive work of the group are upended and reversed in work with socially noncompetent persons in an intending group, occurring in an inverse order to that recognized as normal social group processes.

The book makes visible the pregroup processes of socially unskilled populations and highlights the nature of the professional role and tasks in work with nonsocial processes in entities less developed than group. In addition to providing a methodology for work with socially unskilled persons in the context of their participation in an entity—collectivity or group—the book contributes to practice theory, elements of practice with individuals, judged to be underdeveloped or missing from the Social Goals and Reciprocal models (Papell and Rothman 1966). Although the text is focused on practice with socially unskilled persons, it contains materials relevant to all social work practice with groups.

Part of the Specialized Methodology contains materials missing in the Mainstream Model. These have been evolved in relation to socially unskilled populations and are specific to enabling individuals to achieve social competence, function socially, and become able to form group. Despite being located in the Specialized Methodology, the materials have relevance and applicability for Mainstream practice with mostly competent members, in groups that may include some socially less able members and in groups whose members have yet to accomplish all the social tasks leading to the achievement of a mature social group form and functioning. Thus the Specialized Methodology is capable of contributing back important methodological directives to the Mainstream Model.

In being defined as a separate practice, the Specialized Methodology can be seen to have redefined the Mainstream Model, articulating elements not specified in the original formulations of this practice, and extending the range of its applicability and use. The Specialized Methodology and the Mainstream Model *together* define a practice employable broadly with many populations and provide important knowledge and technique for all practitioners. The text itself reflects this, particularly in the theoretical materials contained in part 2, which are relevant to the range of practice represented by the Mainstream Model and the Specialized Methodology, and in the materials in part 3 focused on work with individuals in the context of their group membership.

Many social workers who work with socially unskilled persons in groups and grouplike entities are encouraged to contribute to the literature portraits of their practice adapted to these populations.

Some Preliminary Considerations

A Continuum of Social Functioning

On a continuum of social functioning, all persons can be seen to possess some range of social competence and some inadequacies or ineptness, displaying both strengths and weaknesses in social interaction. As reported in the literature review in chapter 1, the "modal state of affairs is relative competence," such that "we are competent in interaction some of the time in some situations" (Bradac 1989, in Wilson and Sabee 2003:4). At the lower end of the continuum, social competences may be less developed, fewer, less manifest or in use.

The capacity to form group, to engage with others socially and relationally, appears to be one very precise marker of social competence, developed and in use; it may be the definitive element, the divide separating relatively socially competent from socially less competent persons on the continuum of social functioning.

The Strengths Perspective in This Practice

The practice represented in this book subscribes fully to the strengths perspective (Saleebey 2009), its goal being to enable socially unskilled persons to uncover, mobilize, develop, and own their own strengths and competences for living rewardingly in the social world.

Social work with groups has held a strengths orientation inherent in its practice throughout its history, stemming from the nature of the practice.

Although not always articulated specifically, its presence as an enduring focus is contained in the creation of small groups as real-life entities, living out in microcosm a live group experience in interaction together, and within this, fostering needed modifications and improvements to social functioning.

Practice with socially unskilled populations seeks to mobilize the strengths of individuals, sometimes unknown to themselves until the practice situation of the special methodology makes them visible, activated and known. In the problem to be served in this practice, initially the strengths may lie dormant and unknown. One of the tasks of the practice is to enable individuals to discover, mobilize, and own their strengths. Problem focus may be more prominent at the outset, but strengths and social competence are emergent in this practice, becoming established and in use.

Defining Condition Differentiated from Deficit Label

The descriptor "socially unskilled" employed in this book acknowledges an existing condition identified as requiring special help. It is recognized as the initial, defining circumstances for initiating a professional practice designed to alleviate that condition. It is a precise, accurate descriptor, as differentiated from "deficit label," and is intended to create a clear view of a disabling condition that can be addressed and altered. Without adequate social competence, individuals may not be able to know, access, and employ their strengths.

Definition of Social Competence and Social Noncompetence

The central concept of social noncompetence has been derived from an extensive review of literature on social competence, presented in chapter 1. A preliminary definition is presented here as part of the practice explicated in this text. Chapter 1 defines the nature of social noncompetence in greater detail.

Social competence is defined as possessing an adequate degree of capability for interpersonal engagement in social interaction and for functioning ably in the social world: "the ability to interact with other people in a way that is both appropriate and effective" (Segrin and Givertz 2003:136).

Social noncompetence is defined as lacking the characteristics subsumed by the term "social competence": the absence of social skills sufficient to engage well in the social world, and the presence of some behaviors that are dysfunctional to the social task.

Because of complications in how the term "socially noncompetent" has been understood, the term "socially unskilled" has been selected as a substitute. Technically, the term would be "socially nonskilled," to denote the absence of characteristics of social competence, but socially unskilled is employed as a familiar colloquial term. Definitional materials are elaborated in chapter 1.

Socially Unskilled as the Norm

There is some suggestion that "socially unskilled" is becoming the norm in North American society. Behaviors that formerly characterized specific populations lacking in social skills are now seen to be becoming prevalent in previously normative settings such as schools, universities, and community agencies, to an extent that interferes with teaching and learning. Some universities are offering seminars "to teach students how to build social networks in person" and "to learn how to engage with the real world, instead of just the virtual world"; many students are required to take courses in interpersonal skills (Levey 2009:39).

Organization of the Text

The book is organized in three parts. Part 1 addresses the concepts of social competence and social noncompetence and their behavioral manifestations. Part 2 brings together some essential theory for social work practice with both socially competent and socially unskilled populations. Part 3 focuses on the Specialized Methodology essential to working with socially unskilled persons in collectivities and groups. A brief summary of chapters follows.

Chapter 1 reviews multidisciplinary literature concerning social competence and social noncompetence and identifies a developing literature of social work practice with entities composed of socially unskilled populations.

In chapter 2 the importance of social competence is explored as the entrée into successful and rewarding social life, the necessary condition for group forming and functioning. A typology of the social behaviors of children in groups typical of each age-stage is presented. From these materials, a set of social tasks is identified, specific to and worked out at each age-stage, using the group experience to work out each task. Progressions in the capability of the entity are seen as matched to and reflecting the developmental progressions in social competence of the individual members. Thus the small group form is recognized as containing social developmental progressions linked to individual social development, advancing in complexity and capacity with the social functioning level of its constituents. These materials, derived from extensive practice experience with multiple children's groups, provide a tool for assessing the social functioning level at which socially unskilled persons may be arrested, and for indicating the social tasks yet to be accomplished.

Chapter 3 examines the nature of socially noncompetent interaction, which creates a class of threshold entities unable to become group. Populations are identified whose circumstances may account for alterations to normal social interaction. Two typologies are developed: the first portrays a classification of social functioning categories, normative to variant; the second categorizes features and qualities of flawed or aberrational interaction.

Chapter 4 includes a review of social science literature on the potency of the small group, followed by a view of the domesticated small group for specialized professional purposes found in the social work literature. Distinctions are made between self-forming groups reconstituted with a social worker and those that are professionally assisted in their formation.

Chapter 5 identifies the special characteristics of intervention in social work with groups, derived from the necessity of attending multiple aspects of individual and group life concurrently. The interventive pattern is employed in both Mainstream practice and the Specialized Methodology.

Chapter 6 presents a portrait of a set of special norms emanating from the professional function of social work and influencing both the social worker and the group participants. They have the power to create a group form unique to the profession of social work and tend to generate an egalitarian group well adapted for helping purposes. The norms have an impact on purpose, relationships, group structure, and functioning and the ways in which the content of the group experience is shaped.

Chapter 7 presents the Broad Range Model on a continuum of three group forms, each reflecting a range in the social functioning capability of the participants and each requiring adaptations in the role and tasks of the social worker. The range is from allonomous groups to autonomous groups, each requiring a distinctive practice methodology, with an intermediate transitional group form that incorporates aspects of both methodologies. The allonomous group is seen as the most likely form achievable by socially unskilled persons.

Chapter 8 reviews the Mainstream Model of practice in social work with groups, and in chapter 9 the Specialized Methodology to promote social competence is introduced.

Chapter 10 provides an overview of features of the Specialized Methodology. Chapter 11 presents the requirements for the specialized practice with respect to the agency and the practitioner. Professional expectations and technology are examined. Chapter 12 examines the essential elements to be worked with in advancing social competence: the individual's relationship to self and to others. It identifies a class of forerunner interventions in a pregroup period while these two relationships are evolved.

Chapter 13 examines the place of actional modes in engaging socially unskilled persons toward (re)establishing a sense of effectance with their world, the prelude to relating to others. The use of activities as the preferred content form is explored. Chapter 14 explicates the route and processes through which social competence can be achieved in this practice. Finally, chapter 15 provides a portrait of a socially noncompetent entity in its progression toward group.

[Part I]

Social Competence
and Social Noncompetence

Part 1 addresses the concepts of social competence and social noncompetence and their behavioral manifestations. Chapter 1 reviews multidisciplinary literature concerned with defining these concepts and various associated conceptual designations. It explores the literature on social skills, viewed as manifestations of social competence, and identifies a developing literature in social work reflecting practice with socially unskilled populations.

Individual social competence is explored in chapter 2 as the necessary condition for group forming and group functioning. Individual social competence is seen to evolve in the increasingly social behaviors of children's groups at each age-stage. A description of this behavioral progression makes visible a set of social tasks to be undertaken at each age-stage, worked out in successive group experiences. Progressions in the development and functioning of group-as-group are seen to evolve in tandem with the accomplishment of each social task, achieving greater complexity as an entity as the social functioning level of its members advances. The portrait of social tasks is identified as a tool for assessing the social functioning level at which socially noncompetent persons may be arrested, indicating social tasks still to be accomplished.

Chapter 3 identifies a class of threshold entities whose participants lack the social competence to generate group. It identifies a range of populations whose circumstances create alterations to normal social interaction, presents a portrait of features that characterize their social functioning, and discusses varieties of flawed or aberrational interaction.

The Concepts of Social Competence and Social Noncompetence

Social Competence

It may be easier to define social noncompetence than it is to define social competence: competence is more apparent in its absence. Defining social competence is "like trying to climb a greased pole" (Phillips 1984:24); it is said to have as many definitions as there are authors concerned with it (Wilson and Sabee 2003:4).

The concept of social competence is examined in the literature of several foundation and applied social sciences for its relevance to social work practice with socially unskilled populations in groups. The term "social competence" is present in social work literature (Maluccio 1981; Saleebey 1992, 2009). In the social science disciplines, it is not a well-defined, unitary concept. The terminology varies from one discipline to another, alternately referred to as "social competence," "interactional competence," "communicative competence," "interpersonal competence," "relational competence," "emotional competence," "communication competence," or "social skills," reflecting varied levels of conceptual and operational descriptions. The components of social competence are not well specified. Some of the definitional problems for this concept lie in the fact that it is located in several disciplines. It requires a transdisciplinary definition that addresses both individual elements and collective, social, group elements.

Social competence may be seen as an additional way of delineating specific competence, or it may serve as a summary concept, subsuming other particular designations. Alternatively, the term may specifically reflect social approaches as distinct from psychological perspectives and definitions. Wilson and Sabee (2003:29) make this distinction: "Psychological perspectives highlight qualities that enable people to communicate competently. Social perspectives, in contrast, draw attention away from individuals as the primary unit of analysis, posing questions about competent relationships, groups, and interactions."

Rose-Krasnor (1997:123) defines social competence as "effectiveness in interaction, considered from both self and other perspectives. Social competence is viewed as an organizing construct, with transactional, context-dependent, performance oriented, and goal-specific characteristics." She offers a model of social competence with a theoretical level, an index level, and a skills level of analysis.

The variety of terms reflects interest in related concepts among several basic and applied social science disciplines. The range of interests spans the conceptual and the operational, the theoretical and the behavioral. The fields of interest among basic social sciences include psychology, social psychology, child development, communication, sociolinguistics, and, in the applied social sciences, social work, education, psychiatry, speech pathology, clinical psychology, gerontology, and management.

Concerns of authors in these several fields include the need to develop theoretical grounding for the concept; to refine the definition of the concept and its domain; to achieve an integration of ideas about social competence; to refine the operational level of description of social skills; and to identify linkages with other relevant concepts and constructs. Spitzberg (1993:140) proffers the most complex analysis of the concept of interpersonal competence, suggesting that "competence may well be a more complex phenomenon than current conceptions . . . suggest. In essence, interpersonal competence may not consistently lead to positive social and personal outcomes. . . . [C]ompetence possesses certain ideological components, and . . . is likely to involve dialectical complexities that current conceptions have yet to resolve."

Additional work on the definition of social competence is located in socialization theory, child development, and developmental psychology, in particular within lifespan development materials. Developmental psychology is notable for its thrust to look firsthand at humans in interaction, and to evolve theory from firsthand observation. Brownell and Brown (1992:183–200) have provided an outstanding review of literature reporting on the specific social competences of infants and toddlers. There is a need for similar definitive work with other ages and stages. The literature pertaining to older age groups seem to rely on traditional existing descriptive materials that lack an uncontaminated, fresh look at behaviors through new perspectives and suffer from the presence of too many unmanageable descriptive variables.

The components of social competence are described variously. Wilson and Sabee (2003:5), using the term "communicative competence," seek to deal with problems of definition by treating it as a "theoretical term rather than as a construct" and defining it "within the parameters of specific communication theories." "Relative competence" is acknowledged as the "modal state of affairs" (Bradac 1989, quoted in Wilson and Sabee 2003:4): "that we are competent in interaction some of the time in some situations." Wilson and Sabee suggest that "within any situation, not all things that can be said and done are equally competent . . . success in personal and professional relationships depends, in no small part, on communicative competence. . . . [M]ost people display incompetence in at least a few situations, and a smaller number are judged incompetent across many situations" (3–4).

Ideas associated with social competences include that they are learned, viewed as social skills, "developed and refined over time through implementation, [and] do not appear instantaneously, fully developed, . . . ready to be applied" (Greene 2003:51); that they are visible in performance and may vary with situation and context; and that they may be acquired through specific programs designed to teach social skills. There is a division between definers who view social competence as within person and those who view it as reflecting person-in-interaction-with-environment. Distinction is made also between the person's own view of his or her social competence and the assessment made by others of competent behavior.

Klemp (1979:41) notes that "the competence of a person is judged by his performance. . . . [A] competent person is one who can meet or surpass performance standards, either implicit or explicit." Duck (1988:9) sees "significant parallels between certain types of competence, the stages of a relationship's development, and the nature of the development of children's understandings of the basis of friendship." Duck recognizes a four-level hierarchy of types of social competence, "which deals with competency issues at several different levels and can be viewed as a relationally developmental hierarchy in which each skill presumes and builds on the skills of the previous level(s)" (93). Duck's hierarchy runs from social skills to interpersonal competence to communication competence to relational competence.

Perspectives of Applied Social Sciences

It appears that the applied social sciences have an easier time with the concept of social competence, defining it pragmatically in more concrete, behavioral terms as social skill, and viewing it in terms of programs designed to help people acquire necessary skills for social living.

"An overwhelming body of evidence indicates that the possession of adequate social skills is necessary for maintaining social, psychological, and in many cases occupational well-being. People who lack adequate social skills appear to be at risk for developing a truly amazing range of problems" (Segrin and Givertz 2003:135). Segrin and Givertz define social skills as "the ability to interact with other people in a way that is both appropriate and effective" (136). They quote Liberman, DeRisi, and Mueser (1989) as identifying four factors related to deficits in social skills:

- Never having learned to interact effectively with others . . . through lack of an appropriate role model.
- Experiences [of] psychological problems that cause their social skills to deteriorate . . . through disuse . . . or the way that psychological symptoms . . . disrupt social behavior.
- Environmental stressors . . . interfere with socially skilled behavior.
- Social environments may change in such a way as to reduce or take away positive social reinforcements . . . once available.

Segrin and Givertz add two more factors:

- Skilled social behavior is challenging (and complex).
- Circumstances may provide a lack of opportunity to practice social skills, or to receive effective feedback (137).

Klemp (1979:42) defines (social) competence as "a generic knowledge, skill, trait, self-(image) or motive of a person that is causally related to effective behavior referenced to external performance criteria." Although he poses these elements as alternatives, they can be viewed as a combination of components that together are capable of generating social competence.

Social work, psychiatry, clinical psychology, and education share a primary interest in social competence, from both developmental and remedial viewpoints, having specific programs for various populations at risk or socially unskilled. There is an extensive literature on social skill development addressed to persons who lack competences, to those whose acquisition of relevant competences is developmentally related to their age-stage, and to adult students who must acquire competences specific to becoming professionals, such as teachers, social workers, and psychiatrists.

The same diversity associated with the many conceptual terms for social competence is present in the range of specific social skills identified, the number of problems and populations to which they are being applied, and the variety of social skill training programs employed (Segrin and Givertz 2003). Many of the programs for social skill development in education, psychology, and psychiatry are designed as cognitively focused learnings taking place in classroom contexts. In contrast, in the practice described in this text, social learnings occur within a salient primary group experience, at critical moments in social interaction when a particular socially skilled response is needed and is acquired with the assistance of the social worker, as learning in life, in situ, at the moment needed.

Within the profession of social work, several authors have addressed competence in clients. Maluccio (1981:22) emphasizes the person–environmental transaction as a measure of competence "result[ing] from the constructive interaction of a person's qualities and potentialities with a nurturing and challenging environment—an environment providing both support and stimulation." Weick et al. (1989) define an altered practice approach oriented to the person's strengths; Saleebey (1992, 2009) advances this focus in his "strengths approach." Both highlight the competence of persons in a paradigmatic shift in practice. Malekoff (2004) elaborates a strengths-based group work practice with children and adolescents.

The Mainstream practice of social work with groups is focused on the advancement of social competence and the use of strengths, although preceding these precise conceptualizations in time. Coyle (1959:91–94) articulates this focus well in her recognition of the centrality of group experience in the social maturation of juveniles.

Falck (1988), in his paradigm for membership in small groups as the only and essential condition through which and within which human beings live their lives, gives special credence to the necessity of achieving a succession of group memberships throughout one's life. Durkheim (1951) in an earlier time period and in the social science literature also identified the importance of social embeddedness through membership in important small groups as an antidote for anomie and proneness to suicide.

Socialization and Social Competence

Social competence is seen as the capacity to engage effectively and appropriately in social interaction and, by extension, to navigate the social world successfully, to hold a functional place in the society and the culture, and to be accessible to ongoing socialization throughout life. Social competence is socially learned through a continuous socialization process throughout life, in successive social situations, acquired in the context of significant family, peer group, and other relevant primary relationships. Requirements for socialization are relationships combining strong affect, power, and love (Perlman 1967) that carry tasks of preparing the person for functioning appropriately and effectively in the social world.

Basic social learnings for social competence are achieved in childhood, enabling the person to develop significant social competences for living in the world. To these are added ongoing and new socializations to current requirements and circumstances, with the task of keeping the person relevant, connected, and functional in a changing world. Socialization is the product of interpersonal and group influence in which persons who are in relationship together have the capacity for reciprocal social influence.

Social competence has implications both for the person and for the society, each needing competence in place for successful individual and collective societal functioning (Schwartz 1962). Weinstein (1969:755), working with concepts of social psychology theorists such as Thibault and Kelley, Homans, Bleu, Goffman, and Garfinkle, identifies interpersonal competence as "the ability to accomplish interpersonal tasks." He emphasizes socialization for empathy as the basis of interpersonal competence; highlights differences between parental and peer socialization; and defines an "implicit learning model" in socialization for interpersonal competence, stating that "much of the socialization process depends not on direct training but on incidental learning" particularly as the child learns appropriate normative behavior rather than effective or competent behavior, such that "much of interpersonal effectiveness is learned only accidentally" (773).

The accidental nature of social learning for competent functioning in the social world is compounded further by the vagaries of social living circumstances for many individuals. Many of the populations addressed in this book have experienced inconstancy in the provisions of their social situation—undependable, interrupted, erratic, truncated—such that their socialization experience is discontinuous in nature, lacking the smooth progression of a normal socialization process.

White (1963) recognizes the repeated process of engaging with and "having effects" on objects in one's environment as exercising a sense of being effective in relation to them, culminating in a sense of effectance and competence. As the individual becomes effective in dealing with human objects, the sense of competence can be recognized as social competence.

Social competence is the outcome of a series of social learnings accomplished at each age-stage. Social competence acquired at each age-stage can be specified as partial in an ongoing progression throughout the lifespan, fully attained in adulthood.

Although the literature on social competence (and its alternative descriptors) does not specify well the specific elements that make up social competence, it seems possible to identify some critical components. In an early attempt, Foote and Cottrell (1955) identified the constituent elements of interpersonal competence as autonomy, creativity, empathy, health, intelligence, and judgment.

The elements that make up social competence appear to include

- a sense of self and some knowledge of one's capabilities
- a sense of others and some recognition of their capabilities
- a measure of self-management and internalized control
- a degree of self-directedness
- an ability to engage relationally with others, to achieve synchrony and appropriateness in social interaction with others
- awareness of norms of interaction and some recognition of cues and patterns in interaction

- an ability to relate to others empathically, sensitively
- an ability to join with others as a participant in and contributor to a collective enterprise

The achievement of mature object relations (Blanck and Blanck 1974) appears to reflect the capacity of individuals to connect fully with others in the collective enterprise of small group, to be able to merge the self with others in joint undertakings of a collective whole, and to contribute with others to something beyond individual—to a collective process and product.

The Concept of Social Noncompetence

The term "social noncompetence" has been selected as the descriptor for populations lacking social skills sufficient to allow them to enter into the social world well and to generate essential small social groups. The concept contains three elements. First, it designates those competences relevant to social interaction, as distinct from other kinds of competences. Second, it identifies a behavioral realm classifiable as "competent," distinguishable from "noncompetent." Third, the addition of "non" to the term competent specifies behaviors other than those recognized as competent.

Webster's Dictionary makes a clear distinction between non- and un- or in-. Non- is recognized as "lacking the usual characteristics of the thing specified; the absence of" while un- and in- are seen as "having a meaning positively opposite to that of the base word." Thus *noncompetent* reflects an absence of skills necessary for negotiating the social world, implying the possibility that they can be acquired; while *incompetent* reflects inability to do and implies the presence of nonfunctional behaviors, possibly not able to be adapted.

The designation "socially competent" is recognized as the outcome of a socialization process that generates social skills learned through interaction within significant relationships. "Social noncompetence" defines populations for whom this process has been inadequate, incomplete, insufficient to enable the development of skills for living successfully in the social world. Social noncompetence thus reflects on the inadequacy of basic socialization processes, and on circumstances less than adequate in the environment.

Individual Social Competence

The Necessary Condition for Group Forming and Collective Group Functioning

The chapter explores the association between individual social competence and the capacity to engage in group formation and to function as a participating member. It is focused on social competence essential to the functioning of social groups. The materials examine the prevailing behaviors of children in groups at each age-stage, identifying social behaviors of developing complexity, which move progressively toward the capacity to engage in group and function within it.

From the portraits of children's behaviors at each age-stage in groups, a set of *social tasks* is identified as defining the work of children and adolescents in their age-stage-related progression to social competence for social life in groups. The accomplishment of each social task moves the individual progressively toward more complex social functioning in group life, making group capability more possible.

Papell and Rothman (1980:119) highlight the connection between individual social competence and collective social functioning. In defining the Social Goals Model of practice with groups, they state that "the model assumes that there is a unity between social action and individual psychological health." The concepts of individual development, individual psychological health, and social competence are somewhat entangled in the literature, but all point to the capacity of the individual to function socially with others.

There appears to be a profound, dramatic, observable shift from individual to group functioning when social competences are put in place, are in process of developing, or are reactivated, and perhaps most especially when they are called upon for use. The pattern of individual functioning changes when individuals become able to merge their individual selves in the larger complex whole of group. Social workers who work with groups may be particularly aware of the transition from individual to group functioning, both for socially competent populations who are able to make this shift rapidly and for socially unskilled populations as they acquire competence sufficient to be able to merge with other selves in group enterprise.

This chapter undertakes to identify several facets of social competence, to explore the ways in which they can contribute to the formation and functioning of group, and to identify the ways in which components of individual social competence enable the transition to group constituent, membership, affiliation, belonging, and groupness. The chapter posits that certain individual competences must be developed and in place in order for group-relevant competences to be employed, and for group to form and function. From the normative functioning in the group life of children at each age-stage, a typology of group functioning is developed, which characterizes the group life of children and adolescents as evolving group forms.

A progression of social tasks is identified in the group life of children at each age-stage, leading successively to cumulative social competence and to more complex group forms. The social task progression addressed in group life matches the tasks of individual development at each age-stage. The portrait of advancing complexity in group form and of competences to be practiced at each age-stage is seen as a preparatory and practice circumstance through which, progressively and gradually, participants acquire the necessary social competence for group life, and for living in the social world. In that process, the group experience that they are able to have at each age-stage advances in complexity and specificity of social competence.

Individual Social Competence, Group Forming, and Nature of the Entity

This section explores the link between individual social competence, the *capacity to form group*, and the *nature of the entity* created. Social competence evolves gradually, appearing as successive skills accrued at each age-stage in human development (Greene and Burleson 2003:51; Newman 1976:19). The capacity to form group and the nature of the resulting entity are determined by the level of social competence of the members. Thus the social competence level of the individual members is reflected in the complexity of the entity they are able to construct together. The entity group, then, must be viewed as having varying characteristics determined by the functioning level of its membership.

These features in the variable entity group are located at the outer edges of social development theory and small group theory and have been beyond the mandate of either specialization to specify. In small group theory the thrust of research has been in the study of adult functioning under lab conditions in which temporary, ad hoc collectivities are convened and assumed to be equivalent to enduring groups in their functioning. A missing piece in small group theory has been the study of groups composed of persons at various age-stages. Hence we do not have a normative portrait showing what group life consists of from childhood to adulthood. The best materials in the literature are those from lifespan social developmental psychology, which looks firsthand at the social functioning of humans from infancy through early childhood, documenting actual behaviors indicative of social competences. These materials stop short of documenting the nature of the group as successive skills of social competence are accomplished.

There are a few attempts to acknowledge differences in groups composed of persons at various age-stages or with different populations with varying competence for group life. Early writers in social work with groups have given some visibility to the functioning of children's groups at various age-stages, through the presentation of process recordings of group sessions. The lines of analysis associated with these glimpses into interaction in children's groups are focused on aspects of group development or sociometric analysis of relationships (Coyle 1937a, 1937b; Wilson and Ryland 1949; Konopka 1949; Garland, Jones, and Kolodny 1973). The sociological work of Newstetter (1930) and Newstetter, Feldstein, and Newcomb (1938) is singular in its focus on individual–group interaction and group adjustment.

Newman (1976) has created a developmental portrait of the essential features of social interaction and of interpersonal skills during six life stages, in an article that is almost unique in the literature on small group theory. This material approaches but does not specify the nature of group at each stage.

Lang has identified collectivity (1987) and group forms ranging from allonomous to autonomous (1972a, 1972b) as efforts to delineate groups with varied attributes, classifiable as collectivities of various kinds, and as groups with distinctively different features and needs. In the small group theory literature, Delamater (1974), Mills (1967), and Tuckman (1964) all recognize different orders of groups, of varying complexity and differentiating characteristics.

Social workers who practice with groups have experiential knowledge of a range of groups, distinguishable in their functioning. This is likely to be a mixture of knowledge about normative, age-stage groups and about groups shaped by the particular aberrations or social difficulties of the members.

This chapter develops a portrait of normative groups, each having particular features generated by members' social competences at each age-stage. This typology will lend itself to identifying the features of entities composed of socially unskilled members, as a guide to the nature of anomalies in entitative functioning. The typology will make visible the ways in which a particular entity composed of socially unskilled persons mirrors the features of a normatively developed group at a particular age-stage. Recognition of the features of anomalous groups may assist the practitioner in planning for how to work with the group. The normative typology will also contribute to the interface between developmental psychology and small group theory.

The typology of typical behaviors of children in group at each age-stage is presented below. From this typology, a set of *social tasks* is abstracted, which characterize the functioning of children in groups at each age-stage. The tasks appear to be preparatory and practice modes designed to acquire successively a set of social competences relevant for functioning in social life in groups. The social tasks that appear at successive age-stages portray the learning and working out of key elements in group functioning and the acquisition of a specific competence at each stage. Thus it is possible to characterize the nature of the *entity* at each stage, at the working out of each social task, and to portray the element of group life coming into place in an advancing order of complexity and completeness—from partial to total, from incomplete to complete, from simple to complex.

In the final section, a way is proposed of assessing the functioning of socially unskilled populations using the social task typology to locate and recognize "where members are" in their social functioning; with what social task they are struggling; and hence the desirable nature and focus of their group experience.

Normative Behaviors of Children in Groups at Each Age-Stage

While descriptions of children's individual behavioral characteristics at each age-stage exist in literature, the portrait of their behaviors together in group is incomplete. This appears to be an undeveloped piece at the boundary where developmental psychology, social psychology, and small group theory might interface but have not done so. The section begins with a description of typical behaviors of children in their group life at each age-stage. This portrait is generated from experiential knowledge of social work practice with children's groups.

There is a developmental progression in the predominant behaviors at each age-stage, and in the activation and use of groups, visible to practitioners who have worked with an array of ages and stages of participants in and members of groups but little known to those who have not had this extended practice experience.

In some agencies in social work, there is opportunity to work in groups with children and adolescents at varied age-stages, serving either normal social developmental needs or the special needs of particular populations at risk. Settings include settlement and neighborhood centers, youth-serving agencies, schools, child welfare agencies, family service agencies, and other agencies serving particular populations and problems. The intent is to offer group services that provide opportunities for normal growth, development, and socialization, and special help in acquiring age-stage-relevant social competence to populations with special needs. Practice in both normative and specialized settings has generated for its practitioners in-depth knowledge of the functioning of individuals in groups, and the functioning of group-as-group, at each age-stage, particularly in practice that makes full use of group processes. Such experiential knowledge needs to be gathered and formalized as a contribution to the portrait of social development of individuals and groups, and as an informational guideline for practitioners working with particular age-stages in groups.

A Typology of Social Behaviors

The typology presented in table 2.1 describes typical children's social behaviors in group at each age-stage. At a descriptive level, the typology highlights normative behaviors of children at each age-stage in their group life, in social work groups, as experienced by their social worker. In several of the categories, the materials represent an amalgam of characteristic behaviors accumulated from extensive experience with many groups of a particular age. The behaviors are presented under headings that identify critical elements of group functioning as these play out differently at each age-stage of group life: presocial, part-social A, part-social B, social A, social B, and social C. In each category, a single element of group life predominates, with new elements being added cumulatively from one age-stage to the next. A graphic portrait of these elements is presented in figure 2.1. The identified elements are interaction, relationship, purpose, structure, operation (group functioning), and technical competence (members and group developing skills for group functioning). Table 2.1 is presented in the next four pages, followed by figure 2.1, which summarizes the social tasks and evolving entity at each age-stage.

Social Tasks

Emergent from the descriptive typology is the discovery of a set of social tasks, specific to and worked out at each age-stage, in group life, using the group experience for the working out of each task. Social tasks are tasks relevant to social life and central to the functioning of small social groups. These are tasks to be learned experientially, practiced and accomplished in the social situation of the small group, and incorporated as social equipment for subsequent social living in small groups.

At each age-stage of individual functioning, there appears to be a social task to be encompassed (see fig 2.1). The tasks represent a *social progression in learned and practiced competence* in the collective domain of small group. In part, the progression reflects a transition from membership in a familial group to one in which peer relationships are worked out and social competences learned in the family group are reworked for use in the context of the egalitarian relationships of peers. Lidz (1968:265) highlights the new circumstance for children of having to establish and earn their place in nonfamilial groups as distinct from being accepted because one is a member of the family, that is, "achieved versus ascribed status."

Juveniles are seen to be employing behaviors intended to work out specific social tasks at each age-stage. The tasks appear as successive and sequential, such that the accomplishment of each task furthers social

TABLE 2.1

A Typology of Social Behaviors in Groups at Each Age-Stage

1. PRESOCIAL CATEGORY: 4–5 YEAR OLDS

The group life of young children age 4–5 years is somewhat volatile because elements of group life that could sustain togetherness are not yet in place.

Interaction	Variable, unstable, ad hoc, occurring in shifting subunits, short-term, brief, episodic. Has features of impulsivity, contagion, and imitativeness and is prone to swift chaos. Participation is variable.
Relationships	Unformed, transitory, rudimentary, dyadic only. Peers are viewed as objects. Interpersonal awareness and observing are present, defined behaviorally.
Structure	Provided by worker through routine, regulation, scheduling, patterning. Fluidity and unpredictability of interaction requires routine, guidance, and management.
Norms	Not activated. Inner controls lacking or partial, variable from child to child; dependence on the adult for control, maintenance of order, routine, for patterned repetitive ways of doing; rule establishment.
Activity	Flows in short interest spans, unorganized, characterized by individual, parallel, side-by-side action. Activity provides means for being and doing together and gives specific direction for engaging together, often contained in the activity form itself, e.g., the singing game.
Operational	Modes instituted by worker, in design and direction and patterning.
Worker role	Active, central, directing, creating structure and regulation through use of activities that support, sustain, direct interaction, anticipate relational ties in play form.
Nature of the entity	Unformed, undeveloped, an early context for social experience, a preliminary pregroup collectivity, allonomous form, worker directed.
Elements of group life in place:	Interaction is central ingredient in place, first element essential to group life, but insufficient to constitute group.

2. PART-SOCIAL CATEGORY A: 6–7 YEAR OLDS

Interaction	In transit from portrait of presocial entities. More sustained, stabilized, becoming patterned. Sociality is emergent, some impulsivity, variable participation, becoming more stable.

(continued)

TABLE 2.1

A Typology of Social Behaviors in Groups at Each Age-Stage (*continued*)

Relationships	Some beginning relationships, shifting, short-term dyads, emergence of "best friend," trying out relational connections. Interpersonal ties are partial, not encompassing all the members, but each connecting with one or two others.
Structure	Worker-directed and play-form generated. Externally created, regulated, patterned by worker. Less required than in younger age group, but still necessary.
Norms	Ways of going evolve, beginning norms established by worker and recognized.
Activity	Parallel play, turn-taking play forms, "It" games. Activity supports and sustains being and doing together, directs the action. Enormous creativity.
Operational	Ways of going become patterned, habitual.
Worker role group.	Active, central, directing, but less than in presocial
Nature of the entity	Partially formed, unstable shifting relationships; a pre-group collectivity, evolving, allonomous form.
Elements of group life in place	Interaction, and relationship (partial) in process.

3. PART-SOCIAL CATEGORY B: 8–9 YEAR OLDS

Interaction	Becomes sustained. Participation is stable. Interaction involves more of the members. Ability to engage collectively advances.
Relationships	Developing, becoming more sustained, dependable. Attachments are visible. Sense of self and sense of others evolve.
Structure	Evolving as relationships develop and stabilize. Some reliance on worker to provide needed structure. Rudimentary roles begin to develop.
Norms	Are established and activated. Members may struggle to accept, abide by norms, singling out breaches of norms by other members. Progression is toward inner controls.
Activity	Central and involving, alters to include wider array of activity forms that are more interactive, less turn-taking, parallel in nature. Practice in performing "It" games, perfecting individual place in group. Significant creativity and productivity; emergence of personal standard for products, some frustration in generating wanted outcomes.

TABLE 2.1

A Typology of Social Behaviors in Groups at Each Age-Stage (*continued*)

	Sense of self measured by adequacy of products. Pleasure in related play.
Operational	Ways of going as group become established.
Worker role	In transit as member competences grow. Worker less directive.
Nature of activity	Collectivity becoming group. Transitional toward more self-directing. In transit regarding group-relevant elements.
Elements of group life in place	Interaction, relationship, and structure.

4. SOCIAL CATEGORY A: 10–11 YEAR OLDS

Interaction	Characterized by emergent capacity to merge self in larger whole, to act together, to concert, to immerse oneself in the interaction of group. Enthusiastic participation, sometimes chaotic, irrational, swift. Peer initiative begins to direct interaction. High energy as a collective. Behavioral.
Relationships	Extend, consolidate. More members differentiated. Pattern of relationships is clear, stable.
Structure	Social structure develops, reflecting relationships, some roles assumed.
Norms	Become established and act as effective guides to behaviors, strongly invoked by members.
Activity	Characterized by joy in doing together and in collective action. Activity forms extensive.
Group purpose	Emergent with establishment of relationships.
Operational	Group ways of doing are established. Social tasks previously learned singly are now implemented together.
Worker role	Worker adapts to less central and directing, to guiding and managing nonrational group process.
Nature of entity	Practice at becoming and being group, testing the limits of the entity, finding what group can do.
Elements of group life in place	Interaction, relationship, structure, purpose.

5. SOCIAL CATEGORY B: 12–14 YEAR OLDS

Interaction	Interaction for its own sake—progression from doing to simply being together; joy in togetherness and in endless interaction, processing relevant issues.

(*continued*)

TABLE 2.1

A Typology of Social Behaviors in Groups at Each Age-Stage (*continued*)

Relationships	Elaborated, extended to most group members, members differentiated. Relationships revise, stabilize. Sense of individual self redefined, in context of group. Members individualized.
Structure	Complex relationship, role, task structure.
Norms	Well defined but more relaxed, incorporated. Breaches tolerated, inner controls more effective.
Activity	Verbal form predominates, activities less necessary. Talk replaces action.
Purpose	Growth as adolescents is primary purpose.
Operational	Well-established group ways. Roles well developed.
Technical	Members contribute individual competences to the functioning of the group. The group develops technical competence for pursuing group goals.
Worker role	Guide; stimulator of discussion.
Nature of entity	Elements of group are developed, consolidated. Collective competence in place to advance entity and use it. Practice at using group.
Elements of group life in place	Interaction, relationship, structure, purpose, operational.

6. SOCIAL CATEGORY C: 15–16 YEAR OLDS

Interaction	Becomes more focused, still predominantly verbal, stable in nature, dependable.
Relationships	Well established, relaxed, deepening, recognition of member capabilities, contributions.
Structure	Present but less essential.
Norms	Inner controls effective, group norms less crucial.
Activity	Verbal processing of topical issues; task focus as entity.
Purpose	Group purposes emergent.
Operational	Well functioning as entity.
Technical	Competences for group life well developed.
Worker role	Resource, stimulator.
Nature of entity	Elements of group life in place and operational. Use of group to pursue collective goals, achieve elegant solutions. Trying out what group can do.
Elements of group life in place	Interaction, relationship, structure, purpose, operational, technical.

Age-Stage	Social Task	Portrait of the Entity	Group Element in Place
Presocial: 4-5-year-olds	Learning to interact in group		Interaction
Part-Social, A: 6-7-year-olds	Learning to relate in group		Interaction Relationship
Part-Social, B: 8-9-year-olds	Forming relationships Exploring commonality of purpose		Interaction Relationship Purpose
Transformational Point—From Collectivity to Group			
Social, A: 10-11-year-olds	Practicing being a group, using the social tasks in combination Learning joined action Collective doing		Interaction Relationship Purpose Structure
Social, B: 12-14-year-olds	Revising and elaborating group operation Collective being Learning to be members		Interaction Relationship Purpose Structure Operation
Social, C: 15-16-year-olds	Developing technical skills for group life Finding what group can do Pursuing group goals		Interaction Relationship Purpose Structure Operation Technical

Figure 2.1 Principal Elements of Group Activated with Each Social Task: Portrait of the Entity

development and social competence at every age-stage and enables progression to the succeeding social task. At the same time, the preceding social tasks may continue to be worked on or reworked along with the relevant new task predominant at each stage. The complexity of social life in small groups requires the consolidation of these several social tasks such that they can function effectively both singly and in concert.

The social tasks include practicing to engage in interaction; practice in forming relationships; forming actual relationships; finding commonality of purpose; articulating and pursuing common purposes; evolving ways of being and doing together; exploring how the entity group works; forming group and evolving group structure and group ways of operating; and acquiring and practicing the technical skills needed for functional group life. Because each task is central to the functioning of groups, at each progression members are occupied with encompassing the task of each age-stage. Successively, social competences are attained that will advance the individual member toward full competence for social living through small life groups, and the entity toward full life as a complete, effective, mature group in society.

The progression in the *capability of the entity* is matched to and reflects the developmental progressions in social competence of the constituent members. As individual social competence evolves, so too does the nature and capability of the entity. The nature of the entity is shown graphically in figure 2.1, to portray the progression from incomplete to complete as each element of group functioning is put in place in turn.

In the succession of social tasks, there is a progression from learning a specific task separately at each level to a point at which the tasks, learned individually, must be practiced together and integrated as complex social functioning. The social task at each age-stage is reflected in the functioning of the entity at each level. The capability of group-as-group—as entity—is limited to the social tasks already accomplished and by those yet to be addressed.

The *developmental progression of group-as-group* is visible in the social functioning of participants, at each age-stage. It can be recognized as a progression from incomplete to complete functioning as an entity, from immature to mature social functioning, paralleling the tasks of individual growth and development. Thus, at the 4–5-year-old level, the primary feature of the entity is *interaction*. In essence, the social task at this age-stage is to learn to interact—to practice interacting with one's peers. The competences in place at this age-stage are insufficient for generating groupness. Interaction is the principal feature of the collective; while this is the central feature of all groups, by itself it is insufficient to generate and form group. Convening in the collective provides opportunities to practice interacting, to experience the unanticipated outcomes of interactional exchanges, to learn about the process of engaging with peers, to know experientially interaction that is contained and manageable or chaotic and out-of-hand, and to discover the impact of one's individual behavior on others, and of others' behaviors on the self.

When the tasks associated with interpersonal interaction have been accomplished, group members are ready to engage with one another on a new level. The new social task is to *use interaction to relate*, to build connections with other human beings, to construct relationships. At the 6–7-year-old level, this task emerges in the formation of beginning ties with another individual. Again, the practice element is visible, as dyadic ties are tried out, in a shifting pattern of not-yet-stable connections. "Best friend" may be reworked with new personnel, as relational possibilities are tried out and tested, disregarded and reformed.

At this age-stage, the entity will contain two primary elements, *interaction* and *relationship*. Relationship, not yet stabilized, is manifest as members test out and practice new connections that recognize "the other" in a preliminary way, acknowledging characteristics of "the relatee" as having commonality, consonant with one's own ways of being and doing. Practice at becoming related characterizes the collective at this level—a time for trying out, testing, engaging, discarding, reforming, which is the forerunner of a set of relationships likely to be formed at later stages. These two elements, interaction and relationship, are each vital to the functioning of group-as-group, but as the sole elements developed, they reflect an incomplete entity, lacking in essential group-relevant dimensions.

At the third level, 8–9 year olds, relationships form and stabilize but are partial and incomplete, that is, they exist between persons whose commonalities produce comfortable ties. The connections do not extend to and among all the members yet, but those relationships that have formed become dependable and stable. The social task of constructing stable and rewarding ties extends the period of practicing relatedness to one in which actual significant relationships are constructed.

It is this task of constructing ties that moves the participants into the next stage, that of identifying "what we can do together." Recognition of commonality in new relationships evokes the possibility of common, *shared purpose*, propelling the entity into a domain of concerted action. In the 10–11-year-old age-stage, the entity becomes suddenly important, and being and doing together in the collective domain achieves centrality. This is the *transformational stage* in which group-as-a-whole can be realized from the accumulated accomplishment of successful tasks in the prior stages. Participating members can recognize and differentiate the entity group-as-group. Joy in being and doing together emerges, thrusting the members into collective action.

Sense of self and other, each delineated and reflected in the relationship-developmental stage, now progresses to recognition of the group-as-a-whole, emerging through collective engagement in the life of the entity. Doing together propels the experience of groupness. Pleasure in collective purpose and action pervades this stage and is reflective of a progression in recognition from individual, to relational, to awareness of a larger whole into which the individual selves are merged and submerged.

Now the elements of group life are extended to include interaction, relationship, collective action, delineation of common purpose and recognition of the entity. Group forming and functioning are visible, but the collective functioning, like the interaction at the first level, is being explored, experienced, and recognized in its nature and is likely to flow in enthusiastic, impulsive episodes, unruly, nonrational, perhaps chaotic in nature. The sense of entity and its capabilities is being learned at this stage. Ways of going in the collective emerge through doing together. The separate social tasks previously learned are experienced in a consolidated form of practice. The task of the 10–11-year-old stage is to learn what doing together can produce, what collective capability (generally and specifically in this entity) can yield. This is *experiential knowledge of the capability of group*, generated actionally in swift interpersonal engagement with relevant and salient activity.

Hence, it is in the adolescent group of 12–14 year olds that the entity group achieves its fullest realization. Here, the members rework relationships, purpose, and interaction, revamping collective doing to *collective being*. Their group-forming capability is in place and more rational in nature. Purpose can be contemplated. Learning to be group members may extend in this stage to learning interpersonal adaptation and role-taking, of concerting competences and contributions, of finding ways to recognize and use what each member can contribute, of becoming competent in the operation of the

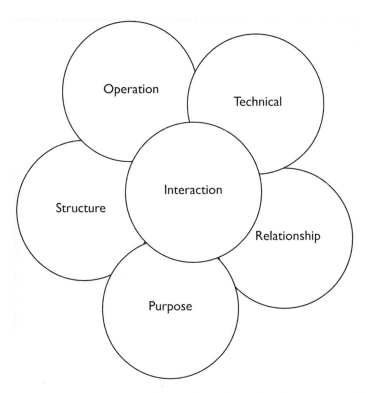

Figure 2.2 Portrait of Group Complexity When All Social Tasks Are Accomplished

entity, and of undertaking significant purposes together. At the 15–16-year-old level, group capability is advanced with the achievement of technical competences in role-taking and skill in working together to achieve group goals.

Implications for Practice

The recognition of social tasks worked out in small groups accomplishes several things. First, it makes visible the group life of juveniles as a locus for developing and exercising social competences. The group is a preparatory and practice entity, a learning modality, and is not fully developed as a complete entity until the social tasks have been accomplished. Children's groups are the nursery, the context and the means through which social competences are acquired, practiced, and used. Cooley (1918) said it well when he described the small group as "the cradle of human nature," the *locus for becoming humanized and socialized.*

The social tasks to be learned are preparatory for living competently in the social world through living successfully in small groups. Hence the group life of children is incomplete because they are involved in learning and practicing how to be and do as a group, at each stage working out a particular aspect of group life. The maturing child faces a set of social tasks that can be encompassed socially only with others in group and that require social engagement in order to be worked out.

The recognition of social tasks legitimates the activity of juvenile groups focused on a specific task to be encompassed and points to worker activities relevant to assisting members in working out each social task. It also provides a portrait of the entity that can be attained at each age-stage, highlighting the progression from incomplete to complete group. Pictorially, this progressive evolution of the entity is portrayed in figure 2.1, which reflects the degree of completeness of the entity toward a fully developed group. Entities having only some of the essential components of a developed group are reflected clearly as collectivities progressing toward group as each element is added.

Wider Implications of the Typology of Social Tasks

There are special implications of the social task progression evolved through and in groups. In particular, socially unskilled populations may appear to be arrested at the point of working out a particular social task. For some persons, lack of opportunity for successive small group belongings across several age-stages may alone account for failure to surmount the several social tasks leading to developed group.

> Young single mothers were convened as a support group in a child welfare setting. Although they were adults parenting young children, in their group life they functioned as young children. They were not autonomous as a group and were content to have their worker plan and prepare content for each session. Over time they began to transform in their group life. At the beginning of their third year together, they suddenly took charge, directing the worker to open the group membership

to other single moms "who need this group," and indicating that one of the members should be present with the worker in meeting new candidates "because we can describe what the group is about better than you." These women had not had the opportunity to grow in group experiences since childhood and required time to progress through uncompleted social tasks to a group capability that matched their current stage as adults.

In the author's practice experience with emotionally disturbed 10–12-year-old boys, she recognized in the chaotic nature of their interaction features in common with a group of 4–5 year olds with which she had worked as a social work student. This recognition enabled an understanding of the tasks facing the boys belatedly, and of needed components in worker role, focus, and activity.

Both of these examples point to the need to recognize the functioning level of socially unskilled members and the social task they must address. For some populations, it may be necessary to encompass the full range of social tasks, while for others, some of the tasks may have been surmounted partway through the progression.

The typology, then, and the pictorial portrait of developing but not yet complete group, should be serviceable in recognizing "where the members are," selecting a matching worker role, and assisting with the addressing and completion of relevant social tasks. The significance in making this match is the recognition that persons who are chronologically adults may be facing the social tasks of young children—those of learning to interact or to relate and to use the group to practice the competences emanating from these social tasks.

The contribution of this small piece of theory is, first, to enable practitioners to comprehend the delayed, unaccomplished social tasks facing socially unskilled persons and to plan the group experience accordingly; and second, to serve as a new guideline for understanding the social tasks that normally developing children grapple with in becoming socially competent.

The Gold and Kolodny (1978) and Brooks (1978) articles are excellent examples: the first because it shows out-of-control adolescents learning to interact successfully—their first need—through the media of hockey and basketball; the second because it represents the restoration of lost competences through media of exercise and swimming, to the point where interaction and relationship accomplishment overcame their fear of communicating outside the group and within life in the fearful setting of a single-room-occupancy slum hotel.

It becomes evident that the entity group advances in step with the group members' social task accomplishment at each age-stage. The group-as-group is incomplete and partial through several age-stages, with elements being added at each stage. Figure 2.1 portrays pictorially the gradual advances toward group formation in a way that heightens the view of the partial, incomplete nature of the entity gradually acquiring all the necessary components for group life. When all the social tasks have been surmounted and all the elements of group are in place, the portrait of the group (fig. 2.2) takes on the appearance of a complete flower, with each of its petals identifying a significant element of group life.

In essence, the complete flower can be seen as a pictorial representation of social competence as manifest in group, reflecting the achievement of all social tasks that enable group to form and to function fully. The floral portrait can stand as representative of *social competence in its collective, group form*, as distinguished from individual social competence, but also reflecting the necessity for individual social competence as the fundamental basis for the achievement of collective social competence.

[3]

Forms of Socially Noncompetent Interaction Requiring Special Adaptations to Social Work Practice with Groups

Our society does not of itself train us in the social skills which its complex relations require.

—Elton Mayo, 1945

The means of social growth, development, socialization, and the acquisition of social competence are through membership, belonging, and interaction in a succession of small primary social groups. In general, through this process most of the population turns out reasonably well socialized, equipped with social competence sufficient to live their lives and to maintain the society and the culture.

For a minority of persons, this "social process in organized small groups" (Coyle 1930) is inadequate or unsuccessful, producing members of society not equipped to function effectively in the world. The phenomenon of socially unskilled individuals is reflected in ineffective social interactional processes.

The dilemma for this subgroup of the population is that, lacking achieved competence, entry into a succession of small groups is difficult and problematic, may not result in the formation of group, and thus may deny continuing access to the very social processes that have the ongoing capability of advancing social competence.

The capacity of individuals to form group is dependent on social competence developed and in place. When this is lacking, the group-forming capability of persons is limited, and the resulting entity must be recognized as other than group, less than group, and having less than the normal capability for contributing to the social growth of its members (Lang 1987).

The purpose of the chapter is to identify and give visibility to populations whose lack of social competence produces interactional forms that do not lead to the formation of group. The chapter focuses on the nature and characteristics of flawed social engagement and social interaction displayed by persons who lack social competence, identifying ways in which these act to prevent normative social processes from proceeding. It identifies features of interaction in collectivities composed of specific populations whose social competence has been undeveloped, underdeveloped, interrupted, truncated, discontinuous, impaired, divergent, marred by illness, or atrophied through environmental deprivation and limitations.

The chapter recognizes the connection between individual and group functioning, viewing the lack of social competence of individuals as a condition that limits the capacity to form a social group. Lack of individual social competence reflects itself in inadequate, incomplete social forms, such that it can be seen as a limiting condition in two domains: individual and group. Many individuals, despite anomalies in social functioning in their primary social, familial unit, nevertheless achieve social competence sufficient to maintain social ties and live rewardingly in their social worlds. It is to those individuals who are unsuccessful in acquiring social competence, and who require a remediative social group experience in order to advance in social competence, that the practice described in this book is addressed.

The literature on social work with groups contains a number of descriptions of practice with populations who lack social competence sufficient to form groups. Yet it appears that no effort has been made to bring together these separate portraits of incapacitated, disabled, intending groups, which, despite their wide diversity, share this significant commonality.

A Class of Threshold Entities

The chapter is intended to heighten visibility for a range of populations of socially unskilled persons by viewing them as a *class of threshold entities* whose participants lack the social competence to generate group and to enter the realm of group life without major assistance of a social worker skilled in practice with groups. They stand on the threshold of group life, unable to enter. The sections that follow identify the range of populations involved, present a portrait of features that characterize their social functioning, and develop a typology of forms of flawed or aberrational interactions. The intent is to give visibility to populations in need of special help in forming and functioning in social groups.

The Populations

Because the populations in the class labeled threshold entities are so diverse, it is initially difficult to see the commonalities between them. The populations reflect anomalies of some kind in basic socialization processes in primary social units, mirrored in the lack of achieved social competence. Deficits in social competence may be visible in the social interaction patterns of children and adolescents, or they may be enduring in the social interaction of adults whose juvenile years have not enabled adequate social competence to be achieved.

Conditions leading to social noncompetence may derive from inadequacies in the social functioning and socializing process of the primary social unit; from the presence of a particular form of anomaly in the primary social unit itself; from failure to establish and maintain an enduring social unit; from variations in the personal endowments of individuals that influence how they are able to interact socially; from inherent or acquired elements that limit or restrict the social functioning of individuals; or from inadequacies in the environing context within which persons must make their way socially.

A typology of kinds of aberrational interaction in collectivities and groups is developed below. The populations represented in the typology include

- normally developing young children who are presocial in their interaction
- persons who have experienced serial family units through placements in multiple foster families
- persons whose primary group constellation has had an altered duration, size, and composition, for whom socialization has been brief, truncated, or discontinuous through divorce and remarriage
- persons from families who experience violent interaction

- persons from families with an alcoholic parent
- persons from families with a mentally ill parent
- persons whose primary social unit functions inadequately, creating anomalies in social functioning
- persons who are either overendowed (gifted), anomalously endowed (learning disabled), or underendowed (developmentally disabled), whose intellectual capacity interferes with socially competent functioning
- persons whose social competence is inhibited by some physical anomaly, disability, or impairment
- emotionally disturbed children whose emotional and social development may be arrested or divergent, and who may have acquired as well a repertoire of dysfunctional behaviors
- mentally ill adults whose behaviors are primarily illness-directed rather than social
- adolescent gangs whose social organization and structure work against socially competent functioning of participants in society
- institutionalized populations whose social competencies may have atrophied
- isolated and undomiciled populations whose struggle to survive supersedes all else, and who lack social settings in which to exercise social competence

The pervasive descriptor by social workers undertaking group service with these assorted populations is the absence of social competence adequate for the generation of and participation in group life. A concomitant descriptor is low self-esteem; the two appear together.

The commonality among these diverse populations is the anomaly in how they engage and interact with others. A delineating distinction of socially unskilled populations is the failure to advance, unaided, beyond a pregroup phase, to social engagement, interaction, relationship, and group formation.

A specialized form of practice in social work groups related to these populations is essential if they are to be enabled to access the social group processes that can advance their social competence. The entry point of this specialized practice is the recognition of nonnormative kinds of social interaction, and the requirement for the social group worker to design ways in which socially unskilled persons can be together usefully and productively and can be enabled to enter into processes that will advance their social competence.

Developing a Typology

The task of developing a typology capable of portraying characteristics of these widely diverse populations of socially unskilled persons has been challenging. From many possibilities, two typologies have been developed.

The move from the concrete descriptions of socially unskilled populations to their abstracted features led to the construction of a first classification system built around the term "social," enabling comparison of disparate populations (table 3.1) and portraying a range from presocial and social to variations producing altered social functioning.

TABLE 3.1

A Classification of Normative and Variant Social Functioning

CONDITION	CATEGORY	DESCRIPTION	POPULATION
Normative social functioning	Presocial	Developmentally incomplete, in transit; normal progressions for age-stage; limitations to social competence expectable	Young children
	Social	Social competencies in place, developed, appropriate, in use, and advancing	Normally functioning older children, adolescents, adults
Variant social functioning	Truncated-social	Discontinuities in primary group experience result in partial, disjunctive, or incomplete social competence, some elements present or absent	Children/teens in foster care; in serial family units through divorce, remarriage; or in communities lacking in provision of primary social groups

(continued)

TABLE 3.1

A Classification of Normative and Variant Social Functioning (*continued*)

Divergent-social	Dysfunctional or altered socialization produces anomalies in social competence, some competences absent or at variance	Children/teens from violent families; from families with alcoholic parent; from families with mentally ill parent; or from single parent families
Arrested-social	Emotional development noncontinuous, basic needs unmet; neglect, abuse	Emotionally disturbed children and adolescents
Diverted-social	Some element in the person alters social competence	Persons who have a severe physical disability or who are physically incapacitated (sight, hearing; speech); learning disabled; mentally ill; cognitively impaired; or gifted
Atrophied-social	Social competencies in disuse	Homeless; isolated persons lacking social contexts; or institutionalized populations
Asocial	Social competencies not developed or inaccessible for use	Persons who are mentally ill
Antisocial	Social competence undeveloped or underdeveloped, deviant	Adolescent gangs

The first two categories, presocial and social, represent normative social functioning, with social competence already in place or developing. Social competence that has been altered in some way from normal progressions is identified under categories of variant social functioning.

In the condition labeled *truncated-social*, socialization is partialized in nonsequential units as individuals are moved from one family group to another through foster home placement; or as the family group of origin is altered, re-created, or replaced by subsequent modifications of personnel, through divorce or remarriage. In both circumstances, socialization may be truncated by altered living circumstances, such that instead of continuous social development, the individual may experience in each time period disjunctive and partial social units, with the social experience in each discontinuous from each other. Social competence evolving in the primary family unit may not continue to be addressed in subsequent replacement units, and new socializing elements may take precedence. In the same truncated-social category are individuals for whom successive socialization groups are not available, such that social development that should have continued in peer groups is missing.

Divergent-social identifies family units containing an element that alters significantly and enduringly the nature of family social interaction and the evolution of social competence. Families whose interaction escalates habitually to violence are mirrored in the aborted interaction attempts of adolescents whose learned pattern of engaging with others rises toward threatened violence and falls back short of its realization, replaced by disengagement and withdrawal, broken interaction reflecting social noncompetence of a particular self-protective kind (Sullivan 1996). Similarly, the interaction and relational pattern originating in families with an alcoholic or mentally ill parent are reflected in ineffective, unsustained social engagement; shallowness in relationships; uncertainty of the dependability, continuity, and rewards of social connection; and social noncompetence.

A family came to the park for an event that promised free hot dogs and soft drinks. They were seated together around a picnic table, refreshments in place, hot dogs partly eaten. All family members had their heads down and were sitting motionless before their meal. The mother and two girls seemed to be masking their faces behind long hair. The boy stared at the uneaten food in his hand and was still. One of the girls sobbed quietly behind her hair. The man was ranting at the girl and seemed to be out of control. His reaction seemed excessive, his face contorted with rage. The woman and children sat as in a still life, stunned.

As I walked past their picnic table, I wondered what could have precipitated such a violent outburst and noted that the family members' reaction was equally excessive. What should have been a pleasant occasion had become a disaster: familiar to them.

In the single-parent family unit, the strength and power of the only adult may create a reactive interaction pattern in the juvenile(s), intended to mitigate and counteract the power of one adult unmoderated by interaction with a second parent. In the absence of the moderating effects of the two-parent relationship, the juveniles appear to create their own ways of mitigating the power of the single parent, developing social interaction patterns functional to this task within the family unit, but dysfunctional in other external social situations, and appearing as socially noncompetent interaction.

> In a group of children from single-parent families, the children created an enduring uproar, such that it was difficult to bring order sufficient to initiate the program for the group session. Over the din, the social worker described how to proceed with the chosen craft, thinking that it was improbable that anyone would hear what to do. Presently the group members engaged with the craft *as though they had heard her*, and she understood their uproar as an individual strategy, pooled in the group, for managing the power of the adult.

Arrested-social is a category reflecting arrests in social and emotional development emanating from neglect, abuse, and failure to meet basic human needs, such that individuals may be arrested at an early age-stage emotionally even though they are housed in a half-grown or grown body and therefore, in social development and the acquisition of social competence, may be several years behind expected social functioning for their chronological age. While individuals in this category may have been the product of circumstances in the truncated-social category, they are given a separate category in recognition of the special dilemma they face in being out of sync with normal social development and mistakenly assumed to be age-stage developmentally appropriate.

In the *diverted-social* category, some element in the person alters or limits the capacity to interact socially and to develop social competence and may alter the capacity of others to engage well with him or her. Included are conditions such as physical disablement; altered sight, hearing, or speech; intellectual overendowment or underendowment; cognitive impairment; and mental illness.

Atrophied-social identifies a category of persons whose social competence is not in use, through homelessness, social isolation, or the effects of institutional living where social needs are not recognized or addressed.

Asocial identifies a category of persons whose social competence has not been developed, or for whom social competence is inaccessible for use, due to illness or mental health problems that impede social functioning.

Antisocial identifies a category of persons whose social competence is only partial, and who may function at odds with societal norms.

A further typology was constructed to portray the features of interaction generated by socially unskilled populations. This typology, presented in table 3.2, is intended to characterize the feature of aberrational or flawed interaction and to highlight that there is a range of interactional patterns. One of the tasks of practitioners is to recognize the collective features of interaction created by socially unskilled populations, as a diagnostic tool in determining an appropriate technology to use with a particular threshold entity.

The pervasive features of interaction in the class of threshold entities lacking social competence to form group are likely to include brief, unsustained, episodic, fractured exchanges among small subunits, primarily dyadic. Within each socially unskilled population there appear to be clearly distinguishable types of interaction, each characterized by a particular quality along the following range: thin, disengaged, and short-lived; negatively engaged; impulsively chaotically engaged; limited in engagement; dysfunctionally engaged; and oppositionally engaged.

TABLE 3.2

A Typology of Aberrational Interaction Patterns

FEATURE OF INTERACTION	INTERACTIONAL QUALITIES	POPULATION
Paucity	Interaction is inadequate, distant, withdrawn, disengaged, disconnected, intermittent, brief, limited	Institutionalized populations; isolated populations
Negativity	Interaction is negative, disparaging, insulting, antagonistic, defensive, hostile, negatively engaged, poorly connected; a pattern that counters group formation	Emotionally disturbed children and adolescents; gang groups
Impulsivity	"Simply behaving" (Mills 1967), impulsive, disconnected noninteractive except as contagion, nonengaged, nonpurposive, aimless, chaotic	Emotionally disturbed children and adolescents

(continued)

TABLE 3.2

A Typology of Aberrational Interaction Patterns (*continued*)

FEATURE OF INTERACTION	INTERACTIONAL QUALITIES	POPULATION
Wannabe	Thrust to be interactive is present; social competence is partial or absent. Meagre interaction, random, limited, unsustained engagement, partial or not developing, dyadic, brief, immature, inexperienced, tentative	Adults who have not had group belongings since childhood
Marred	Interaction is brief, episodic, escalates to critical moment and aborts; avoiding, nonsynchronous, nonprogressive, held back, thin, dysfunctionally engaged, short-circuited, shallow, withdrawing	Persons from violent families; from families containing an alcoholic parent; or from families with a mentally ill parent
Oppositional	Interaction is counteractive, partial, resistive, self protective, autonomizing, camouflaged, seemingly inattentive, intermittently synchronous, deviously engaged	Children from single-parent families

The two typologies presented in this chapter identify populations whose social competence is compromised in some way through a variety of conditions and recognize a range of interactional patterns typical of socially noncompetent performance in threshold entities unable to become groups. Knowledge of the etiology of social noncompetence and of the aberrational interaction patterns generated by socially unskilled persons is essential to shaping the technology of social work practice with collectivities and groups serving these populations

[Part II]

Group Work Practice Theory Essential to Practice with Both Socially Competent and Socially Unskilled Populations

Part 2 is focused on elements of practice theory that are relevant to all group work practice but have particular importance to practice with socially unskilled populations. The materials begin with an acknowledgment of the multiple influences activated in small groups and the view of the capability of small group use in the profession of social work. To these fundamentals is added a description of the unique interventive pattern characteristic of social work practice methodology with groups. The materials then focus on a set of professional norms relevant both to normative practice and to the specialized practice described in this book. The norms influence both the social worker and the group members and tend to create or approximate an egalitarian group form, serviceable for group work purposes and practices of the profession.

The chapters in this part identify the theoretical source materials that inform the Specialized Methodology of practice with socially unskilled populations and introduce the methodology, its context, and its contribution.

Chapter 4 reviews the social science literature on the potency of the small group, followed by a view of the domesticated small group for specialized professional purposes expressed in the literature of social work with groups.

The chapter distinguishes the capability of the professionally formed group from that of the self-formed group, reconstituted with a social worker.

Chapter 5 identifies the special characteristics of professional intervention in social work with groups, derived from the necessity of monitoring and attending multiple aspects of individual and group functioning concurrently. The interventive pattern is employed in both Mainstream practice and the Specialized Methodology, with greater demands for social worker action in the latter.

Chapter 6 presents a set of special norms emanating from the profession of social work and influencing both the social worker and the group participants. These norms have the power to create a group form unique to the profession. They tend to shape the group as egalitarian, a form well adapted for helping purposes. An egalitarian group form is desirable, permitting optimal access between members and the resources of the group and the assistance of the worker to each member. The norms, scattered through social work literature, are brought together in chapter 6 to assess their composite impact. The norms have an impact on purpose, relationships, group structure and functioning, and the ways in which the content of the group experience is shaped.

Chapters 7 and 8 present theoretical materials, identified as the Broad Range Model and the Mainstream Model, that together contribute to the Specialized Methodology of this text. The Broad Range Model defines a continuum of three group forms, each of which reflects a range in the social functioning capability of the participants, differences in the nature of the entity, and associated adaptations to the role and tasks of the social worker. The range is from allonomous groups, which require major assistance from the social worker in order to function, to autonomous groups, which function well with limited professional assistance. Between these two is an intermediate, transitional group form with some features of both allonomous and autonomous groups and incorporating aspects of the practice methodologies associated with both. The allonomous group is the most likely form achievable with socially unskilled persons.

Elements in the Mainstream Model are described. Selected features are identified that are incorporated into the Specialized Methodology as essential elements enabling the practice to be effective.

In Chapter 9 the Specialized Methodology for practice with socially unskilled populations is introduced, and its relationship to Mainstream practice is explored. The chapter identifies the context of the Specialized Methodology and its contribution to practice knowledge pertaining to work with individuals in group.

[4]

The Small Group in Life and in
Social Work Practice: Forms and Functions

This chapter begins with a brief summary of the potency of the small group; explores literature pertaining to the domesticated small group in social work and elsewhere; and examines variance in practice between self-forming and professionally assisted forming of groups in social work.

The Potency of the Small Group

The small group has been identified as a beneficial social form by a number of social and behavioral sciences. Its potency is documented in the literature of psychology, social psychology, sociology, anthropology, and organizational behavior theory, as well as being acknowledged in social work, education, and other helping professions.

Small groups in society are credited with carrying significant functions, such as providing

- humanizing and socializing experiences
- opportunities for psychosocial growth and development

- social nurture, sustenance, and support (Cooley 1909)
- an arena in which to earn peer acceptance based on performance and to acquire multiple scales on which to evaluate one's own competence, thereby developing greater complexity as a human being (Lidz 1968)
- a locus for affiliating, experiencing belonging, and maintaining the sense of social embeddedness necessary to survival (Durkheim 1951)
- a sense of identity, self-definition, self-esteem, and personal identifications
- the source for developing attitudes, values, and behavioral referents (Krech, Crutchfield, and Ballachy 1962; Verba 1961)
- specialized forms of peer socialization not available elsewhere (Elkin 1960)
- opportunity for resocialization in preparation for new roles (Brim and Wheeler 1966)
- replacement personnel who can serve as "significant others" over a lifetime (Coyle 1959; Seguin 1972)
- ongoing social influence through successive belongings in small groups across a lifetime
- intergenerational transmission and modification of culture (Wilson and Ryland 1949)
- social maintenance, social stability, and social control functions in society (Wilson and Ryland 1949)
- a context and means for collective thinking (Coyle 1930), decision making, collective problem solving, task accomplishment, and social action
- a training ground and vehicle for responsible citizen participation in society (Coyle 1959)

The small group is seen as the fundamental unit linking the individual and society, the building block of society, and the locus both for maintaining stability and for producing change in both the individual and society (Blitsten 1955). The small group, in and of itself, is also recognized as a powerful social unit, of such importance in human lives that none of us can survive long or well without such fundamental social belongings.

All these group functions can be found being employed for specialized purposes with selected populations within the profession of social work, usually in circumstances where the ordinary small group at large in society has not been effective in realizing one of its important functions (Inkeles 1969), or where social work endeavors are intended to contribute deliberately a particular small group function at a specially needed point to a vulnerable population grouping or in a vulnerable society.

Conceptions of the potency of the small group described in literature of the social and behavioral sciences appear to be normative in nature; that is, they reflect an array of social and developmental progressions presumed to occur with socially competent populations who are able to use the social influences generated within significant social group belongings. They identify the possible, when conditions enable social influence to occur, with socially able or socially developing persons in groups. The portrait of the influences of the small group on human development and social functioning highlights the loss of access to the rich benefits of group belonging for populations lacking the social skills to construct group.

The profession of social work advances the view of group use to populations with special needs. The practice methodology in this book extends it further, to populations unable to engage with others in group without special help in developing social competence.

The Domesticated Small Group for Specialized Purposes

The notion that the beneficial potential of the small group can be harnessed and deliberately maximized is present in the literature of both the social sciences and social work.

Cartwright and Zander (1968:23) suggest that

> groups mobilize powerful forces that produce effects of the utmost importance to individuals. . . . [G]roups may produce both good and bad consequences. . . . A correct understanding of group dynamics permits the possibility that desirable consequences from groups can be deliberately enhanced. Through knowledge of group dynamics, groups can be made to serve better ends, for knowledge gives power to modify human behavior and social institutions.

In the *Social Work Year Book* of 1937, Grace Coyle (1937a:2) described group work as the domesticating of the group process for educational ends. . . . The control of the group environment is concerned with . . . the development of persons through the interplay of personalities in group situations and [with] the creation of such group situations as provide for integrated, cooperative group action for common ends.

Helen Northen (1967:13) notes that

the social worker recognizes the potency of social forces that are generated within small groups and seeks to marshal them in the interest of client change. Although groups have the power to support and stimulate their members toward accomplishment of individual and corporate purposes, positive results are not necessarily achieved. The group may have very little influence on its members, or may have potent influence that is destructive for its members or for society. The development of the group therefore must not be left to chance.

Vinter (1974:5) states that

the treatment group is conceived as a small social system whose influences can be guided in planned ways to modify client behavior. The potency of the social forces generated within small groups is recognized and these forces are marshaled deliberately in pursuing goals for client change. The composition, development, and processes of the group are influenced by the worker in accordance with his purposes. The worker attempts to initiate a series of transactions, through the processes of the group, and through his own interactions with the clients, which can effect behavioral, attitudinal and other changes.

Tropp (1969:3D, 4D) states that

the natural forces of the group hold the key to individual growth and . . . the worker's main role is to help the group use these natural forces. . . . [I]f groups have the capacity, as systems of mutual aid, to help people in such fundamental and powerful ways, it behooves a social worker who wants to lead a group to view this phenomenon with . . . a healthy appreciation of the central fact that people can and do help each other in vital ways through the group experience; and that if he wants to help people through the group method, he must learn how to help groups to be effective.

Vinter (1967:16) defines the group in social work as "a deliberately structured influence system in which changes are effected by social interaction with others. . . . The practitioner attempts to develop a group which has a maximum potential for influencing [members] in desired directions." Vinter acknowledges the worker-member interactions as being of special importance in the treatment group but adds that

> potent influences are also exercised through member–member interactions, through the group's activities or program, and through its structure. All of these can be mobilized by the skilled practitioner to implement his treatment objectives [but] frequently it is the group that is implementing treatment [or] influencing the individual in directions compatible with treatment goals. . . . The worker must be concerned with every point in the group's movement, and must participate actively to guide its process in desired directions. . . . He is also concerned with the group's organization and the governing procedures it develops, as well as the quality of interpersonal relations among all the members. (17)

Schwartz (1961:15) identifies "a [symbiotic] relationship between the individual and his nurturing group . . . each needing the other for its own life and growth, and each reaching out to the other with all the strength it can command." He defines the social work function as

> to mediate the individual-social transaction as it is worked out in the specific context of those agencies . . . designed to bring together individual needs and social resources . . . the person's urge to belong to society as a full and productive member, and the society's ability to provide certain specific means for integrating its people and enriching their social contributions. . . . [T]he social worker's job is to represent and to implement the symbiotic strivings, even where these essential features are obscured from the individual, from society, or from both.

The recognition in the social sciences of beneficial group forces capable of intentional activation is operationalized in the social work concept of worker function in the group. Every author who has written about social work practice in the small group has emphasized that a major portion of the social worker's function is related to the development and functioning of the group itself. Throughout the literature on social work with groups, perhaps the most pervasive idea is that of a social worker consciously affecting group processes toward the improvement of individual functioning in group, group functioning, the accomplishment of group goals, and the realization of the beneficial by-products of individual member growth.

Elsewhere it has been observed that when the small group is deliberately employed as a helping instrument, a variety of collectivity and group forms can be identified (Lang 1979b), shaped by the nature of the profession, its ethics, its goals, and its technology.

Among the various domesticated uses of groups, group use in the profession of social work has its own distinctive features, with its emphasis on fostered and facilitated group processes, the achievement of a fully developed group, the activation of group autonomy, the mobilization of mutual aid phenomena, and the requirement for an effective, influential group capable of being dually focused on generating benefits for individual members and on the accomplishment of effective action by the whole group in the wider community (Lang 1979a).

Self-Forming and Professionally Assisted Forming of Groups in Social Work

Two distinctly different types of groups can be identified in use in social work practice with groups. The first is a type of group having conventional, natural, or *self-forming* processes, normatively developing and functioning like other groups at large in society. All aspects of the process of group formation are left to the group members to shape in typical ways, the outcome resembling all other small groups in society, with one adaptation: the contribution of the worker in the form of mediation in interaction. In this type of group, the worker does not act to influence the group form itself but enters the group interaction process at points where his or her differentiated contribution is needed. His or her sphere of influence is limited. Self-forming groups are more susceptible to inequities in the structures and processes of group life, as the more dominant and aggressive members tend to construct themselves into central positions at the expense of less able members; hence the benefits of group belonging may be distributed inequitably.

In the second type of group employed in social work there is a *professionally assisted*, deliberately influenced formation process. The contribution of the worker during the formation of the group results in an entity altered in ways characteristic of the profession of social work. Possible disparities and inequities in the structures and processes of group life are moderated through special norms that are able to rebalance the process of group formation toward a more egalitarian group form. It is an entity in which certain beneficial components of group life are activated and ensconced in unusual measure or degree, through professional help directed to the construction of the group itself. This distinctive entity is distinguishable as the Social Work Group, a unique social form capable of being replicated, once the components and processes that contribute to its development are understood.

The Concept of a Specialized Group

Our ideas about a specialized entity developed in particular ways for the accomplishment of specialized professional purposes are mixed up with ideas from small group theory about how groups in general form, develop, and function. Rosenthal (1970:53–62) identifies a problem in practice theory in the assumption of some writers that the group forms spontaneously or automatically, independently of the worker and without experiencing any influence from the presence or actions of the social worker. He suggests that in social work the group's "career" is different from that of groups at large in society; developmentally it follows a course that is at variance with those groups accounted for by small group theory.

In a general way, this difference is conveyed graphically in figure 4.1. The figure conveys the idea that special influences at work during the formation process lead to the formation of a specialized entity; when the special influences are those typically introduced by a social worker, the resulting entity will be that unique social form, the Social Work Group. The figure is intended to suggest that the entity undergoes transformations at the same time that it is engaged in the process of forming. When group formation occurs without the influence of the social worker, the need is generated for professional influence on group processes that are inequitable.

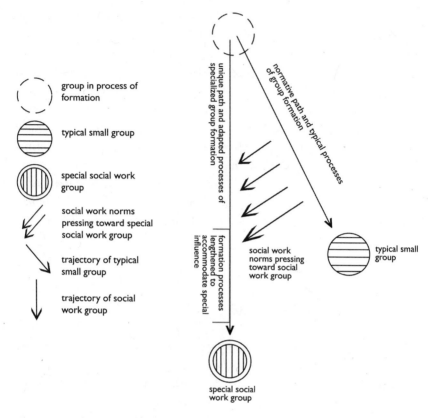

Figure 4.1 Effect of Special Influences Introduced by the Social Worker on the Formation of a Specialized Social Work Group Form

Sources of Technologies for Working with the Social Work Group

The social work technology that pertains to professional help with the formation, development, and functioning of the group itself has developed in two distinct time periods, in two distinctly different practice contexts, and in two distinctly different kinds of groups.

The earliest professional technology, related to the group itself, developed in practice in community settings, in self-formed and often preexisting groups (Wilson and Ryland 1949; Coyle 1948; Trecker 1949, 1955, 1972; Phillips 1957; Konopka 1963; Klein 1972; Tropp 1969). The social worker faced the tasks of establishing himself or herself as a part of the group, but with a differentiated role; developing relationships with each member; becoming familiar with the state of the group; monitoring its processes; and contributing in ways that might improve the structure and function-ing of the group and the position of members and opportunities for them to benefit from the group experience. The tasks were challenging when the group had existed prior to the addition of the worker. The process of reconstituting it as a social work group was frequently difficult, capable of upsetting the group structures. Because such revision could be upsetting to the group members, a technology developed for working with the group to facilitate such change in gradual, evolving ways. The clear purpose of this technology was to rearticulate the member-group relationship in ways that would allow each member to benefit from and contribute to the group experience; and to correct skews in structure and process that supported domination, isolation, scapegoating, exclusion, and other group malperfor-mances that distributed opportunities and acceptances unequally.

As remedial forms of practice developed, a second professional technol-ogy emerged, related to the group itself (Vinter 1967; Glasser, Sarri, and Vinter 1974; Northen 1969). Practice in clinical settings tended to convene strangers in formed groups in which the worker was a constituent from the outset; the group could be professionally assisted in forming. The influ-ence of the worker was stronger in this circumstance, and the time frame within which to establish an influential professional role was shorter. It was discovered that certain aspects of group life, difficult to affect in the earlier form of practice, here become accessible to worker influence as they develop: the group composition, the construction of relationships, the development of norms, the establishment of a role system, and the cre-ation of structure and operating procedures. With professional assistance in its formation, the emergent group might possess attributes supportive of a helping endeavor as it came into being.

Significantly, both of the technologies pertaining to professional help to the group itself are concerned with similar phenomena: the achieve-ment of an optimal form of group with egalitarian structures and balanced opportunities for members, and capable of influencing its members in beneficial ways. The differing technological routes emerged because dif-ferent forms of groups were employed—the self-formed and preexisting group, and the newly convened, professionally assisted formed group.

When professional assistance is contributed to reconstituting the self-formed, preexisting group for helping purposes, it enters a phase comparable to the newly convened group undergoing formation with professional assistance. These two differing technologies, the one creating disruption and revision to existing group structures, the other helping to create group structures, both lead to one specialized group form—the Social Work Group, formed or reconstituted with a worker for helping purposes and structured in ways supportive of the helping endeavor.

An examination of the literature pertaining to the two technologies for professional help in the formation, development, and functioning of the group highlights the commonalities of intent and equivalencies in technique of the worker, whether the group is formed or reconstructed for helping purposes.

Figure 4.2 portrays graphically the two routes to the Social Work Group; the one reconstituting with a social worker a preexisting, self-formed

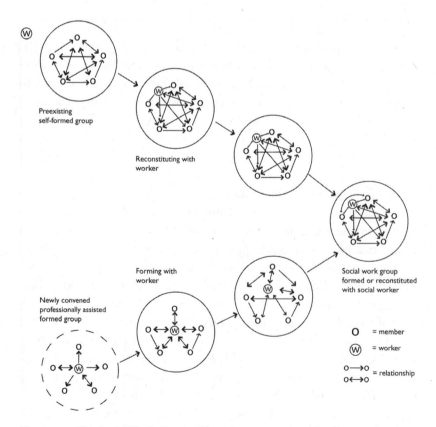

Figure 4.2 The Social Work Group: Formed or Reconstituted with a Worker

group, and the other generating a new group with professional assistance to its forming. Note the location of the social worker. In the preexisting, self-formed group, the social worker begins as an outsider with the task of entering the group's processes, establishing himself or herself as a constituent, and exerting professional influence on inequitable group processes. In contrast, the social worker is central in the initial stages of group formation in the professionally assisted formed group, exerting influence on the establishment of equitable group processes. In the professionally assisted formed group, the worker faces the tasks of facilitating group formation that is equitable and of moving out of the central locus to facilitate the functioning of the group's processes. Both routes lead to comparable outcomes in the establishment of the group, whether reconstituted or formed initially with a worker.

Social workers may not have the opportunity of forming new groups in their practice, thus facing the tasks of reconstituting preexisting groups for helping purposes. The tasks of reworking inequitable group structures and interaction processes may lengthen the time frame of the practice: it may take longer to rebalance ineffective preexisting group processes than it would to construct effective interactive patterns with participants in a new group, professionally assisted in its formation.

Concurrent Interventions
in Multiple Domains

The Essence of Social Work with Groups

This chapter characterizes the mainstream methodology of social work practice with groups in a new way. Important characteristics of this practice are identified, to make its nature clearer and to highlight it as the most complex and powerful methodology in the repertoire of social work practice with groups. The materials recognize a high-risk, ad hoc methodology that works with spontaneous, inventive social interaction of members and worker in an evolving content and group process in a "developing present," rather than employing a preset curriculum as its modality. Intervention in critical or salient moments in situ characterizes this methodology. Practitioners and educators need to preserve and use this special methodology, which is unique to the social work profession and contains the most powerful avenues in our possession for growth and change of members, group as a whole, and community.

As practices proliferate that are short-term, preplanned, curricular, manualized, psychoeducational, or worker-driven, and/or use the group only as context (Vinter 1967), there is a tendency to substitute these simpler

---

This chapter was previously published in *Social Work with Groups* 27, no. 1 (2004): 35–51. ©2004 by the Haworth Press.

technologies for the Mainstream social work group methodology, which is at the top of the repertoire for practice with social work groups. In this shift, the profession loses or eliminates the stunning possibilities of group creating, generating its own unique experience, processing its own issues in its own way, in its own order, in its own time, creating possibilities not dreamed of, and having the inputs of the social worker as a component in that process.

The chapter focuses on intervention by social workers in practice with groups. It examines dictionary and professional definitions of the term "intervention"; reviews terms and perspectives represented in practice theory to describe the activities of the social worker with groups; explores alternative descriptors of the professional contribution of the social worker to group life; and identifies unique features of social work intervention in groups that have received scant attention in the literature. The mainstream, central repertoire of interventions employed by social workers in adequately functioning groups is identified. This repertoire is extended to document interventions appropriate for use with socially unskilled populations who require specific help to function socially, to become able to form group, and to participate in and benefit from group life and group experience.

Definitions of the Term "Intervention"

The verb "to intervene," from the Latin *inter* and *venire*, means literally "to come into" or "to come between." The verb has multiple meanings and uses, of which many are classificatory in nature, and a few are relevant:

- "to come in, as something extraneous, in the course of some action, state of things, etc.; of a person, party or state: to come between in action; to interfere, interpose; also to act as an intermediary; to take a share in (obsolete)" (*Oxford English Dictionary* 1989, 8:2)
- "to come between; to intercept; to interfere with; to prevent, hinder" (*Oxford English Dictionary* 1989, 8:3)
- "to come in or between by way of hindrance or modification" (*Webster's New Collegiate Dictionary* 1977:605).

Elsewhere there is a definition of intervene as "to come into, for purposes of influencing." *Oxford* defines "intervention" as "the action of intervening, 'stepping in' or interfering in any affair so as to affect its course or issue" (8:3). All dictionary definitions of intervention carry the implication that whatever intervenes may be of a different order from that with which it intervenes.

Intervention in the Profession of Social Work

While dictionary definitions make clear that something that intervenes may be neither benign nor beneficial and may be positive or negative in nature, the term intervention in the profession of social work carries a specialized meaning and a positive connotation. Intervention is seen as the activity of the social worker "coming into" practice situations for purposes of influencing, helping, or assisting through inputs designed as beneficial contributions to the problem solving of persons using social work help.

Barker (1987:82) defines intervention as

interceding in or coming between groups of people, events, planning activities, or an individual's internal conflicts. In social work, the term is analogous to the physician's term "treatment." Many social workers prefer using "intervention" because it includes "treatment" and also encompasses the other activities social workers use to solve or prevent problems or achieve goals for social betterment. Thus it refers to psychotherapy, advocacy, mediation, social planning, community organization, finding and developing resources, and many other activities.

Hollis and Woods (1981:5–6) describe intervention as a general term, widely in use in practice, to designate the particular contribution of the social worker to the helping endeavor.

Intervention in Social Work with Groups

Intervention may be an inaccurate term to describe the activity of the social worker in groups. The social worker is an internal participant in the whole group experience as a member with a differentiated role and function and participates and shares in all that takes place as the experience of the group. Thus the contribution of the social worker, in those salient moments when professional inputs are needed, constitutes points at which the practitioner's specialized function is activated as a particular needed input designed to facilitate or enhance the interaction.

Intervention is defined as "coming into" a situation for purposes of influencing it; in the circumstance of the social worker with groups, he or she is already there and may choose to enter or not enter into a particular interactional exchange as it is taking place but shares the experiencing of it. The social worker is aware of and a participant in all that goes on in the life of the group but activates his or her professional contribution selectively, as needed.

The sense, then, is of a professional constituent whose expertise is activated whenever the circumstances require it, but who is also a part of the whole group experience and who monitors the whole, in order to be ready to contribute specialized inputs in salient moments as the group-as-a-whole and its constituent members require specific assistance. The social worker has a share in the life of the group and is seen by the members as an internal constituent. In effect, the social worker is party to everything that happens in the group but may activate his or her professional expertise intermittently.

A second reason for seeking an alternative term for describing the activities of the worker is that intervention carries the meaning of an "extraneous element" that "intrudes" or "interrupts" or "comes between" or "interferes." In social work practice with groups, the social worker's contribution is usually timely, necessary, appropriate, and useful because it arises out of ongoing monitoring of, comprehending of, and participation in the group experience. It may have the effect of redefining the situation and enabling group members to find alternative and superior resolutions, thereby enhancing the life of the group and facilitating its progression.

In effect, the worker "comes into" the entire group experience, then engages in particular moments of group interaction that require professional assistance to resolve. If the group can be helped to function well, its socializing influence on its members can be assured. Because the social worker is part of the action throughout the life of the group, his or her contribution is unlikely to be intrusive or interfering, particularly if it is directed at enabling the group experience to flow more ably and more smoothly, and to resolve what is conflictual, problematic, or impeding the progression in group experience.

Further, every member's actions have the potential to influence the group and its members; worker actions are only one of many contributions, differentiated by the professional role and function.

In the special circumstance of a preparatory pregroup experience, the worker contributions will have stronger influence because the entity begins as an unformed group, exists as a collectivity, and is in use as a *learning and practicing modality*. Because the members are unable to generate groupness until their necessary social competences are developed and in place, elements of individual and entitative influence are not yet functional.

A Special Category of Interaction

In social work practice with groups, intervention may be understood as a special category of interaction, through which the social worker adds an order of input or influence distinguishable from that contributed by the nonprofessional participants. It is contributed with the intention of adding a useful, needed component, capable of improving something in the person, the interaction, and/or the situation. It is this difference that distinguishes the interaction between the professional worker and the members of the group from the interaction among the members, and between member and group.

Conceptions of the Technology of the Social Worker with Groups

In the literature on social work practice with groups, intervention has been described in a variety of ways. The list below reflects designations over time, beginning with early descriptors, and moving to more complex conceptions. The early descriptors address the actions and activities of the worker, later defined in terms of tasks and related skills. Over time, the descriptors became more abstract conceptualizations, and eventually more definitive.

acts	skills	means of influence	procedures
actions	tasks	helping media	techniques
activities		practice principles	technical skills
		strategies of intervention	

The earliest descriptors are expressed in *actional* terms, describing the actual things that the worker does in the concrete, live moment. *Tasks* specify the things the practitioner must do; *skills* are the competences with which the professional tasks are carried out. *Means of influence* identify direct and indirect forms that interaction can take (Vinter 1967). *Helping media* identify the locations within which worker action can be staged, as well as specifying *content forms* capable of influencing the group. *Practice principles* are abstracted, conceptual directives intended to guide the practitioner in his or her actions; *procedures and techniques* address ways of doing. *Strategies of intervention* imply an approach or design for a practice. *Technical skills* highlight a repertoire of capabilities to be acquired. *Intervention* appears to be an umbrella term, subsuming worker actions.

The complexity of group life may be a strong factor in determining how intervention has been conceptualized. The existence of several frameworks for practice has also played a part in how intervention has been defined, as have a range of supporting theories. Most pervasive in all the definitional efforts is the view that if the social worker assists the group with its group processes, the group itself will implement its own powerful influences on the members; that is, to facilitate the functioning of the group itself is the primary function of the social worker, activating the group's own significant capabilities for affecting its members and the wider world (Coyle 1948; Wilson and Ryland 1949; Trecker 1949, 1955, 1972; Phillips 1957; Konopka 1963; Tropp 1969; Klein 1972; Schwartz 1961; Vinter 1967; Papell and Rothman 1966; Falck 1988; Garvin 1981; Lee 1994; Steinberg 1997; Northen and Kurland 2001).

Northen and Kurland (2001:80) state that "the primary task of the social worker is to facilitate the group process, so that the group truly becomes a prime influence on the behavior of its members." Coyle notes that

> the primary skill is the ability to establish a relationship with a group as a group. This involves the capacity to feel at ease, and, in fact, to enjoy the social interplay among members and to be able to perceive both individual behavior and its collective manifestations (for example, to be aware of the morale of the group or its network of interpersonal relations) as well as to become a part of the relationships and to affect them. (Murphy 1959:100)

Probably Middleman stands alone in her efforts to identify practitioner skills in relation to group-as-group and group-in-action, in her articles on

"Think Group" (Middleman 1986, 1987) and in the joint efforts of Middleman and Goldberg Wood in their book *Skills for Direct Practice in Social Work* (1990). These skills are described concretely, actionally, and specifically in relation to particular professional tasks.

Characteristics of Intervention in Social Work with Groups

The materials in this section examine the nature, features, and patterns of social work intervention in group. The special features of this practice derive from the necessity of attending multiple aspects of member and group life *concurrently.*

The requirement of the social worker is to be oriented and attuned at the same time to all aspects of group life: the individual members and their needs; their interpersonal, interactional engagement at individual, subgroup and whole group levels; the functioning of the group as an entity; the interaction of the group with its wider environment; and the full content and process of the group experience. This represents a considerable demand on the worker's conscious awareness of, sensitivity to, and comprehension of everything that goes on in the group. Within the enormity of the professional task in social work groups, the social worker is protected from overwhelming demand on his or her expertise by the fact that not all parts of the group system require intervention; that needed interventions do not occur simultaneously; and that as group life plays out, the interventions of the social worker are located variously, when and where needed. The interventive domains have boundaries within the systems of the group, which limits them to a manageable universe.

Nevertheless, the demand on the social worker is that he or she monitor and track sensitively and with conscious awareness, and comprehend all the interactional processes taking place in the group, so that an appropriate actional response can be made at critical or salient moments. The necessity is to be attuned concurrently, moment by moment, to a compound of individual and group needs in multiple domains.

Readinesses to act (White 1963) are generated from sensitive monitoring of group interaction processes and from accumulating knowledge and understanding of the group and its members, converting to an operationalized, appropriate actional form at critical moments when worker input is triggered.

The progression from preoperational to actional occurs as an intuitive, preconscious, rapid response, probably right-brained, and informed by knowledge of persons and situations. It appears as an unpremeditated, swift response, in place before it can be deliberated, but flowing from comprehension of the persons and processes involved.

This pattern of intervention is essential in social work practice with groups, which enables the group to become a living, manageable microcosm of life in the larger world (cf. Erikson's [1963] concept of play as a miniature, manageable domain where life events can be reworked by the child). In the group-as-life, life events are played out in miniature, in ways available to modification, improvement, growth, and development, through the impact of member, group, and worker input. This is the mainstream of our practice, in which events engage the members and group as life experienced, reality, as distinct from practices that engage the members reflectively about their lives elsewhere.

The primary benefit of groups in which the lived experience of group events becomes real life to the members is that the social worker is present, involved, and ready to intervene at optimal moments, in ways that may be crucial to the participants. Such moments when problems are manifest can be seen as unusually open to new learnings, new ways of doing, new competences to be tried out in the situation. The small, timely interventions of the social worker in real-life events, happening here-and-now, add a special dimension to the experience, intended to improve, augment, moderate, and modulate what is going on, to the benefit of individual members and group as a whole.

The Nature of the Social Work Contribution

Interventions in social work groups are of two orders: those that are lodged in the group's interactional processes, occurring as impromptu responses to episodes of group life; and those that are *planned, larger responses*, flowing out of knowledge of group and member need, and presented as a particular, staged provision to particular group and member needs that can be addressed programmatically and in a more premeditated way.

Interactional Interventions

Worker contributions flow from professional knowledge of individual and group development and functioning, the nature of the problem condition, and from specific knowledge of these members in this group in this situation with these dynamics in this moment. Readinesses to act derived from this knowledge provide the social worker with near-operational inputs that quickly convert to operational, actional form as needed.

Interventions in interaction in this practice may appear to be ad hoc, impromptu, spontaneous, unpremeditated, and unplanned, except that they are informed by and flow out of the social worker's understanding of individual and group current needs and are lodged in moments that are recognized as being needed. It is a *moment-seizing* kind of intervention.

Each intervention is located in the moment, in the situation, in the concrete, in the here-and-now, as it happens. Interventions can be seen as a continually adjusting, process-enhancing, outcome-altering process, contributed in small, concrete moments within small events. Each intervention may be small, partial, piecemeal, as responses to concrete occurrences, contributed as small inputs, in process, in situ, in multiple domains, and having incremental, cumulative effects for individual members and the group as a whole. Intervention is seen as a differentiated input, not otherwise present, in response to immediate circumstances and situations in group life. Interventions are individualized and tailored to particular aspects of member and group need and lodged in arising, salient, teachable moments.

Interventions are lodged in multiple domains of group life as they present themselves as needing professional input, occurring in relation to an individual member, in response to subgroup interchanges, the whole group, or the content of the group experience.

The pattern of intervention derives from concurrent awareness of all parts of the group's systems, portrayed in differentiating responses to multiple parts of group life concurrently. This means that the social worker is balancing awareness of events throughout the group's complex systems and adding professional inputs when and where needed. Thus, the social worker may act successively in many interventive domains, now attending to individual need, now to subgroup interaction, now to the content of the group experience, now to the functioning of the whole group.

As the group and its members grow, change, and adapt throughout the group experience, there is a constantly changing set of interventive responses as the social worker keeps abreast of changes and progressions in individual and group functioning through the task of monitoring the interactional flow and the performances of individual and group. Actual interventions are continually changing, as one set of dilemmas is taken care of and new ones present themselves in individual and group growth and development. Each intervention may be complete in itself, adequate for the specific moment in which it is generated, but inadequate as an overriding, encompassing response to the situation(s) or person(s) for which it is delivered.

Progressions are built through simple single actions in small, concrete moments, cumulating over time, repeating or advancing with changing circumstances, and totaling to a multitude of inputs capable of guiding the group and its members to new competences and performances. The nature of the practice requires time, multiple experiences, and multiple contributions from both members and worker for socializing effects of the group experience to be fully effective.

The technology of social work with groups, then, is a moment-seizing strategy, delivered in a pattern of interventions that are distributed, partial, and concurrent, lodged in multiple spheres of individual, interpersonal, and group interaction. Each intervention may be a small input, one of many, each complete in itself, and totaling cumulatively to a powerful contribution to the social functioning of individual member and group as a whole.

The challenge to the social worker in social group work practice is to be concurrently aware of and keeping track of the whole and all the parts, to know how each is doing at the present moment, and to be ready to contribute appropriate inputs on demand in multiple parts of the group system at necessary moments.

Planned, Programmatic Intervention

Planned, designed, premeditated interventions are presented as content specifically related to or in response to known needs of the group and its members that can be addressed programmatically and, frequently, in the collective. These will be content forms that are preexisting or specifically designed or adapted by the worker in response to particular needs and are capable of delivering relevant experiences to all the members.

These may be programmatic provisions related to age-stage, circumstance, problem, or situation, capable of meeting common needs of the group as a whole. Brooks (1978) provides an excellent example in her work with isolated, reclusive older men living in single rooms in a slum hotel. She designed a group for them initially to operate as a health club, using activity and exercise as a means of attracting them out of their rooms, eventually triggering a flow of communication and "a stream of mutuality" (61) in the swimming pool so powerful that it transformed the group.

Programmatic intervention that is more individualized is also a possibility:

Worker had written a play using the ideas of the group members and incorporating some possibilities for advancing individual members in their social development through the performances of their puppets in new roles. The play cast Bruce, an extremely isolated, withholding child, as a genial host, welcoming people into his home. When Worker read the play to the group and came to the part about Bruce's puppet as the genial host welcoming people, Bruce abruptly put down his work and came to stand beside Worker. "Read that part again," he said urgently, leaning against her arm.

Besides serving as an illustration of a planned, programmatic intervention, this vignette reveals a rare moment in which the deeper hopes of a socially isolated group member become visible.

Programmatic planned interventions can take many forms and represent the best understandings of the group and member needs, uniquely operationalized by the social worker at critical moments of group life in forms accessible to the participants.

In a group composed of children of single parent families, the interactional pattern of the members was one of continual uproar. Everyone talked at once, no one listened, and it seemed impossible to bring to and sustain order in the interactional arena. The worker instituted a program of game playing, using those social games that can contribute so much to the social constraint of extraneous, dysfunctional behaviors as well as engendering a game-related cooperativeness and the possibility of collective action. Within the games, members behaved like normal children, abandoning dysfunctional behaviors in the excitement of the play. Games, which create their own boundaries, their own demands for functional, disciplined performances and the sharing of roles, played a major part in moving the members forward to a more functional group life.

The Pattern of Intervention in Social Work with Groups— Carpe Momentum

We tend to see the *defining unit for intervention* as a single incident or episode involving one or more group members, containing something problematic, and joined by the social worker for purposes of contributing a specific intervention designed to enable a good resolution. When intervention is viewed only as a single action taken in response to a single incident and each incident is viewed only one by one, the pattern of intervention is not fully visible.

The pattern of intervention in social work groups highlights an extraordinary methodology in its scope, range, differentiation of parts, individualization of response in many domains, demand for multiple interventive competences on the part of the practitioner, requirement for readinesses to act in any of several spheres at any moment, and necessity to comprehend changing situations moment to moment to moment, and to respond usefully as needed.

The necessity to see the whole and all its parts at one and the same time; to track each, moment to moment; to make swift judgments about where intervention is needed, when and in what way; and to be ready to act, unrehearsed, ad hoc, in multiple domains concurrently, characterizes this practice. The pattern of intervention, in its collective manifestations, portrays a complex, sophisticated mobile methodology, capable of responding to the whole and to all its parts, to the here-and-now and to new, transforming, progressing, changing moments.

The practice does not belong only to social work practitioners with groups. It is comparable to the functioning of parents with young children, of teachers with students, except that the group session may be defined as requiring "full performance mode" for the practitioner, to the extent that the participants require social work expertise to be "at the ready," at "red alert" throughout the time-limited period they are together. In contrast, parents and teachers will have benign periods with their children over extended time periods when no particular intervention is required and the interactional system is self-sustaining.

At its best, it is a methodology that creates a compound of responses, tailored to the needs of individuals and group. Novice practitioners may recognize in the "data" of group life possible interventive points while not yet having in place all the near-operational competences to act when needed. The recognition of "intervenable moments" is a first step to becoming a skilled practitioner. Experienced practitioners will have more responses ready in place at the moment needed but in the complexity of group life, and in practice with new populations and problems, will continue to face moments and situations where interventive response is a challenge.

Learning to work first with socially competent individuals in "sufficient" groups provides opportunities to know what normative crises are likely to precipitate intervention in social work groups, and of what these interventions consist. This experience provides a normative base from which to recognize and comprehend the anomalies in the functioning of entities composed of socially unskilled persons.

"Sufficient" Groups

A sufficient group is one whose members have the social competences to evolve groupness, achieve group formation, and develop appropriate relational, normative, structural, operational, and technical components of group life so that the group experience can proceed normatively. Members possess social competence. The conflicts and struggles occurring in sufficient groups are amenable to being worked out by the members, with the intermittent assistance of the social worker being activated when needed.

Social Noncompetence

Social noncompetence is manifest in three spheres: in individual functioning that is presocial in nature; in ineffective interpersonal interaction between members; and in the inadequate formation and functioning of the entity as a whole. Social noncompetence refers to the absence of essential social skills and to the presence of dysfunctional behaviors that impede the construction of relationship.

Inexperience with Group Life

Populations that have had insufficient experience with group life may appear initially to be socially unskilled, but the provision of group experience may advance them quickly to adequate social functioning in groups. Currently, our society makes better provision for group experience for children than for adolescents and young adults. Even children's groups have become focused on specific sport or computer competence rather than on growth-producing group life.

Social noncompetence may be reflected in a compound of behaviors that may be inadequate, inappropriate, ineffective, or unrewarding. It may reflect deficits or incompleteness in individual social development, some divergence in socialization, manifest in dysfunction in social engagement and interaction. Social noncompetence presents itself as a lack of, ineptness in, or absence of necessary means to navigate the social world successfully.

Social noncompetence is the indicator of some failure in previous primary relationships to experience connection capable of nurturing, sustaining, and enabling, through which progressive social competence can be acquired. It may be reflected in flawed, marred, limited, or nonsynchronous interaction. There may be multiple types of social noncompetence, mirrored in behaviors that indicate competences that are partial or not yet learned; absence of knowledge of rules of social relationship and interaction; absence of motivation to be connected interpersonally; or absence of empathy in interactional response to others.

Personality formation and development is the precondition and means for the construction of interpersonal relationships and the evolution of groups. In practice with socially unskilled populations in intending groups, intrapersonal matters may impede sociality in some of the participants, a fact that generates a requirement for a level of intervention not usually needed in practice with groups, and for extensions of the practice methodology to meet needs preceding and preliminary to interpersonal engagement. When intrapersonal matters are settled, interpersonal connection is facilitated along a social growth continuum.

Social noncompetence is a limiting condition, both for interpersonal connection and for group belonging and group functioning. It calls for a specialized use of the interventive patterns described in this chapter, amounting to a second distinctive methodology of practice in which the whole interventive response is stepped up, in frequency and foci.

The chapter has characterized the nature of the Mainstream social work practice that makes full use of group processes, highlighting the nature of the intervention of the worker as ad hoc, spontaneous, in critical moments of group interaction, as well as in planned, improvised responses to known needs of members and group as a whole. The chapter recognizes the need to extend the methodology beyond use with adequately functioning groups to use with socially unskilled populations who require special help to function socially, form group, and participate in group life.

6

The Social Work Group
as Unique Social Form

Influence of Professional Norms

The materials in chapter 7 on small social forms will portray the nature of the entity created by populations of varying social competence, the level of individual member competence being reflected in the ableness of the resultant social form. While the extent of competence of the members for social life in small groups determines the nature of the group they are able to create—whether allonomous, transitional, or autonomous—the social worker may activate a set of influences that will shape the group form in special ways, with particular distinguishing characteristics and functions.

An earlier version of this chapter, entitled "Some Defining Characteristics of the Social Work Group: Unique Social Form," was presented at the First Symposium of the Committee on the Advancement of Social Work with Groups, Cleveland, Ohio, 1979, and published in *Proceedings 1979 Symposium*, ed. Sonia Leib Abels and Paul Abels, 18–50 (Hebron, Conn.: Practitioners Press, 1981). This committee of caring practitioners and educators, the forerunner of the Association for the Advancement of Social Work with Groups, was concerned about the absence of any forum through which people engaged in the practice and teaching of social group work could communicate. Following the establishment of the journal *Social Work with Groups* in 1978, this loose collectivity of social work professionals initiated its first symposium in 1979.

This chapter examines the special group form created by the establishment of a set of professional norms that define how the members can be related and how they can function together usefully. The norms are seen to create an opportunity for members to learn experientially and to practice good ways of being related, functioning well together, knowing the benefits of belonging, experiencing social growth and acquiring or advancing social competence, through participation in this specialized group form; and discovering what they can do together as an entity.

The form itself is seen as having socializing effects on both individuals and the group, through the implementation of the set of norms pertaining to how members can be and do together. The special norms are examined as they affect the social worker, individual member, and group-as-a-whole. The activation of norms is acknowledged as generating the most specialized form of group in social work, identified as the *Social Work Group*, a social form unique to the profession of social work and differentiated from other groups used in social work that do not attain these special features.

The Social Work Group is seen as the most complex social form employed in social work practice with groups because it activates and uses group processes as the primary means of service delivery. It combines with this technology the implementing of special norms that create a group form well adapted for helping purposes. It is a group form that is particularly functional in advancing socially unskilled persons to the acquisition of social competence; as well, it is a serviceable form for social work practice with socially competent people.

Norms That Shape the Social Work Group as a Specialized Entity

The Social Work Group can be characterized as an *optimal group,* in which certain positive elements of group structure and group process, present in some measure in all groups and capable of having beneficial effects, have been activated and made operational to an unusual degree. The element that shapes the Social Work Group as a unique social form is a set of special norms that define requirements for an entity beneficial to its members and serviceable for helping purposes. Northen and Kurland (2001:40) define a norm as "a generalization concerning an expected standard of behavior in any matter of consequence to the group. It incorporates a value judgment. A set of norms defines the ranges of behavior that will be tolerated within the group and introduces a certain amount of regularity and predictability in the group's functioning. . . . Norms serve as the principal means of control within a group." Mills (1967:7) states that norms "help orient persons to each other by providing guidelines as to how certain universal interpersonal issues are to be managed."

The norms are scattered through the literature of social work with groups and have been identified singly in the writings of many authors. The ways in which they contribute together to the shaping of a special form of group were explored initially at the first symposium of the Committee for the Advancement of Social Work with Groups (Lang 1981).

The chapter brings together these special norms to examine the contribution of each to the creation of a special form of group; to trace the outcome of each as it functions as a variable, influencing the way the group forms and functions; and to explain their combined potency. The special norms that shape the unique entity the Social Work Group are examined as they apply to the social worker, the members, and the group, and the impact of each norm is identified. The power of the norms to socialize individual members to functional ways of going, as well as to shape a special social form, functional for social work purposes, is explored. Finally, the special function of the norms for socially unskilled populations is examined.

The special norms that shape the Social Work Group are activated in the purposive, relational, structural, operational, and programmatic aspects of group life, operating at variance in particular patterns not typical of, or occurring accidentally in, small groups generally. They appear to derive their variant form from the specialized professional purposes for which the group has been convened, and in turn they contribute to the development of a specialized egalitarian structure that makes possible the entry of the group into a productive realm comparable to that of a mature group. In this respect, the Social Work Group may be seen to follow a developmental course that differs from that described as phases of development of small groups at large in society.

The norms appear as paired or matched requirements that are intended to influence the functioning of both members and worker in similar ways. Wherever there is a specialized requirement for worker engagement or performance, there appears to be also a similar requirement for the group members.

Norms that have been identified as "specializing," which contribute to the construction of a special kind of group, are listed in table 6.1 and treated one by one in the discussion that follows. The table is intended to show the norms for group life occurring in the Social Work Group that lead to its formation as a unique social form, distinguishable from other groups and capable of replication. It identifies features that both singly and in interaction with each other lead to the development of an egalitarian structure. It is difficult to separate them for purposes of analysis because they are so intertwined and interactive. The table highlights five aspects of group life that occur differently in the Social Work Group and appear to be essential to the construction of a specialized group form for helping purposes.

Purpose

The purposes for which social work groups are convened are more specialized than those found in small groups outside of the profession. The domesticated small group in social work may hold purposes not unlike those of groups at large in society, but the implication of being convened by or reconstituted with a social worker under professional auspices is that the group may not be able to accomplish its purposes, or may accomplish them badly, without the specialized contribution of the professional worker. In some sense, the combining of normative group processes with the specialized contribution of the social worker may be seen as ensuring beneficial outcomes that otherwise might be left to chance.

The small group in social work is shaped by this special purposive dimension and by the context in which it is convened. It is created or constituted for special purposes, with particular goals, in the context of a social agency with a professional person; its life span is shaped by its purposive nature; it is terminated when the special purpose is accomplished, or reconstituted as an ongoing group with a new purpose (Greenfield and Rothman 1987).

The social worker brings to the group a differentiated professional purpose, a *helping* purpose, addressed either to assisting the group in the accomplishment of the members' collective purposes, to helping members achieve their individual purposes, or to achieving purposes that the professional holds for the members and for the group, and which reflect his or her understanding of the special needs and deeper hopes and aspirations of the members. Professional and member purposes are combined in a compound unlike that occurring in groups without a social worker. The

TABLE 6.1

Special Norms That Contribute to the Formation of the Social Work Group

COMPONENT OF GROUP LIFE	SPECIAL NORMS RELATED TO WORKER	SPECIAL NORMS RELATED TO GROUP MEMBERS AND GROUP
Purpose	Differentiated helping purpose for worker	Differentiated group purpose under professional auspice
Relationships	Professional norm for acceptance in worker–member relationships	Norms for open relationship system Norm for acceptance, tolerance of difference in member-member relationships Norm for mutual aid
Structure	Professional norm for activation of group autonomy Professional norm for constraining worker power Professional norm for activation of democratic group processes	Norm for open communication system Norm for open, flexible role system Norm for distributing members' power Norm for egalitarian group process
Operation	Professional norm for worker mediation in group interaction	Norm for participating Norm for participating togetherNorm for effective participation and productive work Norm for development of technical competence of members for group functioning
Content	Professional norm for worker mediation in interaction between content, group process, and individual members	Norm for open, flexible program content forms and range

addition of a helping purpose to the purposes held by the group and its members inevitably transforms the entity from a small group in society to a specialized small group under professional auspices and can be expected to activate a specialized function, role, and contribution for the worker. These dimensions will not be present in groups at large in society. Even if the worker has no other purpose than that of helping the members achieve their purposes, this helping purpose will activate worker behaviors and contributions that distinguish the group from other groups in society.

The establishment of a specialized group containing a constituent with a special helping purpose sets the stage for a number of dimensions of group life to be evolved in ways unique to the Social Work Group.

Rosenthal (1970: 54, 74–87) identifies the differences from the members, personified in and represented by the social worker's presence and initiatives in the group, and seen as the source of an initial dynamic capable of creating strains that press the members toward "a special form or type of social process," a group formation distinguishable as a social work group. He cites factors through which the worker's differential involvement and response are manifest in terms of agency and profession, rather than as a coparticipant with similar interests and needs.

> What distinguishes the *social group work group* from every other group [is the fact that it] is constrained by the focus of the social worker and consequently its career, particularly during the formative period, is quite different (or only accidentally similar) to other groups during their Beginnings. Further, the creative "by-product" of the *social group work group* is only present incidentally, if at all in other groups and then by accident. . . . It is the accident that the social group worker seeks to install as the regular through the use of the social group work method. (Rosenthal 1970:81–82)[1]

---

1. Rosenthal (1970) employs the term "social group work group" to designate this specialized entity in the profession of social work. This designation derives from the descriptor of practice of social group work, our earliest label, later redefined as social work practice with groups. Although this is certainly the most accurate descriptor of the entity employed in social group work practice, it is semantically confusing. For this reason, this book uses the simpler designation "Social Work Group."

Groups convened in social work may reflect an additional purpose that has the effect of differentiating the group from other groups, from the perspective of the members. The group may be defined explicitly as having a *specialized group purpose* of being employed for the benefits of members or of the larger community. In this sense, a specialized group purpose may exist in the minds of the members as well as in the mind of the worker.

These specializing features may account for the need of groups convened for or with a professional purpose to give more attention to the articulation of purpose, and for the need to combine professional and member purposes in a compound purpose unlike that occurring in groups without a social worker. Variance in all subsequent components appears to stem from the specialized nature of purpose in the Social Work Group.

Relationships

Several authors identify relationship components that are distinctive to the Social Work Group. These are discussed below in terms of the differentiated relationship between worker and member, and in terms of the specialized relationships developed between members.

The Worker–Member Relationship

The worker–member relationship is the one specialized, differentiated relationship (Lang 1967) within the group, replicated between the worker and each member and expressed also between the worker and the group as a whole.

The worker brings to and reflects in this relationship with each member of the group professional convictions about the worth, value, and uniqueness of the individual; the capacity of the individual to grow, to be self-determining and to achieve self-realization, to contribute usefully and responsibly to the larger endeavor of the group as a whole and through the group to the larger society beyond. The worker deals with the group as an entity within this same framework. This stance is directed by an important professional norm for acceptance and valuing of the individual.

This single component, the differentiated relationship, makes for a species of relationship in which the member feels valued, worthy, nurtured, supported, and held in esteem. The member responds to the worker's favorable reflections of himself or herself with an impetus toward growth and toward identifying with the group in which these favorable reflections are experienced (Perlman 1957:69).

As this set of worker–member relationships develops in the group, it constitutes a matrix of specialized relationships all characterized by components of acceptance, understanding, and the valuing of the individual. At the same time as members are experiencing the worker's valuing of them as individuals, each also sees the others being valued similarly by the worker. Over time the members may incorporate this *modeled relationship* and re-create it in an additional dimension—the member–member relationship. Relationships among members may then be characterized by unusual acceptance, respect, and interpersonal valuing.

The Member–Member Relationship

The beneficial potential of the small group seems to arise and become activated when a set of positive interpersonal relationships is constructed and the damaging potential of negative, conflictual relationships is suspended. Indeed, the group itself cannot come into being without "a preponderance of positive ties" (Northen 1969:48) born of mutual acceptance.

Schwartz (1961:18) defines the need to develop a mutual aid system containing "many helping relationships." Northen (1969:25) emphasizes the importance for the social work group of a set of mutually accepting interdependent relationships.

This recognition of the "acceptance process" (Rosenthal 1970:83) not only as a key dynamic in the formation of the group but also as a necessary condition for the generation of beneficial effects in the group has been formalized in the articulation of a specialized norm for the Social Work Group. Northen (1969:40) identifies this crucial norm for the acceptance of difference, for interpersonal tolerance.

The norm is established in several ways: it may be *articulated* as such by the social worker; in the worker's own relating to members, interpersonal acceptance and tolerance of difference will be *demonstrated*; and the social worker, hoping to assist the members in achieving effective group processes and in experiencing balance and accommodation in interpersonal exchange, may *mediate* in interaction in ways that foster interpersonal tolerance and acceptance.

This norm signals the expectation that this will be a special kind of group. Such a norm has the effect of moderating the natural likes and dislikes that normally take shape among the members of a group at large, constraining members to form a special kind of relationship in which particular efforts are made to accept, tolerate, and differentiate each member.

Interpersonal patterning is made more rational and purposive by this norm: members are constrained to go beyond natural interpersonal reactions to achieve a more moderated form of interpersonal ties. Members are invited to extend themselves beyond their customary ways of relating, to stretch their capacity for interpersonal tolerance and acceptance, to extend their capacity to individualize and differentiate one another, and to try out a new species of relationship.

The outcome of this norm is the emergence of an *altered affective structure* in which members attempt to be satisfactorily related to each other. Subgroups may be less prominent, less fixed, with less rigid boundaries, and interchange across the larger whole may be more typical. The possibility is increased of interpersonal relationships being developed between and among all the members, and of the interpersonal relationships being characterized by acceptance. The affective structure of interpersonal relationships may become *horizontally structured* rather than vertically or hierarchically structured, with a reduced need for status strivings when each member is individualized, accepted, and appreciated for what he or she is. This relationship structure could be characterized as an *open relationship system*, in a designation comparable to that of the open communication system described in the social work literature.

Colleagual help may arise when a network of caring, valuing relationships has been established; in some groups in social work it may be fostered as well by the articulation of a second specialized norm for helping one another.[2]

---

2. I have coined the term "colleagual" to convey the precise meaning "of colleagues or peers."

Structure

In the Social Work Group, certain adaptations to group structure are
sought. These arise out of the variant operation of certain components of
group life.

Specialized Structural Components Related to Group Members

The first structural component is the requirement for an *open communication system* (Lang 1967:4–5; Northen 1969:18). It follows from the establishment of a set of relationships in which each member is acknowledged,
valued, and respected that each member's contribution to the group will
also be valued. The communication system of the group therefore needs
to be structured to allow each member to be heard and to make his or
her contribution, with every contribution received, valued, and used by the
group. Northen identifies the open communication system as one that provides for the "achievement of a pattern that is predominantly one of integrated interaction."

A norm for an open communication system may be articulated as such,
or the mediation of the social worker in interaction may demonstrate it
visibly. An open communication system evolves in the group as the open
relationship network brings acknowledgment of each member's inputs,
and as the group members are encouraged to achieve a pattern of communication capable of involving everyone.

The outcome of the development of an open communication system
is the establishment of *access channels* between the individual member
and the group as a whole and between and among the members, channels through and along which there can be a two-way flow of resources
from individual to group and from group to individual, and among worker,
group, and individual.

These channels represent a structural adaptation from those typically
found in groups at large, where the distribution of opportunity to be heard,
to contribute to, and to receive from the group may be inequitably patterned, excluding some members, limiting others, and giving a disproportionate hearing to still others.

A second structural adaptation suggested by several writers might be
identified as an *open role system*, that is, a circumstance in which role

entry, occupancy, and exit are fluid rather than fixed, and role sharing and interchange are possible. Schwartz and Northen both suggest this in their descriptions of the role of the members as a collaborative one in the explicit sense of members becoming both helpers and helpees to one another (Schwartz 1961:18; Northen 1969:31, 48).

In a wider sense, however, the multitude of roles required for effective group functioning is defined both in social work and in small group theory as being capable of being shared and distributed among the members (Cartwright and Zander 1968:304–5).

Better outcomes for group and members are envisioned when there is equality of opportunity for role occupancy and role alternation: for the group in terms of its being able to access the maximum possibility for multiple members' contribution in a given role; and for the individual member in terms of having full opportunity for extending competence for performing in a range of roles.

A key notion expressed in the literature about the open role system is that a *delay in group formation* may prevent premature structuring and avoid the establishment of the more aggressive and domineering members in a fixed role network. A critical moment is passed in the progression toward the formation of the Social Work Group when the initial role occupancies typical of most small groups are bypassed in favor of a more open role network, resulting in a more equitable structuring of the group (Sarri and Galinsky 1964:29–30; Rosenthal 1970:80).

The thrust of the pressure to form an open role system is to establish a power-distribution and power-sharing structure, establish flexibility in the functioning of the group, and extend the hierarchy-free relationship structure to include that of the role structure (Bundy, Lang, and Klein 1954; Klein 1972:94–95).

Specialized Structural Components Related to the Worker

A pervasive ethical idea in the literature throughout the history of the profession is expressed as a requirement for the employment of democratic group processes (Lindeman 1939; Coyle 1947; Wilson and Ryland 1949; Trecker 1949, 1955, 1972; Klein 1953; Konopka 1963; Tropp 1971; Somers 1976). Historically, this concept was important in North American society at the time that early forms of practice with groups were being developed, and it became constructed into practice modalities as a central concept (Somers 1976; Papell and Rothman 1966).

Several ideas appear to be contained within the concept of the democratic group, including acknowledgment of the group as an autonomous, self-governing, and self-directing unit; the conception of the small group as a training ground for contributing to a democratic society through experiencing the little democracy of the small group; "the idea that the individual can influence, manipulate, change or even control his environment" through collective action taken by the small group (Somers 1976:335); the notion that the democratic form allows for every individual to participate, contribute, and benefit more fully than do totalitarian forms (Konopka 1963); and the notion that the society is stronger when all its constituents can contribute and when society is structured to receive their contribution.

When the forms of group practice in social work became diversified, the concept of democratic group functioning seemed difficult to incorporate, particularly in practices focused on the treatment of individuals, which do not develop the group as group; and those practices that are cognitively focused and curricular in nature, not attuned to group processes and the development of a functioning group. In these practices, "group" is nominal, in name only, serving only as context (Vinter 1974). In the author's own practice, the goal of achieving a developed group to the extent possible, functioning equitably, was central to the treatment group, in recognition that the group contributes elements that the social worker cannot. Levine (1979) reaffirms the notion of an autonomous group in the group treatment sphere, asserting that individual growth cannot occur unless the group members are enabled and encouraged to achieve an autonomous group state and take control from the worker, who must be prepared to cede it. While he recognizes the need for group autonomy, he does not address the issue of democratic group processes.

The ideological aspects of the concept of democratic group functioning seem to have obscured the more central nonideological component: namely, that a particular kind of social structure lends itself to enlarged and enhanced opportunity for members to give to and benefit from the group experience, to contribute to the larger community through the group, and to take back into their individual selves the increments to individual growth arising from that experience.

A professional norm of activating democratic group functioning is realized in the achievement of an *egalitarian structure* in the social work group. A related concept, which reflects the influence of social work values on the practitioner role, is present in the literature over time but finds its best articulation in the writings of Rosenthal.

Rosenthal (1973:61) suggests that the social worker may be active and directive in the formative period of the group, helping it to become a social work group rather than just a group, but that he or she is constrained by twin professional norms to encourage and foster group autonomy, and to curtail his or her power and "shield individuals from his or her (possible) domination, inadvertent though it may be," through performance in a professional role that defines his or her involvement as an instrumental, non–personally engaged, non–self-seeking constituent.

The specialized structural component of the social work group thus is reflected by the presence of a social worker in an influential structural position without personal power, constrained not to dominate the group, but rather to assist it in its autonomous and democratic functioning through performance in an enabling, instrumental, participating role. The constraint of undue constituent power is thus the outcome of the specialized structural adaptation for both the worker and the members, achieved through the development of an egalitarian structure.

Operation

Specialized Operational Requirement for the Worker

The professional task of the social worker is to *mediate in group interaction*. This term is intended to describe the entry of the worker into the group interactional processes with the intent of offering assistance at points of difficulty. This use of "mediation" is somewhat more specific than that employed by Schwartz (1961) and Shulman (1968), although it could be viewed as a particular example of the mediation between individual and society described by Schwartz (15).

Mediation in interaction in social work groups is uniquely related to knowledge of small group processes, of the problems of small group functioning, of the problems of individuals as they endeavor to be part of the group, and of the struggles of the group to be appropriately related to its larger environment.

The social worker learns to recognize in the raw data of group interaction the possibility that the dynamics of a particular critical incident in the life of the group are being insufficiently or inappropriately resolved and therefore are in danger of being structured into the group's ongoing functioning as a harmful, inefficient, or useless recurring dynamic or needless obstacle. The social worker learns to project forward in his or her mind the concrete, problematic dynamics of the present moment in the life of the group, against the more abstract knowledge and experience he or she holds about group functioning, exploring the import for the group if these are not resolved (Bloom 1975). Knowledge of such group phenomena as isolation; domination; scapegoating; nonparticipation; exclusion; and inadequate mechanisms for conflict resolution, agenda processing and decision making provide the framework for the professional judgments that shape worker actions intended to mediate, moderate, modulate, and facilitate group processes that are problematic for the group and its members.

Worker mediation in interaction has two major effects on group functioning. First, it assists members to find improved ways of working together, more skilled means of processing the "data" of the group experience, and superior solutions. At the same time as mediation in group interaction assists in dealing with moment-to-moment challenges arising when members of a group interact with one another around content significant to them, it also establishes through demonstration the means to the accomplishment of improved forms of handling interactional difficulties and inadequacies. Thus, as members are processing vital issues with the assistance of the worker, the group is also evolving toward expanded and improved technical skills for handling the content and process of group life.

Mediation in group interaction produces a moderating effect in interpersonal and group interchange, leading to a group process that may be both more rational and more interpersonally attuned, characterized by skill in processing group issues and in functioning effectively as a group. Inequities in interaction are rebalanced by the contribution of the worker.

Specialized Operational Requirement for Group Members

In addition to the influence of a worker mediating in interaction, there appear to be specific norms activated in the social work group that are concerned with the nature of member and group functioning. Sarri and Galinsky (1964:30) identify one such norm as a norm for *effective participation*. This norm recognizes the infinite number of problems in engagement and participation that can be manifest by group members as they struggle to be part of a larger whole. It implies that an effective group in social work will be one in which problems in the activation and regulation of member participation are faced and solved. For some socially unskilled populations, a simple norm for *participating* may precede the norm for effective participation. Both young children and some socially unskilled adults may face the necessity of engaging and sustaining participation as a first step. For others, relevant and productive participation may need to replace bizarre and socially dysfunctional behavior (Gold and Kolodny 1978). If the open communication system regulates the ways that members will share the opportunity to communicate and participate, this norm for effective participation is addressed more particularly to the quality, quantity, and nature of the actual participation.

Related to this norm is one, either implicit or explicitly stated, for the *development of technical skill* (Lang 1972) on the part of group members for the adequate processing of the content of the group's experience. This expectation matches the thrust of worker mediation in interaction and acknowledges the possibility of a progression in the competence and effectiveness of individual participation and group interchange.

An *expectation for participating together* in a shared content may also be established in the Social Work Group. Engaging together in a *common content* is seen as contributing to the effective functioning of the group, and as defining the primary interactional sphere to be in the collective space of the group as a whole, with expectations for the give-and-take among members that Coyle (1930) describes so eloquently. The thrust of this norm is similar to that encouraged by the formation of a special set of relationships, which also tends to move the interactive arena into a collective realm.

A norm for the *accomplishment of productive work* (Wilson and Ryland 1949; Phillips 1956; Schwartz 1961; Northen 1969; Tropp 1969; Lewis 1983) may be seen to contribute to the specialized components of the social work group: it defines a *generative function* of the group and its members, establishing an expectation that the group will develop to a point of integrated achievement. This norm may have the effect of mobilizing and operationalizing for use the autonomy of the group, setting in motion a recurring cycle of productive work and group accomplishment, with beneficial increments to group and member growth as the by-product.

An early form of productive work occurs when members engage as individuals in a craft, each generating a product individually, but also experiencing a sense of the collective products of all the members, as a forerunner of producing together.

Content

Specialized Content Requirement for Group Members

A norm for what might be designated as an *open-program content* dimension is important in the Social Work Group. It incorporates the possibility that the group experience may play out through a wide variety of program content forms and media (Middleman 1968) and is the source of yet another dimension of open options and flexibility constructed into the group.

Group members are encouraged to risk themselves in a variety of forms of content, each capable of engaging different facets of the individual and of engaging the group as a whole in a variety of ways (Middleman 1968; Whittaker 1985; Vinter 1974; Boyd in Simon 1971). In this process, individual members can experience, discover, and evolve facets of their individual competence previously unknown.

An open content requirement also provides for members themselves to evolve the content of the group experience out of potentialities spontaneously arising in the group's interaction, reflective of member interests and needs, and through the worker seizing the possibilities presented by members and transforming them into content useful to all the constituents. In this process is reflected one way in which the individual member can find hidden commonalities with other members and make significant individual contributions to the experience of the larger whole. An open content requirement offers a superior possibility for constructing content that is closely related to the needs of the members and of the group as a whole.

The open content requirement also makes it possible for some of the group experience to be played out through artful, actional, activity, and analogic means, which engage parts of the person not tapped in verbal and cognitive content, and which may be central in daily functioning. "Doing" modes evoke the creative, holistic right brain functioning of human beings, enriching the development of individuals and group, and providing rich and useful channels for processing individual and group goals. Varied content forms, and group participation in these, are thus the objects of specialized norms for the engagement of group members.

Specialized Content Requirement for the Worker

For the worker, there is a specialized requirement in relation to the content of the group experience. It is quite similar in nature to that expressed in the requirement for worker mediation in interaction, but it is located in relation to substantive content of the group experience. This requirement, expressed in early literature in such terms as "the purposeful use of program" (Coyle 1949; Wilson and Ryland 1949; Phillips 1957; Konopka 1963; Middleman 1968; Vinter 1974; Whittaker 1985; Shulman 1971), is defined here as the task of *mediating in the interaction between the content, the group, the members, and the group processes*: of adapting the "fit" between the content and the group; of enabling the content to be useful and used by the group; of assisting the group in capturing those lines of potential content development that arise spontaneously in group interaction and present themselves as possibilities to be elaborated; and of introducing some forms of content that seem appropriate.

In this specialized requirement, the worker monitors the interaction between the content, the group, and the members as it occurs, observing the interplay between content and members, and playing these observations against his or her specific knowledge of the capabilities, tolerances, and needs of the group and its individual members, and of groups and individuals generally with similar age-stages, purposes, and problems. This reflective activity, which is like a test of the "goodness of fit" between content and personnel, leads to professional judgments expressed in worker actions intended to adapt usefully the interaction between content, group process, and individual members.

The effect of this requirement is an ongoing adaptation in which the content itself, the group processes arising in the playing out of content, and the interaction between the two are continually adjusted through worker mediation, rendering the content–process connection more beneficial to the group and its members. This contribution of the worker not only produces modifications in the content and the group's uses of content, making it more usable by the members; it also tends to generate a *flexibility in the handling of content* by demonstrating that the way in which the content dimension of the group experience takes place is not necessarily fixed but can be adapted for an improved fit to the needs and requirements of the group. The worker models an adaptational stance in relation to this component of group life, demonstrating that content can be shaped and modified for the benefit of the group and individual members. Individualization of the group and its members, the establishment of flexibility in use of a range of content media, flexibility in evolving and adapting each content medium to fit the group and its members, and mediation of the content–process–member connection are the products of the specialized requirements of members and of worker.

Effects of the Specialized Norms on Development of the Social Work Group

The outcome of these specialized norms, operating both separately and interactively in the Social Work Group, is the evolution of a *rationalized group* structurally and operationally developed for the maximal flow of resources between the constituent members, the group as a whole, and the environing community.[3] Table 6.2 portrays in summary form the specific effects flowing from each component.

This specialized group form is characterized by *egalitarian structures and processes*, flexibility and adaptability in its functioning, and the activation of all its constituents as participants and contributors. It is a specially designed group that creates equity in access to resources and opportunities and maximizes the activation of functioning of all its parts.

Alterations in Phase Progression

In the social work group that is professionally assisted in forming, the progression through phases of group development appears to be altered in significant ways by the activation of the specialized norms. The overall effect

---

3. The term "rationalized" is used here in the sense of "made more rational."

TABLE 6.2
Effects of the Special Norms on the Development of the Social Work Group

COMPONENT	SPECIALIZED NORMS FOR THE WORKER	SPECIALIZED NORMS FOR THE GROUP	EFFECTS OF SPECIALIZED NORMS
Relationships	Professional norm for acceptance in worker–member relationships Professional norm for helping		Development of a matrix of differentiated worker-member relation ships characterized by acceptance, valuing; a modeled special form of relationship; a modeled helping stance
		Norm for open relationship system, acceptance and tolerance of difference in member–member relationships	Development of network of accepting member-member relationships Altered affective structure—relationships elaborated among all members; flexible, less prominent subgroups; interactional sphere in collective locus of whole group Nonhierarchical structure of relationships; reduction of status strivings
		Norm for colleagual helping	Relationships characterized by cooperation, caring; mutual aid; modeled worker–member relationship replicated in member–member relationships
Structure	Professional norm for activating group autonomy		Entitative capabilities established; group energies mobilized and integrated for group-directed functioning Development of egalitarian pattern for handling and processing interaction

(continued)

TABLE 6.2
Effects of the Special Norms on the Development of the Social Work Group (*continued*)

COMPONENT	SPECIALIZED NORMS FOR THE WORKER	SPECIALIZED NORMS FOR THE GROUP	EFFECTS OF SPECIALIZED NORMS
	Professional norm for activating democratic group processes Professional norm for constraining worker power		Worker contribution bounded within instrumental role; constraint of undue worker power
		Norm for open communication system	Development of channels of equitable access; establishment of opportunity-sharing; establishment of expectation for every member contribution
		Norm for open role system	Development of pattern of of role-sharing; flexibility in role entry, occupancy, and exit; role interchange
			Regulation and constraint of undue member power; power-sharing
			Delay in group formation
Operation	Professional norm for worker mediation in interaction		Development of egalitarian ways of working together; a rationalized process established
			Development of skills in processing the group's agenda
			Achievement of superior solutions/resolutions
		Norm for participating together	Engagement of all members in interaction;
		Norm for effective participation	participation in a collective realm

(*continued*)

TABLE 6.2

Effects of the Special Norms on the Development of the Social Work Group (*continued*)

COMPONENT	SPECIALIZED NORMS FOR THE WORKER	SPECIALIZED NORMS FOR THE GROUP	EFFECTS OF SPECIALIZED NORMS
		Norm for development of technical skills for group participation	Development of improved ways of working together; predisposition to recognize member contributions
			Development of member skills in processing group agenda
Content	Professional norm for worker mediation in interaction between content, group processes and members		Establishment of flexibility in choice and use of content Adaptation of content for improved fit to group Evolution and development of content
		Norm for open content range and possibilities	Development of flexibility in content forms and uses
			Development of content evolving out of and close to member interest/need/ competency, rather than precast

appears to be that the formation process is lengthened, the development period shortened, and the phase of productive functioning extended.

Differentiation and individualization of members are activated in the beginning, and power and control issues are mediated by specialized norms. Structural features that may evolve in other groups over time are initiated from the beginning in the social work group, and entry into the productive realm of the mature group may occur sooner.

The Social Work Group thus appears to provide a means of entering the realm of the mature, autonomously functioning group, and of accessing the benefits of it, without having to spend an undue amount of time and energy en route or running the risk of becoming either stuck in the passage through phases or hierarchically structured or power-centralized in ways that would render the group ineffective for helping purposes.

The activation of specialized norms that shape the social work group may be seen as providing an alternative route to entry into productive functioning, with a shorter time in passage and a greater assurance of arrival.

Natural but Mediated Group Processes

At a conceptual level, some of these ideas tend to suggest an ideal type rather than a real group with all its struggles. The raw material of group interaction in this specialized group will be typical of all groups, except to the extent that the specialized norms moderate it. The same struggles and conflicts are present in social work groups as in groups at large in society: these may be handled differently in the Social Work Group. Indeed, the way in which these struggles are resolved will determine whether the group will advance into the specialized form identified as the Social Work Group.

The mediation of the worker in the evolution of the substantive content in the life of the group will tend to move the group toward a *pattern of improved issue processing* resulting in better solutions and resolutions. As well, the members experience the processing of issues as a kind of training ground for problem solving in all groups, and as a locus for learning to contribute to and take from the group experience—an "arena for coping" (Maier 1965:29). Such experiences in being usefully related and in handling issue processing adequately may provide a model or prototype for members to carry with them to other groups.

A Continuum of Development as a Social Work Group

The activation of the Social Work Group represents the most specialized capability of the profession of social work's group use. It may not be achieved, however, or it may evolve only partially, depending on which components are activated.

At one extreme, if all the specialized components that create a maximized group are activated but group autonomy is not fostered or not possible, the outcome may be a partially developed collectivity (Lang 1979b), in which there is unusually good access between the worker and each member, but no group autonomy to safeguard the entity from domination or manipulation by the worker.

At the other extreme, if the group has been self-formed without activation of the special norms and the only professional input is that of worker mediation in interaction, inequities in structure and negatives in relationship may make it difficult for the worker to help enough, and for each member and the group as a whole to give and receive the benefits they need.

In the middle range of this continuum, some groups in social work may approach the specialized features of the Social Work Group without fully realizing them, such that the potentially harmful components of groups at large may become merely benign in the group, and group structures will show some modification in the direction of activating the group's beneficial potential.

The formed group in which members and worker begin together without prior relationships to each other may be seen as an especially desirable circumstance for activating the special dimensions of the Social Work Group whenever the members, if unassisted, are likely to re-create severely dysfunctional, destructive, or hostile relationships and inequitable structures that are extremely difficult to modify, once established.

The Usefulness of the Social Work Group for a Range of Practice Purposes

The Social Work Group in which egalitarian structures have been achieved and entry into autonomous, productive group functioning is possible presents itself as a superior entity for use across the practice continuum. Its characteristics make it a superb instrument for providing beneficial group experiences to individuals with particular problems, as well as an extremely useful entity for the addressing of collective goals, task accomplishment, and social action.

Recognition of and trust in the efficacy of the group itself, and definition of an instrumental role for the social work practitioner in relation to the group, have produced a specialized technology for the social worker, expressed in professional help in the forming and functioning of the group qua group. The intent of social work practice is to assist in the construction of an optimal entity, in the knowledge that beneficial effects will flow from the group itself and from the activation of colleagual forms of help.

Special norms uniquely activated and combined in the group practice of the profession of social work appear to account for the emergence of a specialized group form for helping purposes: the Social Work Group. Acknowledgment of this specialized entity with its powerful potential appears to have been delayed until the special norms that shape it could be brought together from scattered locations in the literature and their contributions examined. Until Rosenthal clarified it, an ideological inhibition also may have prevented the profession from reconciling the directiveness of social worker influences on the formation of the group with the instrumental role of the social worker in an autonomous, democratically functioning group.

The justification for professional intrusion on natural processes of group formation, and for introducing a professionally assisted route to the achievement of egalitarian structures and productive functioning of the group, lies in our professional intent to facilitate the creation of a highly useful entity in an efficient time frame. The professional purpose remains instrumental; there is no intent to co-opt the group but only to help the group members shape and use a superior entity.

Creating the Social Work Group with Socially Unskilled Populations

When the constituents are socially unskilled, the entity they are able to develop will be limited by absent competence and by present dysfunctional behaviors. It will be a partially developed or incomplete group form, lacking capacity for collective functioning and action, because particular competences vital to group functioning are not yet in place and operational.

The Social Work Group form, with its fostering of accepting relationships and its provision for open systems of communication and participation, is very well suited to serving socially unskilled populations. It provides a safe, comfortable, protected place, an ambient and sustaining social experience within which the skills of social competence can be learned and practiced.

All small groups begin with energy invested in the tasks of generating the social-emotional connections of group life; when these are achieved, there can be a sudden shift in energy as the entity, now established, addresses the tasks of the group's life (Thelen 1958). With socially unskilled groups, the energy shift to group task may not occur because the energies of the participants will be focused on learning individual social competence. Socially unskilled persons may not reach the task-relevant phase of collective group life but can benefit from belonging in an ambient and emotionally supportive group experience, directing their energies to being together successfully.

The thrust of the special norms that shape the Social Work Group is the creation of an entity articulated to maximize the innate positive potential of the small group through the establishment of accepting relationships, egalitarian structures and processes, flexibility in functioning, and activation of all constituents as participants and contributors.

Norms provide guidelines for how the group members will function together as a group and may serve as the indicator of the progression from individual to group functioning, that is, the shift to behaving as a collective, as an entity, to group-as-a-whole, to social organization and social order (Mills 1967). Norms also serve to direct and contain individual behavior. The norms that generate the Social Work Group serve an additional, particular purpose for socially unskilled persons: they provide specific guidelines for how to be and do together and constitute a blueprint for achieving social competence.

In the case of socially unskilled persons, norms can carry a more profound function, that of *instructing* in social behaviors. Norms can be the avenue through which socially unskilled persons can learn and practice essentials of social functioning. The special norms thus carry a deeper, more powerful set of directives, which go beyond defining appropriate behaviors for a particular group, serving as life lessons for persons who need *social knowledge* of how to go in any or all group and social situations.

The Social Work Group thus becomes a specialized entity, acting as the context in which social competence can be learned and practiced, as well as creating an exemplar of the possible, as egalitarian small group functioning can be experienced and incorporated by the participants.

The social worker carries a double function in establishing norms that will be functional in enabling the participants both to acquire and advance their social competence and to experience equitable group functioning. Norms alone do not suffice to achieve socially competent functioning: the activities of the social worker mediating in interpersonal exchanges act as specific experienced moments containing directives for how to go—interpreting the norms behaviorally. The norms create the expectation for behaviors functional to the individual and the group; the actions of the social worker help members to know how they are manifested behavior-ally, to perform them, and to incorporate them. Invoked in situ, in concrete moments and in episodes that offer opportunities for on-site teaching and learning, the norms are made visible in the particular, teachable moment, directing how to go competently. .

Norms, then, are two-edged, affecting individual behaviors and generat-ing one of the necessary conditions for constructing group and activating entitative elements of collective life.

7

A Broad Range Model of Practice
in the Social Work Group

Group Forms and Worker Technology

The Specialized Methodology developed for work with socially unskilled persons in groups is derived from two major sources: the Broad Range Model of Practice in the social work group, and the Mainstream Model of social work with groups. The two are described in this and the following chapter.

The Broad Range Model

The Broad Range Model of practice in the social work group was generated by the author (1972) as a response to the articulation of several models of practice in the model-building period of theory development of the 1960s. Models constructed during this period arose

> when social work practice in groups no longer seemed to be encompassable within one descriptive framework. As reflected in the writings of Schwartz (1961), the NASW Frame of Reference Statement, Hartford (1964), Vinter (1965, 1967), Papell and Rothman (1966), Tropp (1969) and

---

An earlier version of this chapter was published in the *Social Service Review* 46, no. 1: 76–89. ©1972 by the University of Chicago. All rights reserved.

Klein (1970), model-building represented an attempt to acknowledge and deal with problems of complexity and disparateness by ordering the elements of dissimilar practice into separate conceptual frameworks. [T]he models have constituted a major step in theory formulation—provid[ing] ways of looking at practice differences with a wholeness and a coherence not possible before the parts were ordered into differing perceptual realities. . . . [T]he structuring of practice differences according to various models create[d] some new problems while [solving] others. (Lang 1972a:76–77)

The author developed the Broad Range Model as a response to elements, copresent in her practice with socially unskilled populations, that had been assigned to separate models in other formulations (Papell and Rothman 1966). That practice experience informed the conceptualization of the allonomous group form.

The Broad Range Model undertakes to define a continuum of group forms reflective of the social competences of the members and indicative of variances in social functioning at both the individual and group levels. The model is analytic in nature, providing a framework within which a range of groups can be classified, their features recognized, and an appropriate practice role and tasks identified for the social worker. This is a compound, dynamic, three-stage model of practice in groups in social work. For comparative purposes the model is presented in summary form in table 7.1, in which the various components are set forth as they appear in three orders of groups.

Previous model formulations have failed to differentiate various orders of group and have assumed all groups to be alike in their group aspects, even though composed of a wide variety of persons brought together for a range of purposes. The Broad Range Model formulation begins with the notion that there are different orders of group in social work, for each of which a different group form is appropriate.[1] These different orders of group are expressed in the terms "allonomous," "autonomous," and "transitional."

---

1. Mills (1967:59) also uses the notion of different orders of group, which he defines in terms of five levels of interpersonal process, of ascending complexity, through which members of a group pass. Tuckman (1964:473) demonstrates in a research study four orders of group system, each having distinguishable characteristics with regard to the nature of group structure and decision-making mechanisms.

TABLE 7.1

The Broad Range Model of Practice in Groups in Social Work

COMPONENT	GROUP FORM		
	Allonomous	Transitional	Autonomous
Unit to be worked with	Individuals	Individuals and group-as-whole	Group-as-whole
Focus of service	Individual social development and functioning	Individual social development and functioning; achievement of group social goals	Achievement of group social goals; individual functioning instrumental to group goal-achievement
Levels of social process addressed	Monadic, dyadic, subgroup	Dyadic, subgroup, group-as-whole	Group-as-whole
Form and nature of group	Instrumental socialization medium; immature group form	Instrumental socialization medium and intrinsic social reality; maturing group form	Intrinsic social reality and instrumental task medium; mature group form
Group formation and structure	Agency-constituted, with worker as central constituent; group formation and structure around worker in locus equivalent to indigenous leader; group fully developed in allonomous form	Agency-constituted, with worker as significant constituent; semi-autonomous structure, with worker moving between central and peripheral locus; group fully developed in semiautonomous form	Agency or autonomously formed, with worker as contributing constituent; autonomous structure with shared leadership, and worker locus peripheral; group fully developed in autonomous form
Nature of worker role	Primary in the functioning of group; surrogation in group processes	Variable, pivotal between surrogation when necessary and facilitation of autonomous functioning when possible	Facilitative of autonomous group functioning and social goal accomplishment

(continued)

TABLE 7.1

The Broad Range Model of Practice in Groups in Social Work (continued)

COMPONENT	GROUP FORM		
	Allonomous	Transitional	Autonomous
Nature of member	Developmentally, experientially, or circumstantially lacking capacity and skill for autonomous group engagement	Partial capacity for autonomous group engagement, not fully developed in all areas	Capable and skilled in autonomous group functioning
Group processes dealt with	All group processes extensively influenced by worker so that group formation, maintenance, and functioning are possible	All group processes dealt with by worker, with group-directed procedures to the extent possible	All group processes dealt with by worker, indirectly, with emphasis on maximum individual contribution to autonomous group functioning
Means of achieving goals of service	Worker-mediated Interaction; behavioral conditioning; ego-developmental and ego-strengthening experiences; socialization; worker management of group processes; role-modeling	Worker-mediated Interaction; behavioral conditioning; ego-development and strengthening; socialization; worker active in group processes; role-modeling; facilitation of mutual aid	Ego-strengthening; role-modeling; worker facilitation of group processes toward goal achievement, task and procedural definition and resource

"Allonomous," defined by *Webster's* (1957:70) as "controlled by stimuli acting on an organism from outside" and as "opposite of autonomous," is here used to signify "other-governed," that is, governed by the worker. "Autonomous" is here used to mean "self-governed," or, more precisely, "group-governed," with the worker in a more peripheral role. "Transitional" is used to describe a group in which there is some blend of allonomous or worker-directed group functioning and of autonomous group functioning.

"Autonomous" is a term used in the literature to describe the functioning both of the individual organism and of small and large social units; it is the assumption of the author that "allonomous" can be applied with equal appropriateness to the functioning of the individual organism and of the small group. Together, allonomous (worker-governed), transitional (worker-and-group-governed), and autonomous (group-governed) groups comprise the three orders of group contained in this model.

The prototype of these three orders of group may be found in the family, a group that is first an allonomous one in which the adult, parenting members exert primary degrees of influence and control in a governing capacity. The allonomous group form is appropriate to the personality development and socialization of its young family members, and it is the critical contributor to the subsequent autonomous functioning of its members both individually and in groups.

The normal progression for young family members is from other-directed to self-directed functioning, in stage-successive transition. In tandem with this individual developmental and socialization process, the form of the family group changes, first to a semiautonomous one in which the juveniles have a larger voice, and ultimately to a relatively autonomous group form. Since the family group's goals are met in part when the children can function autonomously and independently, the total family unit may not be sustained intact for long in the autonomous form but may be reconstituted as autonomous pairs when the maturing family members depart and establish new familial units.

It is not suggested that the allonomous group in social work is a symbolic reenactment of the family, as is held in the psychoanalytic conception of the group. Rather, it is suggested that, for certain people, an allonomous group experience may be a necessary requisite to participation in an autonomous group.

The model is based on developmental rather than clinical and remedial considerations. It is posited that, if the individual is not at a developmental or circumstantial point at which he or she can maintain a measure of minimal autonomous individual functioning, he or she will be unready and unable to be a participant in an autonomous group. Lack of readiness for autonomous group participation may stem from age-stage developmental level; inexperience in social groups; inappropriate experience in primary groups;

incomplete, faulty, or arrested psychosocial development; incomplete or faulty socialization; or need for resocialization to new circumstances.

Preautonomous individual functioning sets limits on the nature of the interpersonal engagement of the members, the readiness of the individual for emotional integration into the group, and the nature of the entity that can be created. For example, in the author's own practice experience, emotionally disturbed children of latency and preadolescent ages, poorly socialized and arrested in their psychosocial development, had much in common, in their group life, with a group of preschool four- and five-year-olds who were developing normally but on the threshold of primary socialization experiences. Their groups were distinctly similar in some respects: both were allonomous in nature, and both created similar role requirements for the worker. In some of the descriptions of neighborhood block groups organized for social-action purposes, it seems possible that the reported failure of many such groups to move beyond primary group functioning to the assumption of social action goals may be explained in terms of the members' prior need for an allonomous group experience (Turner 1968).

The Allonomous Group

Unit to Be Worked With

In the allonomous group, the individual is conceived of as the unit to be worked with. The service is focused on individual social development and on the social functioning of the individual members.

Level of Social Process

The level of social process (DeLamater, McClintock, and Becker 1965) addressed primarily is "subentitative"; that is, the necessities of the group life create monadic, dyadic, triadic, and subgroup interactions, in particular, mediated interactions engaging the worker and one or two members at a time. Worker activities with members in interaction are instrumental to the continuance of the group process; they may serve as linking pins between members not able to invest themselves in something as abstract as the group as an entity. This point of engagement with units smaller than the group as a whole is inherent in the need of the group members for a species of support and control for their functioning together, which they cannot yet achieve unaided.

FORM AND NATURE OF GROUP

In a sense, this is an immature group form, one in which the entity is a context for interaction and a means for the growth of members' capacity for entitative functioning. In nature, the group is an instrumental socialization medium rather than an intrinsic social reality, although it may take on the latter meaning to its members.

The allonomous group is likely to appear in agencies serving preautonomously functioning clients in agency-formed or reconstituted groups, with the worker as a central constituent. Something akin to the allonomous group form may be found elsewhere in society: in the school classroom, where the teacher-centered form of instruction is regarded as efficient for certain kinds of learning; in the interactive play of young children whose interactions call for intermittent mediation by a parent, teacher, or supervising adult; and perhaps in the peer group, which is sometimes characterized by having a fairly controlling, directing, indigenous leader who is more advanced than his peers in developmental level and in capacity for functioning in a group.

GROUP FORMATION AND STRUCTURE

The allonomous group is formed and structured around the worker, who is in the central locus, in a position somewhat equivalent to that of an indigenous leader. The group is fully developed in all its structures and processes but is characterized by certain evidences of the allonomous form. In particular, the worker may have a disproportionate area and degree of influence in all group processes and may be singularly active in much of the interaction. Such a structure is the critical necessity of the group. This allonomous structure has been formulated in the Remedial Model of social work practice with reference to the needs of malfunctioning clients, but without acknowledgment of the nature of the group that such clients are capable of forming. Lack of recognition of the nature of such a group has led to some misunderstanding of the nature of the worker role; it is not caprice or clinical preeminence or the need to be controlling that defines a central, directing role for the worker. His or her actions may be instrumental in maintaining an ongoing life of the group while the members are unable or unready to function autonomously.

Klein (1970:123) and Tropp (1969:14E) both argue that the complexity of group life makes it impossible for the worker to be so engaged, but they do not differentiate that they are describing interaction in a more mature social form, the autonomous group, which is capable of an entitative life of its own, regardless of worker activity.

Group functioning and process in the allonomous group are likely to be rather fragmented and episodic, more susceptible to contagion and runaway acceleration of the rate of interaction, and less predictable, less sustained, and less likely to involve all the members in an entitative fashion.

WORKER ROLE

The role of the worker is crucial to the functioning of the allonomous group. A key notion here is that of worker surrogation, a process by which a worker acts to supply missing pieces in the group process that the group members are unable to contribute. He or she does so in ways that not only bridge a gap in group process as it is occurring, but also serve as a pattern for future group and member functioning. Through surrogation, certain necessary functions and parts of process temporarily become areas of worker activity, by a process of substituting for missing member interactions and roles, activating and supporting needed group processes, and gradually giving these over to members to perform and manage as they become ready. Surrogation may occur in relation to individual role performance, interpersonal response, content, group control, group locomotion, group maintenance, group deliberation, and decision making.

Apart from surrogation in group processes, the worker in the allonomous group is likely to be a great deal more active, directing, and central in the group than he or she would need to be with an autonomous group.

NATURE OF THE MEMBER

The member is an individual functioning at a preautonomous level, lacking capacity, readiness, or skills for participation in an autonomous group.

GROUP PROCESSES DEALT WITH

The worker deals directly with all group processes and exerts extensive influence on them so that group formation, maintenance, and function are possible. The worker may be particularly active in the fostering of a sense of commonness out of similar individual goals; the development of interpersonal relationships that are mediated to minimize enmity; the establishment of norms when the members are unable to express these; the selection of experiences that may contribute to the building of cohesion without demanding intolerable amounts of cooperation; and the creation of opportunities for members to become aware of the group as an entity and to experience satisfaction from contributing to and participating in it.

MEANS OF ACHIEVING GOALS

Service or worker-defined goals seem to be more prominent in relation to the group that is not yet self-governing and self-propelled. The means of achieving the goals of service are very much shaped by the needs of the client, his or her developmental level, and the nature of the entity that he or she can create with others. The means of service in the allonomous group include worker-mediated interaction, ego-developing and ego-strengthening experiences, worker management of group processes, worker role-modeling, behavioral conditioning, and socialization of members through the influence of the group that has been strongly shaped by the worker.

The Autonomous Group

UNIT TO BE WORKED WITH

The autonomous group provides such a marked contrast to the allonomous group that it may be said to be at the other end of a continuum. The group as a whole is seen as the unit to be worked with. The service is focused on the achievement of group-defined social goals in a self-governing unit capable of collective action toward integrated group goals.

LEVEL OF SOCIAL PROCESS

The level of social process addressed is primarily the group as a whole; the point of engagement by the worker is with the functioning entity rather than with subgroup units. The worker's engagement is not instrumental to the continuance of the group, which is capable of entitative functioning without a worker. The group has no problem in forming and developing a viable entity, but its members may have things to learn and experience in order to shape the group into an efficient and effective tool for accomplishing its collective tasks and goals.

FORM AND NATURE OF GROUP

The group may be thought of as a mature group form, in that it is an intrinsic social reality that processes viable group goals and meets the mutual needs of its members. It will be an instrumental socialization medium in only minor degree; the major socialization of the members has been accomplished elsewhere.

GROUP FORMATION AND STRUCTURE

Whether an agency-formed group or an entity that is self-forming, the group is characterized by autonomous entitative functioning, with the worker as a contributing constituent. The worker is located in the group structure as a participant, in a locus and role distinctly different from that in the allonomous group; his or her influence in the autonomous group is somewhat more equivalent in extent to that shared by the members. The group is fully developed in autonomous form, with structures and processes suited to group-governed and group-directed procedures.

WORKER ROLE

The worker role is considerably modified from that appropriate to the allonomous group. The worker serves as the facilitator of autonomous functioning and plays a role in helping the group to develop a suitable entity for efficient handling of selection, processing, and attainment of group goals. A minor part of his or her role may be short-term, temporary surrogation in group processes in order to facilitate the swift development by group members of an effectively functioning entity. This role is in contrast to that of the worker in the allonomous group, who may be creating opportunities for tiny samples of limited autonomous group functioning for the members to experience as part of their learning.

NATURE OF THE MEMBER

The member in an autonomous group is an individual who has developed capacity and skill for emotional integration into the group and for functioning appropriately in it.

GROUP PROCESSES DEALT WITH

The worker may deal with all group processes, but more indirectly, since his or her influence is smaller and less pervasive. There will be less need for his or her engagement in group processes, because of the ability of the group. He or she may address some of the same aspects of group process that concern the worker with the allonomous group, but the focus of worker actions will be on the better adjustment of the individual and subgroup parts to the group as a whole and the better functioning of the entity. Like the worker in the allonomous group, he or she is concerned with individual and group functioning; in the autonomous group he or she works toward the development of maximum member contribution and full group autonomous functioning.

MEANS OF ACHIEVING GOALS

Service or worker-defined goals pertain to assisting the group to maximize its entitative functioning capacity, realize the contribution of each member, and accomplish the goals set by the group. Means of achieving these goals include occasional role-modeling, short-lived temporary or momentary assistance with group processes in an area or moment of difficult group functioning, teaching members how to deal with a particular task, enlarging members' views of goals and the means of proceeding, giving procedural assistance in the management of group processes, making contributions that assist the group in making its own adjustments and adaptations, and serving as a resource in areas in which the group lacks experience.

The Transitional Group

Between these two forms there is an intermediate form, here labeled "transitional," that has some characteristics of both the allonomous and the autonomous group and represents a transition between these two. In such a group, the worker, concerned both with individual development and functioning and with the developing entity, the group as a whole, addresses all levels of social process. He or she focuses on the social functioning of individuals and on the achievement of group-defined social goals. The group is both an instrumental socialization medium and an intrinsic social reality. It is formed with the worker as a significant constituent. It is structured for greater autonomous functioning than is the allonomous group, with the worker moving between a central and a peripheral locus, in keeping with the readiness of members to deal autonomously. The group is fully developed, in semiautonomous form. The worker pivots between surrogation in group processes, when necessary, and facilitation of autonomous functioning, when possible. The member has some capacity for autonomous group engagement, but his or her capacity is not yet fully developed in all areas. The means of service may combine worker-mediated interaction, behavioral conditioning, ego-strengthening and developing, socialization, worker facilitation of group processes, and worker role-modeling. The worker deals with all group processes and attempts to create growth-supportive norms but encourages group-directed processes to the extent possible.

Discussion

The three stages of this model have been developed through the processing and classifying of descriptions of practice of many authors. As such, it is a derived model leading to a different theoretical formulation.

The model seems to offer a way of reconciling some seeming differences in other model formulations, as well as reclassifying and integrating some practice positions that were set apart in previous models. It omits considerations of setting and eliminates the need to think of models in terms of specific goals such as "social" or "remedial" goals. It adds the notion of different orders of group, different group forms, and distinctly different worker roles related to each. It provides a means of assessing which group form and practice modality will be appropriate for which persons. Additionally, it orders the content of practice descriptions in a way that clarifies some notions about worker role. It affirms what has sometimes been viewed as an inappropriately central and directing role in the Remedial Model (Vinter 1967; Papell and Rothman 1966) and distinguishes an appropriate role for the worker in an autonomous group from notions of status and power equalization of the worker role with that of the client member. The model adds, too, the notion of worker surrogation in a faltering group process.

Furthermore, it makes clear what was uncertain in prior model formulations, namely, that in all three group forms the entity is fully developed, but with differing structures, processes, focus, goals, and worker involvement in each.

Moreover, this formulation brings a dynamic dimension into model formulations that is different from the contribution of phase theory. It offers the possibility of a complete group experience in any one of the three group forms (e.g., for some persons the total group experience might have to be allonomous), or of moving, within the life span of a single group, from allonomous to transitional, or through transitional to autonomous, or back and forth in response to the developing capacity and skills of the members for group functioning of an increasingly autonomous nature.

Finally, the model poses an important relationship between the functioning capacity of the individual and the nature of the resulting entity that individuals of a given capacity are able to form.

The Broad Range Model locates socially unskilled populations at the less able end of the group functioning continuum and identifies features of group life for which a particular worker role is necessary. It informs the nature of the practice and points to the predominant features of the social work practice methodology with allonomous groups.

In the next chapter, characteristics of the Mainstream Model are examined, and those features that are incorporated into the Specialized Methodology are identified. The methodology itself is introduced in chapter 9 and elaborated in detail in part 3.

[8]

The Mainstream Model of Practice in Social Work Groups

The Broad Range Model serves to locate practice with socially unskilled populations in the allonomous group form, and to identify a social worker role that is active and directive in response to their needs and functioning level. The Mainstream Model contributes elements to the actual practice that have the capacity to sustain individual participants and the entity in a pregroup, prerelational period. In this chapter, the main characteristics of the Mainstream Model of practice in social work groups are presented. Specific features of the model are identified that are essential elements incorporated into the Specialized Methodology for work with socially unskilled populations.

The Mainstream Model can be characterized as a descriptive model, the central features of which have accumulated from a wide array of practice settings and practice over an extensive time period.

The Mainstream Model

"Mainstream" is a term used by several contemporary authors to describe the predominant form of practice of social work with groups through time, from its beginning specification to the more recent period when additional practice forms have developed. Earlier authors described what has been the prevailing practice of the past half century without requiring this designation—it *was* the Mainstream.

The Mainstream Model of practice, originally conceptualized as social group work by a number of practitioners and theoreticians and sustained as our principal, enduring methodology through time, is recognized as a powerful and effective means to enable social growth and development, as well as a central means to effect change in the wider world. It is a versatile, adaptable practice, serviceable with varied populations in multiple settings.

While some of the more recent practice forms make more limited use of the group as the central means of growth and change, the term "Mainstream" may be used to highlight the prevailing practice as one in which the group and its processes are central. "Mainstream" is a term designating specific elements essential to the practice of social work with groups, as it was originally conceptualized and subsequently elaborated by a number of practitioner-theoreticians who have undertaken the description of the practice. Several authors use the term (Lang 1979a, 1979b; Papell and Rothman 1980; Alissi 1980, 2001; Garvin, Gutiérrez, and Galinsky 2004), and each makes specific reference to the prevailing Mainstream practice in some way.

Lang (1979a, 1979b:207–17), in comparing the central features of group use in social work with the group practices of other professions, identified essential elements of social work's Mainstream practice with groups. These include the use of the social group; use of a developed group; use of natural, nonsynthetic, spontaneous interaction processes; recognition of the group as an authentic social reality; group experiences as an analogic, nonlinear route to change; a practice methodology related to the group and its processes; constraint of worker power and activation of member and group autonomy; and multiple means of growth and change emergent from the group's processes, of which the worker's contribution is one part.

Alissi (2001:5) identified five common elements: "Democratic participation, the pursuit of common goals, the values associated with program content, the power inherent in group processes, and the influence of the group worker all serve as a framework for highlighting traditional ideas and practices that endure in the mainstream thinking."

Garvin, Gutiérrez, and Galinsky (2004:2) acknowledge the use of the term "Mainstream" as the current descriptor in contemporary practice of the traditional and ongoing practice of "social group work." They recognize that "social workers, because of the many ways in which they are asked to provide group services, have had to develop many different group modalities."

Papell and Rothman (1980:6) undertook "to distill some common elements constituting a central identity of social group work." Because the original source materials describing the Mainstream practice of social group work are scattered among several early practice texts, Papell and Rothman provided a special service to the profession in developing their conceptual portrait of its central constructs, which is summarized below.

Papell and Rothman identify "a process of distilling and identifying the central elements of group work in the contemporary period" as having begun with a number of writings by current authors. They recognize "Mainstream" as a term descriptive of "a central identity" and highlight the Mainstream Model of social work practice with groups as "emerg[ing] from the interplay of four constructs: the group, the member in the group, the activities of the group, and the worker with the group" (7). Each of these is detailed in turn below.

The Group

"The mainstream group is characterized by common goals, mutual aid, and nonsynthetic experiences" (Papell and Rothman 1980:7). Papell and Rothman recognize common goal as the outcome of a process of integration of member goals and the professional goals of the worker, yielding a "transcendent purpose that is the product of this interaction" (8). They recognize "spontaneous and meaningfully evolving group processes [as] the instrumental means for realizing group purpose" (7). They introduce the concept of externality, the capacity of the group both "to support its members, and to produce action in human society . . . manifested through the collective power and action of the group to influence, modify, or contribute to its environment, or to assist its members adaptively by developing collective norms with which to respond to environmental demands" (8).

They view the Mainstream group as generating relationships capable of enduring beyond the group, and of the group being internalized as a reference group, a powerful influence group in the lives of its members (8–9). They recognize group development as "embod[ying] a profound understanding of the growth of the group as a whole and the integration of the properties and energy in this change process in relation to purpose" (9).

Papell and Rothman recognize processes in group development that generate group structures, advance the autonomy of the group, and facilitate the contribution of its members to group functioning. They acknowledge a "diversity of the types of groups and target populations . . . relevant to any interpersonal situation within the functions of social work that can be characterized as a human group," recognizing "the flexibility of conception" cited by Roberts and Northen (1976:381) as a central feature of the Mainstream Model.

The Member

Papell and Rothman view the Mainstream Model's focus on the group as generating "particular perspectives on individuals in the group" (9), specifically in the view of the individual as active participant, as holding the status of "member," of having the potential to influence the group, and of experiencing individual growth and change through the exercise of this influence (9–10). "The individual is viewed as a *social learner,* expanding skills in social functioning through the group situation regardless of the primary purpose of the group" (10).

This view highlights the group itself and its processes as capable of influencing the member through its social interaction processes. Further, the Mainstream Model is seen as "concerned with the needs of individuals to belong, to establish affiliative bonds with others, and to develop the capacities for empathy and identification" (Papell and Rothman 1980:275).

The Mainstream Model is seen to recognize "the member's experience of difference, autonomy, and separateness from the group" (Papell and Rothman 1980:10), and to provide a locus for experiencing and dealing with individual differences. The model recognizes and deals with negative experiences in the group, balancing the needs of the individual member against the needs of the group.

The Activities

The content of the group experience is based in present reality, involving a variety of nonverbal as well as verbal forms, and is generated out of the "spontaneous interests and desires of group members implemented in a playful and collaborative process" (10). The use of activities is unique to social work's practice with groups, used comprehensively and imaginatively in the Mainstream Model and "developing reality experience in the here and now" (11).

The Worker

The worker role in Mainstream practice of social work with groups is many-faceted and flexible, in response to individual and group needs, the present situation or moment in which interaction occurs, and the extent to which the group can manage its own life (11). The worker's stance "is intended to heighten identification and role modeling processes in the group" (12). The essential task of the worker is defined as "furthering linkages between members" (12). The worker moderates the use of authority in response to increasing independence of members and group.

Some features of the Specialized Methodology with socially unskilled populations are derived from the Mainstream Model. In particular, the creation of a social group, the focus on working with (sub-)group processes and the assistance to members in their social functioning as members, the use of activities, and the evolution of a "present reality" meaningful to its members. These features are elaborated in part 3.

9

A Specialized Practice Methodology
to Promote Social Competence

In some sense, all practices of social work with groups can be viewed as adapting to the individual instances of a particular purpose, a particular population in a particular group containing particular persons. The adaptability of practice methodology to specific persons and situations is a characteristic within the defined parameters of what constitutes social work's practice with groups, as well as within the framework of particular models of practice. The Mainstream Model embodies this flexibility, perhaps because it does not precast the content of the group experience but fosters its emergence out of the group purpose, members' needs and interests, and group interaction.

When the requirement for adaptations in the practice methodology is too great, the practice can be seen as generating a new model, a new practice paradigm, a paradigm shift, achieving unique new features. The Specialized Methodology of practice developed for work with socially unskilled persons in groups is an operationalized instance of practice with allonomous groups, as formulated in the Broad Range Model. It is based on the special needs of socially unskilled persons for assistance in becoming social, and it is an extension of practice into a pregroup period essential to the progression from socially noncompetent to socially competent functioning.

In the shift from practice with socially able persons to practice with the socially inept, some elements of practice become irrelevant, while others, not needed in work with the socially able or employed only in small ways, become major, essential to work with socially unskilled persons. In particular, work with group processes is replaced by a focus on individual functioning and interaction in small subunits, toward the evolution of social competence sufficient to enter into the domain of group forming and functioning. Some features of Mainstream practice of social work with groups are employed, with modifications addressed to the precise needs of socially less able populations.

In advancing to practice with less able constituents, the focus of worker activity may shift from group processes to the relationship of the individual member to the group and to the achievement of relevant individual functioning in the group. In making this necessary shift, the social worker still maintains the focus on the group as a potential entity and on the activities employed in the group—such that the individual's functioning is viewed in the context of his or her place in the group. In effect, practice with populations requiring greater assistance to achieve and sustain a place in groups has shifted the spotlight to an area of practice needing to be elaborated theoretically—the individual in the group, relationally viewed.

The practice deals with individual and interactional functioning, focusing on nonfunctional behaviors that impede smooth social interaction and relationship. These are of two kinds: individual behaviors that reflect personal problems, and those that mirror an absence of good social tutelage. Both require some management in order for individuals to be able to enter the realm of social interaction, and for that avenue to be opened for them.

The resolution of disrupting and impeding interaction enables the activity to proceed: in this circumstance, it becomes functional to work out difficulties almost as an aside to the main focus of attention, the activity.

There is a continuity between Mainstream practice and this specialized form of practice focused on socializing and/or resocializing populations whose primary group experiences have undersocialized, inadequately socialized, or divergently socialized.

Much group work practice of the 1950s to 1960s with children and youth in youth-serving agencies, settlement houses, neighborhood centers was addressed to the contributions that membership in successive small groups could make to the ongoing socialization of its members: clearly, group workers saw their practice as enabling group members to participate ably in the life of their groups, adding to the social skills already in place, those yet to be achieved. In effect, a Specialized Methodology addressed to unenabled populations, who lack basic social skills for performing competently in their world, carries the same thrust: the practice is more difficult because group members enter at deficit in social functioning, and the tasks of the worker are much more extensive, requiring considerable professional skill.

When group members are socially too unskilled to generate a functional group together, the central focus of group work practice must be on helping members to acquire these social skills, interactively, experientially, in the context of a group life that is pleasurable, fun, satisfying, interesting, and comfortable, and that replicates life (as they may not have known it previously); with the social worker mediating in interactional incidents, interpreting accurately the meaning of behavior (often misconstrued), using teachable moments to instruct members on how to behave toward others, demonstrating and modeling in situ—in life as experienced in this particular group.

The differences between the Mainstream Methodology and the Specialized Methodology are highlighted through comparison of the two. In the Mainstream practice, the potential members are ready to engage together and possess the social competence to do so. In the Specialized practice, the participants are not ready to be members, to engage relationally, to merge their individual selves in the enterprise of a group, to create group.

Essentially the two methodologies share the same objective: to enable group formation and to foster group functioning that can activate the group's own social influences and achievements as the primary means for advancing individual and collective growth in and as the entity. The one works with able personnel capable of forming and progressing as a collective; the other works with persons further back, more limited in social functioning, at an earlier, less able, less competent stage, and attempts to facilitate progression to normal social functioning. In this sense, the goals and methods are similar, but they involve persons at different stages of development and readiness to engage together. The one is normative, the other remediative and promotive of essential social progressions. In the one the practitioner works to enable the participants to advance in social competence and prepare for group experience; in the other it is already present and available for use, allowing the members to engage in a group experience.

The entry point of the social worker defines the practice as either normative or remediative. The task of socializing the members is common to both practices, but at differing points of entry. In the Specialized Methodology the worker is located at the points of difficulty in social engagement; in the Mainstream practice, the practitioner works with persons whose social competences are in place and available: much more in the collective.

The element in social work with groups composed of socially competent persons that distinguishes it from practice with socially unskilled persons is manifest in the ready response to the opportunity to form a group. The novice practitioner sometimes approaches the convening of persons for a potential new group with no expectation that there will be any input other than his or her own and is surprised to encounter individual and collective response, to realize that the professional is not alone, not the sole voice. The potential entity replies to the social worker's initiatives with a clear sense of potential members responding; interaction arises and flows in response to the invitation to create a group together, quickly moving beyond the initial initiative and beyond the social worker's expectations, elaborating purpose and activating relational/interactional processes relevant to the forming of group. There is relief for the beginning practitioner in the experience of members' response, in the sense that the answering voices and the professional voice together will generate group.

In contrast, the sense of a becoming entity responding individually and collectively is not present in the beginnings of collective life with socially unskilled persons.

The "supra" life of the entity described by Simmel (in Wolff 1950) as arising when interaction extends to three or more persons is not manifest when socially unskilled persons are convened for an intending group. Lacking social skills sufficient for engaging together, individual expressions are random, and behaviors are individual, symptomatic, and nonfunctional to the enterprise of attempting to form group.

The Context of the Specialized Methodology

This section locates the Specialized Methodology in relation to existing theoretical materials for social work practice with groups. In the early texts on social work with groups, the tasks of facilitating individual connection to group and of enabling beneficial group processes are documented.

The purpose of the group worker in attempting to help all the individuals within his group to secure from it the maximum enjoyment and growth of which each is capable is obviously not done by a one-to-one approach in which he concentrates first on one and then on another. He has to develop a kind of peripheral vision in which, while he is aware of the group interactions, the esprit de corps and the progress of the program, he is also able to take into his consciousness those of the individual members who for one reason or another require his special attention. . . . [T]his relation between the [worker] and his group calls upon him for a sensitivity to the varying reactions of individuals and for understanding handling of each *within the context of the group.* (Coyle 1948:217 [italics added])

Coyle made this clear statement of mandate in the first full textbook on group practice in social work. The text contains a chapter addressed to the group worker and interpersonal relations, which focuses both on the tasks of enabling an adequate group to develop and on "the relation of [the worker] to the socially inadequate members" (121–22).

Other texts of the period also acknowledge the tasks of working with individuals in the context of the group (see, e.g., Wilson and Ryland 1949; Trecker 1949, 1955, 1972:119–41; Konopka 1963; Phillips 1957; Klein 1972; Vinter 1967; Garvin 1987).

Work with individuals in the context of the group is defined in two places in the literature: as part of work with group processes, and as a separate section specifying work with individuals. In the early materials, some of the writers focus on the limits and boundaries of individual work, particularly the requirements (1) to maintain an adequate connection with every member, rather than an in-depth relationship with a particular member; (2) to work with individual members in a limited way, on the periphery of the group experience; and (3) to make referral to other professionals when more extended help is needed.

The development of remedial practice with groups in new practice domains brought new conceptions of the task of working with individual members within group. Vinter (1967, 1974) identified treatment goals for individual members developed by the practitioner, emanating from the process of individualizing each member's needs and social functioning dilemmas.

Although this was an appropriate contribution to professional knowledge, it was articulated at a time when differing practice modalities were emergent, anticipating the model-building era of the 1960s. Differences among practices were being highlighted, and sometimes misunderstood, such that some new knowledge suffered from the reactivity of theoreticians to one another's formulations.

Papell and Rothman (1966) advanced conceptions of social work practice with groups through their recognition of distinctive models of practice, identified as the Social Goals Model, the Remedial Model, and the Reciprocal Model. Their critique of the adequacy and completeness of each model includes an assessment of how each addresses the task of working with individual members in the context of the group:

> A serious shortcoming of the social goals model is that it has not produced a theoretical design that is adequate to meet the problems facing practitioners in all areas of service. Its underemphasis on individual dynamics and its lack of attention to a wide range of individual needs leave the practitioner without guidelines for carrying out a social work function with client groups where individual problems take precedence over societal problems. (Papell and Rothman 1980:121; see also Cohen in Turner 1968:52–75)

The Remedial Model could be seen as an effort to elaborate this missing piece. Vinter (1974:13) defined treatment goals for each group member as central in a practice focused on "help[ing] individuals through small, face-to-face groups," while cherishing the group's own impacts on members. "The concept of social dysfunction is sometimes used to denote all the problematic states of social work clientele. Treatment goals, then, embody more desirable states of social function."

According to Vinter,

> In addition to the assertions that significant help can be given individuals through experience in groups, and that groups provide both the context and means for treatment, the treatment group can be thought of as a deliberately structured influence system to effect change through social interaction. The kinds of changes sought, as defined by treatment goals, range from acquiring new relationship skills, to changes in self-images and attitudes toward others, to behavioral modifications or integration

into conventional social structures. Although practitioners do interact directly with clients to implement specific treatment goals, potent influences are also exercised through interactions between members, through the group's activities or program, and through its structure. Frequently, the group implements treatment by directly influencing the individual. (15–16)

Papell and Rothman (1980) viewed the Remedial Model as lacking sufficient focus on the group and its processes, focusing instead on the assessment and treatment of individuals through the formulation of treatment goals for individuals by the worker, in advance of convening the group. The model is seen as making theoretical advances in "systematically setting forth . . . guidelines for diagnostic considerations of individual functioning in the group" (126) and "is clearly a clinical model focused upon helping the malperforming individual to achieve a more desirable state of social functioning" (122).

William Schwartz's 1961 Reciprocal Model "advances a helping process . . . intended to serve both the individual and society" (Papell and Rothman 1980: 126). It identifies the "symbiotic need for each other, of the individual and his nurturing group, . . . each needing the other for its own life and growth, and each reaching out to the other with all the strength it can command at a given moment" (Schwartz 1961:15).

Schwartz recognizes a continuum of problems in social functioning,

ranging from the normal developmental problems of children growing into their culture to the severe pathology involved in situations where the symbiotic attachment appears to be all but severed. At all points along this range, the social work function is to mediate the individual-social transaction as it is worked out in the specific context of these agencies . . . designed to bring together individual needs and social resources—the person's urge to belong to society as a full and productive member and society's ability to provide certain specific means for integrating its people and enriching their social contribution. . . . The social worker's job is to represent and to implement the symbiotic strivings, even where their essential features are obscured from the individual, from society, or from both. (15)

Papell and Rothman (1980:129) found the Reciprocal Model lacking in "guidelines in relation to individual dynamics and normative expectations, [without which] there is no basis for assessing the impact of change upon individuals."

The Contribution of the Specialized Methodology

This book may fill in some of the missing piece in the Social Goals Model with regard to work with individuals in the context of the group, contributing a way of going within the processes of the group that enables enhanced social functioning on the part of the members. As well, it has some partial correspondence with the Remedial Model: it shares a view of social dysfunction modifiable through group experience, and it values a species of group formed for special purposes but also recognizes the strengths of a group reconstituted with a social worker, perceiving both as alternate routes to achievement of an entity functional for helping purposes.

The group and its processes are valued and viewed as a main influence on individual social functioning. Engagement with content and process of the group experience is the means through which individual dilemmas of social functioning become manifest and available to assistance and guidance. The group is important in this practice, serving as both context and means for growth and development of individual and group (Vinter 1985).

Professional goals for individuals are not precast or articulated but rather are emergent and extemporaneous in the functioning of the entity; recognized in situ as moments to which a professional input can contribute usefully. The inputs of the social worker are informed by knowledge of good group functioning and of the tasks of individuals in becoming part of the group, and of accumulating knowledge of these individuals in this group, with these dilemmas. As well, individual developmental dilemmas that are presocial in nature and that impede entry into interactional engagement are recognized by the practitioner as needing particular assistance preliminary to individual engagement with others.

As knowledge and understanding of the particular dilemmas in social functioning of each participant evolve, the social worker develops a clear sense of the ways in which individual help is needed and of the needs of each individual.

[Part III]

A Specialized Practice Methodology for Socially Unskilled Populations

Part 3 is focused on the Specialized Methodology developed for use with socially unskilled populations. Chapter 10 presents an overview of features of the methodology. Chapter 11 identifies requirements for the Specialized practice with respect to the agency and the practitioner. The impact of social noncompetence on the practitioner is also explored, and professional expectations that require some modification are noted.

Chapter 12 examines the two essential elements to be worked with in advancing social competence: the individual's relationship to self and the individual's relationship to others. The chapter identifies a class of forerunner interventions in a pregroup period while these two primary relationships are evolved.

Chapter 13 examines the place of actional modes in engaging socially unskilled persons toward experiencing a sense of effectance with their world, as prelude to relating to others. The use of activities as the preferred content form is explored as the means both of engaging individuals and of sustaining the whole entity.

Chapter 14 explicates the roundabout route and processes through which social competence can be fostered and examines the capability of collectivity as a social form suited to the task. Three stages in the pregroup period that precede the possibility of group formation are identified, and the domains of intervention are detailed. Finally, chapter 15 provides an example of a socially noncompetent entity in its progression toward group and social competence.

10

Features of the Specialized Methodology for Practice with Socially Unskilled Individuals and Entities

The Broad Range Model sets out the parameters for practice in three group forms and the characteristics of group and individual functioning, for which particular elements in the practice methodology are identified. The population and problem to be addressed defines the specific theoretical supports and the actual methodology uniquely designed. This chapter presents the particular model of practice in the allonomous group form when the participants lack social competence to generate group. This description of the features of the practice model specifies both its theoretical and philosophical referents and its Specialized Methodology. There may be other populations that classify as functioning allonomously, and for whom other theoretical referents and practice methodologies will be appropriate.

The typologies outlined in chapter 3 make visible a class of threshold entities trying to become group without the social competence to do so. The nature of social incapacity requires a specialized methodology of practice in order for participants in threshold entities to acquire social competence sufficient for entry into group life and to experience the socializing effects of group, so necessary to human social growth. The practice requires significant modification in order to facilitate the development of social competence and the advancement to groupness. This chapter highlights the features of this specialized practice, its theoretical supports, and its relationship to mainstream practice.

The Focus and Goal of Practice

The focus of social work practice with socially unskilled participants needs to be on both the social functioning of the individual constituents and the development and functioning of the entity. The goal of the practice is to enable social competence to be developed and for the members to become able to form group and enter into group life together. The goal is remediative in the sense that it is focused centrally on social dysfunction and on opening the avenues that lead to group, recognizing the powerful influences that group itself will have on its members. The limited social competence of individuals precludes a normal interactional progression to group as the likely social form. The interactional difficulties between and among individual participants create the failure to progress to groupness; hence both individual and entity must be the focus of worker intervention. An altered and incomplete social form requires an adapted practice for the social worker, both in terms of helping the participants to function socially and in terms of supporting the functioning of the whole in the absence of the components of group life that in normal groups would evolve and sustain the entity.

The point of engagement for the worker is with the manifestations of social dysfunction of individuals and entity; that is, the worker must be attuned concurrently to individual and collective functioning.

Purpose

The purpose of the practice is to work with difficulties manifest in interactional process toward improved social functioning and the acquisition of social competence. It is a process model of practice, as distinct from many group work practices that have only a content focus, whether problem focused or serving an identified problem-holding constituency.

It is a practice that may seem to have no apparent identified purpose: its unarticulated purpose is to aid in the ongoing socialization of participants. It may carry such articulated purposes as "learning to get along better, to make new friends," or it may carry an ostensible purpose of bringing people together and engaging them in interaction around a shared or common interest, while its deeper, unarticulated purpose is to advance the participants socially.

Much of our early and current practice in community agencies has this feature, particularly as a socializing practice with children and youth through primary group experience, in which the group life is central to the participants. In current practice, this purpose may also be used to serve socially unskilled populations. Anne Brooks's (1978) practice with isolated, reclusive men living in a single-room occupancy slum hotel is a good example: she used a "health and exercise club" motif to attract the men out of their rooms initially and engage them.

A special element in the purpose of this practice is the recognition by the social worker of the deeper hopes and unarticulated longings of socially unskilled persons to become able to function competently and rewardingly in social life. As the social worker individualizes the participants, he or she is able to identify the social goals of individuals and incorporate these as professional goals for the practice, recognizing those behaviors that interfere with their achievement. This may be misunderstood as "professional goals for individuals," which Schwartz (1971b) once decried as covert and not legitimate. In practice with socially unskilled populations, and with juvenile populations in the process of acquiring social competence, it is inevitable that the practitioner, in individualizing the participants, will discern what is problematic for each and will seek ways of helping individuals to surmount such difficulties. In this, the practitioner joins with the individual in the goal to overcome social noncompetence, making the individual's goals also the goals of the professional practitioner.

The Social Group

The preferred social form for this practice is the social group, recognizing that belonging, relationships, and interacting in small social groups are the source and locus of social nurture and social growth. In contrast to the psyche group, which puts change in the hands of the practitioner, the socio group (Jennings 1950) acknowledges the capacity of social interactional processes to advance social competence, locating change in the participants, in the group's processes, and in the contribution of the social worker through influencing group processes.

The practice is social in nature. It provides for social experience, and social avenues of expression, with adjustments to deal with social dysfunction at the moment manifest. It provides opportunities to learn and to practice social skills.

Limited Social Form

The entity achievable by socially unskilled populations is likely to be limited by the absence of social skills possessed by the participants. Interaction may occur principally between the social worker and each participant, particularly as the worker individualizes and responds to the needs of each, making the worker–member relationship an especially important one. At most, only the three relational-interactional subsystems typical of a constitutionally limited collectivity (Lang 1987:24) may become operational: the worker–member, worker–entity, and member–member subsystems.

A special challenge in practice with socially unskilled persons in small social forms is to work with participants "where they are" while holding to and working toward the possibility of the entity progressing to group. The demand on the worker is to view limited here-and-now interaction in the context of a possible group. This constrains the practitioner to intervene in ways that will not preclude the possibility of the entity progressing to group: group-as-group must be always in the mind of the worker as a prospect, viewing what takes place in the entity as potential for becoming group. This precludes a form of practice that treats individuals in the context of a collectivity where no progression to groupness is sought or desired. In this respect, the practice mirrors the beginning stages of work with groups in social work and is part of its Mainstream practice.

Respecting the boundaries of a potential group constrains worker intervention with individuals within a public domain—dealing with what is visible, manifest, expressed, or displayed by individuals in interaction. The practice is concerned with correcting deficits in social functioning that are the legacy of inadequately performing previous primary groups in the lives of the populations to be served. It therefore undertakes to generate a socialization group or a possible approximation of it, within which social dysfunction can be corrected and social competence acquired.

Socialization Group

A socialization group requires a relationship with the worker character-ized by strong power and love (affect) (Perlman 1967), that is, a worker who cares deeply about the participants and their struggles, manages the group experience, and makes specific individualized contributions to enable improved social functioning of individuals and entity. This relation-ship precedes the socializing effects of the group and enables them to be mobilized. Thus in the early part of the practice, the worker is a powerful influence, while later in the practice, as group emerges, peer and entitative influence replace or lessen the influence of the worker.

Group as Microcosm of Life—An Analogic Practice

The group is intended to be an analogic practice, a life experience whose learnings are readily transferable to the lives of the participants. The pre-ferred form is a life group, one that is viewed as a microcosm of life, closely approximating the social group at its best in life. Its strength lies in its route to assisting its members to become socially able. Using naturalistic social activities that are appealing, appropriate, relevant, and salient to the participants, that provide ways of being together, and that contribute their own innate socializing effects, the worker assists in modifying dysfunc-tional participation of individual participants and entity. Thus, the group experience is being modified unobtrusively as it plays out, and participants receive needed assistance at critical interactional points to perform in new ways, to advance self-esteem, and to acquire social competence. The group is *experienced as real life* by its participants and employs *learning in situ, in salient, teachable moments*.

Although participants will view the group experience as pleasurable and satisfying, they also recognize that it is designed to help them manage better, acquire new social skills, build new relationships. These purposes may not be articulated as such and may be masked by the programmatic content, which provides an attractive entrée into the group for its members, but will be understood by the participants as they experience the guidance of the worker in critical moments of social interaction. (See, e.g., Brooks 1978; Ciardiello 2000; Gold and Kolodny 1978).

On-site social learning in critical moments, as they happen, is the essence of the group experience. It is accomplished imperceptively and is not cognitively or insight-focused, but rather occurs as small moments of guidance and direction, as almost subconscious, sub rosa adjustments made to improve the interaction, thereby facilitating the playing out of the group activities that are the central focus to the participants.

Design for the Group Experience

Given the degree of social dysfunction in these populations, it is clear that long-term groups have a better capability for advancing social competences than short-term groups. The duration of group life may be determined by the intractableness of social dysfunction. A good part or even the entire experience may take place as a prolonged pregroup period.

The Place of Social Activities

Social activities, whether preexisting in the culture or specifically designed for a particular population, have the effect of supporting participants in being and doing together, generate a kind of sociality, which members may not be able to create in social interaction, and make their own demands for functional social participation. Social activities can also generate a group-like sense, important for socially unskilled persons to experience, and may give people a preview sample of what social group life is like. While some current group work practices are solely content-focused, sometimes disregarding important interactional processes, this practice employs the content as an arena within which participants in interaction will demonstrate what is problematic, in moments accessible to alteration. The prototype for this practice is found in the parenting of very young children, for whom social learning and guidance is specific, in the concrete moment, and is preconceptual in nature.

The Grouplike Entity—An Altered Group Form

Because the participants are unable to generate group at the outset, the entity employed in this practice will be an altered social form. It is necessary for the worker to put in place certain elements that will enable group to develop because the members are unable to generate these group phenomena on their own.

The worker must bring structure, order, and direction to the experience; establish norms and controls sufficient for managing to be and do together in the absence of participant contributions in these areas; generate a set of relationships between worker and each member sufficient to hold the entity together until peer relationships can develop; and create content that draws the participants together, creating an illusion or forerunner of groupness and some sense of initial attachment to the entity and its members prior to actual relationship development. Because the worker must provide for these ingredients as a prelude to group life, he or she is in a position to establish them in ways that will be of optimal benefit to the participants. In nature it is somewhat like a sheltered workshop because the practitioner is able to create elements of potential group life in their most balanced and egalitarian form.

The entity is a double adaptation, first because the worker must establish what the participants cannot, and second because in so doing, the worker is able to promote a social form that supports interpersonal acceptance and interactional systems that are open and egalitarian (see chapter 6), activating the beneficent potential of group life.

The Worker Role

One cannot expect socially unskilled persons to proceed together in ways that will generate groupness. Instead they may require an extended period of being together with little or no interactional demand, having compresence and the small togetherness that is generated by doing the same activity individually, side by side. There is a strong requirement for things to be planned, provided, and structured by the worker, and for an enabling contribution to be made toward adjustmental, adapted outcomes, different from those that participants can achieve unaided. The worker must be central, directive, active, facilitating, and mediating to make being and doing together possible and must establish norms for how to go together. In effect, the worker takes on tasks of group life that the members are unable to handle and carries them until such time as the members' social competences emerge and become functional to the life of the group. The centrality of the worker must be functional to the needs of the group.

All groups in their beginnings may show signs of various initial interactional conditions. Most intending groups will move quickly beyond their initial interactional portrait to develop normative interactional patterns and to progress to groupness. Populations that generate aberrational forms of interactions and who, unless assisted, are unable to advance beyond these patterns to form group are the focus of this practice. The portrait therefore reflects ordinary known forms of interaction seen in many groups temporarily or momentarily, but experienced here as the whole, repeated nature of interaction in the class of collectivities unable to form group unaided.

In this order of group, then, *the persistence and constancy of ineffective interaction* are the signals for help with the interaction itself, in order to move into the domain of group life with all its enhancing potential. This is a class of threshold entities, unable to engage, join, belong, achieve groupness, experience the benefits of group life, doomed to remain on the threshold as unrewarding collectivities unless assisted in achieving interactional patterns sustainable as group.

What practitioners know experientially as fleeting, occasional, or temporary critical moments in the life of normative social work groups are the full, persistent interactional patterns for members unable to achieve and sustain group unaided. The assistance then, must be addressed to helping members move beyond nonfunctional forms of interaction to begin to see each other as persons to whom they can become related; to see the potential entity as something desirable and rewarding; and to gain social competences for relational life.

All practitioners with groups are familiar with instances of chaotic or volatile interaction, of periods or moments of underinteraction, of interaction that misses or misconnects, of limited or partial interaction, of interaction that follows a covert direction or contains a dynamic that shapes the interaction in an unexpected way, of runaway interaction that accelerates unbelievably or suddenly derails. It is important that we know these many aspects of group life.

It is when any of these patterns are manifest as the basic way in which a collectivity of persons will interact and continue to interact that the practitioner must recognize a severe condition that cannot proceed to group without exceptional assistance.

The circumstance that may precipitate the need for a specialized methodology of practice with groups can be seen to arise when all members of an intending group are of the same socially unskilled population and, when convened, pool their problem condition in ways that are manifest as some form of aberrational interaction. The practice modifications arising in response to it provide avenues for assisting the least able to become group members, to form group, and to benefit from becoming participants and experiencing the socializing effects of group life.

The activities of the worker are not different in kind from those employed with Mainstream normally functioning groups; but what a worker might do occasionally as fine tuning in normative groups may become a central part of the technology with threshold entities.

Contrasting Mainstream Practice with the Specialized Methodology

Intervention in Mainstream Practice

The central repertoire of interventions in the Mainstream practice of social work with groups is addressed to the functioning of individuals, their interaction, the construction and functioning of group-as-group, and the functioning of the group in its larger context. Papell and Rothman (1966) identify this three-pronged focus of the social worker with groups as pervasive through time.

Intervention in this practice can be seen as a functional professional contribution to the process involved in connecting and integrating individuals into the entity, in enabling the group to form and function appropriately as group, and to have an impact in the wider world as group. These interventions are intended to enhance normative processes for socially able members at points where they require small assists to deal with conflict, to construct relationships, to evolve structures and operational provisions for group functioning, and to achieve group goals.

Intervention with Socially Unskilled Populations

Interventive work with socially unskilled populations is not qualitatively different but is employed with greater frequency, rapidity, and intensity and begins at an earlier point of entry where less is in place. It can be seen as a practice methodology adapted to meet the special needs of socially unskilled populations and as a methodology designed to enable individual social competence to be developed, and for advancement to group to become possible.

In practice with socially unskilled populations, the mainstream practice technology is a misfit because it presumes social competences in place from which group can be formed. When such competences are not in place and available for social use, the methodology must be both modified and extended to serve the very particular needs of populations not yet socially able. The Specialized Methodology recognizes the possibility for individuals to progress from socially unskilled to socially able, acquiring social competence sufficient to experience and use the group. It is designed to fill the gap between noncompetence and competence in social living, and to enable the evolution of social competence. The period of acquisition of social competences can be seen as a period preliminary to group experience, containing particular features specifically designed to enable individual progressions to the beginning stages of group life.

Pregroup Period: A Provision for Socially Unskilled Populations

Pregroup Experience—A "Practice" Modality

A pregroup experience is a specialized provision for persons who lack social competences for forming group and for living their lives satisfyingly in the social world. They require a preliminary, preparatory, grouplike learning experience designed to enable them to acquire basic social competences. It is a "practice" modality in which participants can learn how to be members, socially connected with others, by learning and practicing new and relevant social behaviors and modifying those that are dysfunctional.

This is a practice that employs elements of our Mainstream technology of social work with groups for working with group-as-group and combines it with a specialized technology essential for addressing the needs of individual members within the context of the group experience and assisting them to acquire competence for engaging adequately with others in social interaction. The special feature of this practice is its capacity to advance individuals to social competence through experiences in pregroup life that are guided and adapted, modified as they occur, toward more satisfying outcomes.

The practice does not involve talking about problematics and is not cognitively focused. Rather, it creates a microcosm akin to life, generating experiences that are live and meaningful. Within these, as interpersonal, interactional difficulties arise, it provides small directions and adaptations capable of showing the way and enabling new performances on the part of the participants. Its success rests with *experiential moments* in which individuals learn in live situations how to go in new ways beneficial both to themselves and to the group. The learning is experiential, affective, and social.

The nature of this learning is in situ, in salient, concrete moments, and is specific to each member's need for social competence, individualized for immediate use and incorporation as a way of going, socially. These learnings are not taught cognitively or in the abstract but are achieved through specific guidance proffered in the moment they are needed. The learnings are in the affective domain and are emotional and social, tied to specific concrete moments where the small contributions of the social worker point the way to better coping, performance, and resolution. Provision of assistance at the moment needed gives a special ambience to the inputs of the social worker.

Much of this practice involves interpreting intentionality in the behaviors of others, so that these can be perceived more accurately and responded to in new ways that do not impede the flow of interaction or the functioning of group. In these mini situations, the social worker enables the interchanges of group life to be understood and responded to differently. Multiple moments of this order provide a kind of cumulative blueprint for how to go in relation to one another, how to comprehend another's actions, and how to respond usefully. Discussion of the moments is minimal and simply points the way to normative interactional exchanges that will make group evolution and functioning possible.

This moment-to-critical-moment practice is a means of generating empathy and fostering relationship in populations who tend to view others as threatening, intrusive, offensive, undifferentiated, or irrelevant; and of creating a sensitivity to one another crucial in the functioning of the group. It is an order of help that engenders a capacity to individualize one another, to develop caring and respect for each member, and to view one another as persons. The pregroup experience becomes a microcosm where members learn imperceptibly how to care about one another, how to respond usefully with one another, and how to be social together. This order of practice can be seen as a specialized, preliminary technology, capable of providing members with needed ways of interacting rewardingly.

Special attention to individual functioning in the context of group life appears to be the key to advancing socially unskilled participants to the point of adequate interaction, sufficient for the construction of a group capable of its own powerful socializing effects. As deficits in individual social competence are modified, so too is the capability of group-as-group advanced.

Ethical and Theoretical Supports

Social Work Values

The Specialized practice with socially unskilled populations recognizes as central the worth and value of every individual, and the right to self-realization of each person's capabilities and potential. These values are central to the profession of social work and inform the practice focus on overcoming barriers to adequate social functioning and on acquiring adequate social skills.

Theoretical Contributions from the Behavioral Sciences

The knowledge sources that inform this practice include sociology, socialization theory, social psychology, reference group theory, social learning theory, developmental psychology, the strengths perspective, competence theories, empowerment theory, and Mainstream group work theory.

Sociology contributes the view of the individual's need to take his or her place in society as a productive, contributing member, and of society's need for functional participating members, so elegantly expressed by Schwartz (1961), as a symbiotic, essential connection.

Socialization theory identifies the achievement of a significant strong relationship of "power and love" (Perlman 1965) between socializer and socializee as the context within which socialization occurs. As well, socialization theory operationalizes the need of society for functional participants and the need of its participants to acquire social skills sufficient for living competently as participants in society.

Social psychology contributes the concept of a social group with which an individual identifies and from which "he or she derives norms, attitudes, values, and the social objects these create" (Gould and Kolb 1964:580), thus becoming a reference group. Reference groups are identified as retaining incorporated, influential points of reference by their members after they have ceased to exist as living groups. Social learning theory is a component of socialization processes, reflecting the learning of functional behaviors in interaction in the context of a significant relationship.

Ego psychology contributes knowledge about efficacy, effectance, and the cumulative sense of competence through interaction with objects, both nonhuman and human, in the environment (White 1963), as well as a portrait of ego development through age-stage progressions (Erikson 1959).

The strengths perspective, long a focus of social work with groups without having this explicit designation, now contributes articulated theoretical supports for practice centered on the capabilities of individuals and on the mobilization of strengths, talents, resources, and latent abilities not yet realized (Saleebey 1992).

Finally, the Mainstream Model of social work with groups contributes to this Specialized practice several elements of practice deemed to be essential to working with socially unskilled individuals and groups: the use of the small group as the preferred social form, the use of activities, work with group processes to advance individual and entitative social functioning, and trust in the power of the small group.

11

Requirements for a Specialized Practice with Socially Unskilled Populations

This chapter focuses on the requirements for a specialized practice of social work with collectivities and groups intended to serve socially unskilled persons. The materials begin with requirements of the social agency in which the practice is domiciled, in support of practice with socially unskilled persons.

Some preliminary considerations are presented to orient the practitioner to a practice that will be unlike that of other social work with groups. The materials alert the practitioner to expectable differences in the practice and to the need for developing a content repertoire of activities suited or adapted to the needs of socially unskilled persons. The impact of socially noncompetent behaviors on the social worker and on the practice methodology of social work with groups is also documented.

Requirements of the Agency

Agencies seeking to serve socially unskilled populations must be prepared to support a practice that requires an *extended time frame*: the task of enabling the acquisition of social competence is not achieved in a short-term time period, and no quick fix is possible.

Because the practice employs the social group or the less developed social form, collectivity, as well as a variety of social activities, there must be *good provision for space* and *needed resources* in support of the practice within the agency. Additional spatial and activity resources may need to be contracted beyond the agency building.

While participants are learning to be socially competent through their experience in this practice, the agency needs to be tolerant of noise, levity, mess, and uproar generated in activities that involve being social together, and to view these elements as vital to the practice.

Some activities may require a *budget for supplies and equipment* employed in their use. Agencies must be prepared to provide for items that may be central to and facilitative of the practice.

Finally, an agency undertaking to address the needs of socially unskilled persons must be prepared to *employ social workers competent in this practice* or willing to become so. Agencies must be prepared to provide significant support to the practitioner, in recognition of the stresses experienced in working with these populations, and to provide backup staff when necessary.

Requirements of the Practitioner

A first requirement for social workers who undertake a specialized practice with socially unskilled populations is the recognition that *the practice will be different* from other social work practices with groups. Practice knowledge acquired through professional education and practice experience of social work with groups may not apply in work with entities composed of socially unskilled persons. The differences in practice with populations unable to form group may create a crisis for the practitioner, both in practice expectations and in practice methodology. It is important to recognize the anomalies produced by socially noncompetent functioning and to develop a specialized technology related to the needs of socially unskilled persons and to their ways of functioning in the collective. Not all socially unskilled populations will be so disabled socially as to require a different practice methodology for working with them. Some will achieve restored social functioning as they participate in grouplike experiences and will be able to proceed together to group formation with the help of the social worker. Other populations may require a significant time period in a pregroup experience, within which socially competent functioning may be acquired slowly.

In acknowledging certain predominant differences in practice with socially unskilled persons, the intent is to prepare the social worker to cope with elements characteristic of this practice.

Professional Expectations

Social workers must be prepared to divest themselves of their usual professional expectations for practice with groups and reorient themselves to the characteristics of socially unskilled persons in their individual and collective functioning. The expectation that group will form and develop through phases interferes with the recognition of the actuality of socially noncompetent functioning. As professional practitioners, we are so oriented to normative group processes that professional expectations impede comprehension of social functioning of a vastly different nature, with more limited outcomes. A first task, then, is to shed group-relevant expectations and to attune to the particulars of nonnormative behaviors and interactions; of what is, in the life of a socially noncompetent entity.

Professional Technology

Practitioners working with socially unskilled populations discover early a lack of fit of their practice methodology with the level of functioning encountered and recognize the requirement for an altered methodology oriented to the needs of such populations.

Writers describing practices with socially unskilled persons reflect their efforts to comprehend difference in the functioning of the participants in the entities with which they worked. Brooks (1978) remarked on the slowness of development of relationships and interaction, and the lack of carryover within their wider residential environment, in a group of aging, disengaged, handicapped men who talked with each other in their meetings but not outside the group. Gold and Kolodny (1978) reflect on alterations to the professional role initially, in the face of socially unskilled behaviors of developmentally immature adolescents who require activities as their means to be together. Lang (1962), recording the struggle with the chaotic behavior of emotionally disturbed children, remarked on "the loss of professional skills which could so enrich the lives of these children," leaving the worker "completely frustrated" in efforts to deal with out-of-control behaviors.

Weissman and Schwartz (1989:53–54) noted the necessity for the practitioner to discard expectations for progressions in group development in a practice with frail people, and to look for small gains.

> The worker must recognize that low motivation, high dependency and unresponsiveness are often prevalent in groups of the frail elderly. The difficulty of working with this group cannot be minimized. Because of the frailty and extreme age of its members, the movement of the group will not occur in the same manner as the more traditional group. The consequences of this deviation from expected norms may prove devastating for the worker. Frustration, anger, and feelings of incompetence may take place. . . . The worker looks for gratification from the small behavioral changes that occur from the strengthening of interpersonal bonds between members.

Visible in all the practice literature cited is the struggle of participants and social worker to achieve a viable experience in entities unable to form and use group until some measure of social competence is attained; evidence of the practitioner struggling with the differences presented by socially noncompetent functioning; and reflections of breakthrough when their experience together yields some degree of social progression. In practice with socially unskilled populations, evidence of small progressions becomes the significant reflector of advances in individual and entity.

Content of the Practice Experience

Practitioners must be prepared to acquire for use a range of program activities because of the centrality of this content in sustaining the participants together. It is not essential that the social worker be an expert in the range of activity forms available, but he or she needs to prepare well enough, to know how they work and what the possible pitfalls are in using them, in order to employ them successfully for the benefit of the participants.

The practitioner must employ trial and error in efforts to explore and identify program forms usable by persons of a particular socially unskilled population, and to document the elements of successful ways of working with them. The practitioner may have to discard excellent program media that are social in nature as being beyond the collective functioning level and ability of socially unskilled persons and seek to identify and use activities that are well matched to their needs.

Some particular dilemmas confront the practitioner in the selection of activities appropriate to socially unskilled persons: their level of adequate performance may require adaptations of existing activity forms to make them accessible and usable at a level simpler than that for which they were designed. The social worker has the tasks of simplifying and adapting activity forms to fit the needs of socially unskilled persons and of camouflaging simple forms to make them acceptable to the population, which may be chronologically out of sync with the age-stage for whom the media forms were originally developed.

Socially unskilled populations "may need a great deal of side-by-side activity before they can risk interaction" (Brooks 1978:59). Activity forms involving one-by-one, turn-taking, parallel activity that involves compresence but not interactional demand may be essential forms of content for some populations in the initial period of their being together, and for others throughout their whole experience together as an entity. Usually these activity forms contain life-learnings for young children; for socially unskilled persons, such learnings may be the necessity, belatedly, coming long after they should have been learned.

The Impact of Social Noncompetence on the Social Worker

The absence of normal social interaction in entities composed of socially unskilled persons creates a new and unfamiliar domain for the social worker. When norms for social behavior and interchange have not been learned and incorporated or have been lost, the interactional arena is not moderated naturally and may contain anomalies. The absence of gratifying normal social response will have an impact on the practitioner, possibly subconsciously, perhaps cumulatively, as being outside the pattern of normal, comfortable social interchange. The effect may be comparable to the experience of being in a foreign country where the language, interactive rules, and pattern are unknown. Further, the anticipated progressions in relationships and collective functioning do not emerge in expectable fashion as they would in a forming group composed of socially competent persons. Social workers must be aware of anomalies in personal and interpersonal functioning and be prepared to adapt their practice methodology in response to such differences.

A special requirement of the social worker is the need to *receive difficult behaviors nonreactively* and to learn to connect with and respond to the emotions behind the behavior. With some but not all socially unskilled populations, typical behaviors may feel personally assaultive but must be understood as nonpersonal expressions, however discomfiting they seem to be. Receiving difficult behaviors and relating to the person behind the behaviors is essential if one is to work successfully with socially unskilled persons. A professional task is to extend one's capacity to tolerate a range of difficult behaviors with equanimity.

The assaultive nature of difficult behaviors that operate outside of norms for typical social interchange can have a cumulative effect on the social worker, generating a sense of vulnerability. The practitioner may brace himself or herself subconsciously against the onslaught while still responding nonreactively to the person behind the dysfunctional behavior, seeking ways to respond that will be useful to that person and will preserve the accepting connection between worker and participant.

The process of relating to the person behind the difficult behavior and comprehending the dilemmas faced by socially unskilled persons, as well as experiencing firsthand the vulnerability they project behaviorally to the practitioner, serve to enable practice with these special populations to occur. The engendering of a sense of vulnerability in the social worker by socially unskilled persons is in fact their special gift to the practitioner, allowing him or her to feel as they do, thereby generating a sense of empathy with them. The capacity to feel empathy for socially unskilled persons is essential to working with them successfully.

A further phenomenon common among some socially unskilled populations is the tendency initially to ignore the social worker, proceeding as if he or she were not present, or unable to see or hear or understand them. This too is an unexpected situation for practitioners accustomed to working with socially competent persons in groups who are able to recognize the practitioner's competence and to relate to him or her. With socially unskilled populations prone to ignoring the social worker initially, the practitioner must find ways of inserting himself or herself into the interaction and engaging with the participants.

Specifics of Intervention in the Pregroup Period with Socially Unskilled Populations

Adaptations to the Technology of Social Work with Groups

The previous chapter addressed requirements for a Specialized practice that shape the practice methodology in particular ways. The materials in this chapter focus on the two most essential elements to be worked with in advancing socially unskilled populations. As well, two related tasks for the practitioner are identified: providing professional help to individuals contained within the context of their participation and place in the entity; and staging grouplike elements and experiences as a means of providing samples of what a group is like, and as a means of fostering progression of the entity.

Essential Elements

The two elements to be worked with in advancing socially unskilled populations are *the individual's relationship with himself or herself* and *the individ-*

Portions of this chapter were presented at the fifth annual symposium of the Association for the Advancement of Social Work with Groups, Detroit, 1983; the twenty-fourth annual symposium, Brooklyn, N.Y., 2002; and the twenty-fifth annual symposium, Boston, 2003.

ual's relationship with others, each needing specific help of the social worker in order to become functional for both the individual and the group-to-be. Liabilities in the individual's relationship to self stand as barriers to the evolution of relationship with others, that is, modifications or improvements in the first make possible the second.

The technology to be employed is classed as a *special, preliminary helping mode*, intended to aid socially unskilled populations in their progressions both as individuals and as potential candidates for group belonging, group membership, group engagement, and group relationships. The technology is a precise response to the dilemmas facing socially unskilled persons and may be limited in use to the period preceding group formation, however long this might be. In some instances this will be the whole practice.

The process of progressing from socially noncompetent to socially competent cannot just happen: it requires the specialized help of the social worker who comprehends both the individual and collective dilemmas of these populations, and who possesses the particular professional competence to recognize where individual functioning is arrested, how interpersonal connections are damaged, and how to correct these.

Interventions in the pregroup period constitute a class of *forerunner interventions* that contain the professional task of dealing with parts, part–part and part–whole connections in the here-and-now, while recognizing possibilities for spanning the gap between presocial behaviors and the projected potential of those behaviors for reaching sociality and generating group processes.

The pregroup period is a period that extends practice into a preliminary realm preceding group formation. It is a period not required by socially competent people as they convene to form a new group, but it is an essential time period for persons who lack social competence, and it must be viewed as an *extension of practice* necessary to the progression to social competence sufficient for the process of group formation. It defines both a period of time and activity and a state of the entity prior to achievement of group formation. It is both a presocial and a pregroup period.

The term "pregroup period" is intended to encompass that period in which socially unskilled people are together and experiencing an early form of collective life, preliminary to advancing to the ability to achieve group formation. This term is used in a different way from some of the literature, which describes a pregroup *phase* during which the social worker plans and prepares for a new group prior to the convening of its members (Hartford

1971:67–76; Kurland 1982). Some socially unskilled populations will have their entire experience in a pregroup state, while others will begin as pregroup and later evolve or recoup competences sufficient to form group.

Socially unskilled populations present two major features in their functioning: *low self-esteem and poor sense of self;* and *inadequate social behaviors and response.* The two appear together and feed each other in a circular way. They can be worked on concurrently, as alterations in one begin to alter the other. These two characteristics are the central focus of practice in the pregroup period. If the two can be addressed in ways that will make possible advancement to group formation and group functioning, persons who are commonly locked out of the benefits of group belonging and group participation can be helped to enter groupness.

These two elements of individual functioning—a good sense of self and a capacity to engage socially with others—are of critical importance to the forming of group and are the entrée into the domain of social and personal growth achieved through group experience.

Connections That Initiate Groupness

Initial behaviors in the presocial period of potential collective life are reflected in the particular ambience generated by the discomfort of being together but not connected. Individuals may be uneasy, unsettled, disengaged, tuned out, unconnected, uncommitted, unpredictable, unproductive, subject to swift contagion, or engaging in random forms of individual expression, often chaotic or out of control. In not knowing who they are individually, they are unable to recognize and know each other interactionally. The demand on the worker is to manage the parts that cannot yet form a whole.

In the beginnings of new groups there are several possible connections to be made. Normally developing groups are likely to make use of them all; socially unskilled populations may be unable to initiate any of them. The connections include individual to self, individual to individual, individual to subentity, individual to collective whole, individual to worker, and individual to content.

If relational connections have been damaged in previous life experience, the individual may have difficulty in both connections to peers and connections to worker. This leaves connection to content as the most likely entrée for engaging the individual and altering initial dynamics. The connection to content may also be impaired, as individuals with prior experience of failure in using materials or performing in activities display reluctance to engage, to risk failure, but also to risk succeeding.

Because the social relational route may not be possible, provision of content forms (activities) may be the best avenue for engaging individuals, such that they can experience compresence without having to engage in social interaction and can be assisted in experiencing successful doing. Enabling individuals to overcome reluctance to engage with content will be a particular task confronting the worker.

Relationship of Individual to Self: The First Connection

Deficits in the relationship to self are reflected in low self-esteem, poor self-image, and a lack of knowledge or awareness of one's own capabilities, one's sense of effectance and competence. The lack of these elements in personal functioning makes it difficult to recognize the competences of others and to relate to them. Thus, in the presocial period, individuals may lack the ability to recognize and differentiate others well until they can exercise this ability first in recognizing the competences of the self. When a whole constituency is composed of a number of persons whose relationship to self is incomplete, undeveloped, or damaged, the collective whole is unable to move to those first progressions leading to groupness, which spring from interpersonal recognition and connection, and shared purpose.

Persons with low self-esteem and a poor sense of self require special help in achieving an adequate relationship to self, constructed on experiential knowledge of the self as effective in engagement with the world (White 1963). This relationship to self appears to be central as prelude to social relationship with others and can be addressed through provision of activities within which the individual may be helped to experience success, opening the way to a new self-view, an altered sense of self, and in the process evolving an initial connection to the worker as helper.

A major task of the worker centers on creating comfort in being compresent, preferably through the use of low-demand activities that can engage people individually rather than interactively. The use of program activities is essential in the presocial period to engage, support, and sustain early forms of being together with limited interactional demand. Engaging the individual in media such as crafts creates a *first connection* between the person and his or her process and product, activating effectance vividly in a small, analogic sample of life. Small, repeated experiences at being effective with materials begins to alter the sense of self, contributing to revisions in the persona, the self-image, and new self-esteem. The ambience of this process that engages the person first with nonhuman objects becomes associated positively with the group, the worker, and the other participants. Working side by side, with no demand for interaction, in activities that have a high potential for success, and with worker help to ensure positive outcome, endows the collective and its constituent parts with a positive ambience. The association is strong between the person, his or her experienced effectance in process and outcome, and the context of persons within which the activated sense of being effective occurs.

The growth of self-esteem in one's own productivity and the visible view of other participants' similar process and product begin to create a sense of being and doing together although individually. This is a powerful forerunner to becoming relationally coengaged.

The medium will vary with the population involved. Gold and Kolodny (1978) were forced to use floor hockey and basketball, which initially their "socially dispossessed youth" demanded but lacked the social competence to sustain. Brooks (1978) used the concept of a health club and an exercise program with isolated, reclusive older men in a slum hotel as an initial means to attract and engage them.

Relationship to Others: The Second Connection

In the presocial period, a second major task of the worker is that of dealing with *presocial, untutored forms of interaction*. These are likely to be sporadic, limited exchanges of an order that lack the potential for progression toward groupness in their raw, concrete form. An improved sense of self precedes the ability to recognize others as potential relationships, but the skills of relating must be assisted to enable social ties to form. The yet-to-be entity must be viewed as an arena in which the ways of social interaction and social behaviors can be modeled and demonstrated, learned and practiced.

The view of the enterprise as an *experiential learning modality* defines the nature of a whole class of interventions on the part of the worker. The essential task is to supply guidance to the inept, awkward attempts of participants to connect with one another. Learning how to go, through the direction provided by the worker, allows for social learning to occur in concrete moments of interaction, gradually becoming shaped into positive, relevant exchanges that can contribute small advances toward the collective whole. This is not unnecessary control on the part of the worker (Vinter 1967) but a beneficial addition to the raw exchange, enabling it to play out better and to provide precise, small learnings to the participants.

The small added ingredient that the worker contributes to an interactional exchange provides guidance in how to go in relation to others. The worker contribution may take the form of *interpreting the intentionality* of one person's behavior toward another, creating the possibility of understanding the other. It might come as a *limit set* on how one person is behaving in relation to another, or as a *specific direction* for how to go. It might *provide words* to be said that would resolve a difficulty between persons. It may highlight the effect of one participant's behavior on another.

Through unobtrusive direction and guidance, and assists in specific, small, concrete moments, the worker gradually provides an *experiential blueprint* for how to go together. This action begins to total to an arrival, at the end of the presocial period, at the beginnings of sociality, with individual behaviors reflecting the socializing effects of the worker contribution. In effect, the not-yet-group experience gives direction that can open the possibility of future groupness.

Learning how is like an experience of a peer group with the added ingredient of a worker who guides, helps the interaction to be good and functional, and provides socialization to the untutored interactional response, transforming the experience to one that is positive and beneficial. Without this contribution of the worker, socially unskilled populations simply perpetuate their socially noncompetent ways through successive experiences with others, which could have been good and beneficial had worker guidance been an ingredient.

This task requires that the social worker have a good (or developing) sense of what kinds of social interaction can progress to groupness in order to recognize those moments when interventive help can redirect it to a better course. Practitioners who work with socially unskilled populations recognize this professional task as essential. Without professional intervention to help make the interaction good, and to assist the social learnings to be acquired, the progression from presocial to social, from collectivity to group, may be impossible.

It is here that one sees the Specialized Methodology of the worker most clearly: the necessity of providing *social interactional help* in ways not needed in groups composed of normally functioning persons marks this as a special, essential methodology.

The important feature of this social work practice technology is that it is lodged in significant moments of authentic, meaningful natural life experiences. It is provided *unobtrusively* as specific guidance *in the moment*—in concrete moments—and occurs as a small added component of guidance in real-life situations and experiences. The learnings arising from these interventions are small, specific, concrete: increments accumulating over time, totaling to significant socialization. The practice provides social-emotional learning in situ, in concrete moments as they arise, as distinct from practices that attempt to teach behaviors cognitively or those that attempt to program behaviors.

It is a naturalistic methodology that joins participants in what they are engaged in and is a part of the individual and collective process. This situates the social worker to contribute relevant inputs at salient moments. It is much like the process of parenting very young children through giving intermittent guidance and direction to the child at moments when needed.

Two Special Tasks of the Social Worker with Socially Unskilled Populations

Two aspects of worker technology in the Specialized Methodology have particular importance in work with socially unskilled populations:

- dealing with individual participants in the context of their anticipated membership and belonging in the evolving collectivity or group
- generating grouplike elements in the practice, to enable participants to experience small moments, samples, or equivalents of groupness and know experientially what group is like, in advance of their capacity to achieve it

These two elements essential to the practice are addressed in turn but in actuality will occur concurrently.

Dealing with Individuals in the Context of Their Belonging in the Entity

The context of a collective experience—group or collectivity—establishes a boundary and domain on the social worker's intervention with individuals. The worker must respect the existing and not yet existent, potential relationships among the participants, taking care not to engage with individuals in ways that will supplant, limit, or damage possible or existing peer ties.

This task is essential in all group work practice but holds heightened importance when the populations participating in the achieved entity lack competence to interact socially and to construct group. When interactional processes between and among peers are not in place and the practitioner is fostering appropriate behaviors on the part of individuals, helping them to advance beyond presocial behaviors and achieve self-management, the practitioner faces a huge pitfall. Particularly when social relationships among peers are not yet developed, the worker must maintain focus on the eventuality of peer ties existing and must engage with the individual participant *as if* there were group processes in place or developing.

In their absence, the worker may be tempted to engage with each individual as if there were only one-to-one treatment in the presence of others. To go this route is to eliminate the possibility of group coming into existence, thereby generating a different form of practice and losing the socializing power of the group where it is most needed.

The task of helping individuals to functional performance in an anticipated social entity defines and draws boundaries around what the worker will deal with and how, in the social arena of the possible group. The domain of worker influence defines help to individuals *in the social context of their togetherness.* It requires that help to an individual should not alter the view the members have of one another. The issue is that the worker is not related to one individual but to each individual, to subunits, and to the whole entity and must maintain awareness of these elements while dealing with an individual.

The focus of this practice on assisting and fostering functional personal performance and interpersonal engagement provides the safeguard against falling into the trap of treating individuals in the presence of others. The intention of the Specialized Methodology is to develop group, to the extent possible, recognizing that group belonging and participation are critical to the social growth of the participants. To overstep the boundaries of help to individuals in the context of their belonging in the entity is to deny the potency of the small social form—collectivity or group—as a major contributor to social growth, development, and change of its constituents. Help to individuals in the context of their (potential) belonging thus defines interventions that are unobtrusive, small adaptations, enabling improved individual functioning within the entity without singling out the person unduly.

Generating Grouplike Experience:
Simulations of Groupness

While all social workers who work with groups may employ techniques for fostering groupness, the creation of *grouplike experience* is of special importance for socially unskilled populations. Lacking the social competence essential to generate elements of group life, socially unskilled persons require particular assistance to achieve a sense of being part of a social entity.

Direct interventions with individuals and with interactions between constituents each contribute toward the establishment of an evolving collective life; in addition, there are a number of ways to deliver *simulations of groupness* to socially unskilled populations.

The intent is to deliver experiential moments that are grouplike in nature, and which have the potential of providing glimpses, small samples, temporary moments, of what group belonging is like. Such encapsulated moments, experiences in miniature, can contribute cumulatively to social learning about togetherness, group belonging, and groupness.

Socially unskilled populations may lack firsthand experiential knowledge of what belonging in functional small groups is like and hence may require special provisions to gain it. Such small experiential moments are *externally produced* or *programmatically induced,* rather than evolving inter-

nally, affectively, and relationally in the minds and feelings of the participants, as would be true in a normal, socially competent, developing group.
Simulations of groupness that contribute a sense of being together and
convey what togetherness is like may serve as an alternative route to groupness when normal avenues of relationship to peers and worker are not yet
available and effective.

Grouplike Experiences

Grouplike experiences make use of alternative avenues other than relational-interactional in order to generate small experienced samples of what
group life can be like, and to prepare for entry into groupness. Grouplike
experiences create an *ambience akin to togetherness* and are the vehicle for
delivering experiential, firsthand knowledge of group life, and for evolving
an interior view of the participants as intimates—"us."

There are a number of forms of grouplike experience available to the
practitioner, each intended to demonstrate the possible, to create experiential samples, moments of acting in concert. They include elements that are

- linguistic
- compresent
- structural
- concerting
- instructional-definitional
- environmental extensions
- programmatic
- ritual and ceremonial

LINGUISTIC

Wordings in the plural used as collective designations are intended to establish ways of thinking about the entity prior to manifestations of groupness
emanating among the members. "We," "us." "our," "everybody," and "all"
are terms employed by the social worker that acknowledge the collective
whole before it actually exists and establish the concept.

COMPRESENT

"Being together with" is the meaning of compresence. Compresence may have both a classificatory and an emotional component, a sense of being together, awareness of the whole as fact, but also as an affective sense of the others as constituting a definable entity.

Lacking the relational-interactional component that drives joining, identifying with, and belonging, socially unskilled populations need special provision for experiencing a sense of compresence, of knowing togetherness that is more than simply being in the same place at the same time.

The challenge for the practitioner is to create a sense of "us-doing" while maintaining needed social distance and limiting the demand for interpersonal involvement and interaction. A form of compresence is experienced through collective engagement in one activity in one time period, individually employed by each participant, with both common and unique features in process, productivity, and product from person to person, creating the *effect of collective doing* though separate and individual, with some sense of being part of a larger whole. The use of activities that provide for participating individually but have the effect of collective doing can create a pregroup sense of togetherness. Arts and crafts and many play or game forms also offer this combined effect.

STRUCTURAL

Webster's defines structure as "something arranged in a definite pattern of organization." Structure is viewed as the means of ordering, in ways that provide support for being together while preserving needed distance from one another in the presocial period.

Structure may reflect spatial arrangements that provide some degree of physical distance combined with some measure of limited approach. For example, wheelchairs in a circle may serve to bring the occupants closer, while the positioning of the large chairs maintains distance from one another.

In the author's experience of work with volatile, impulsive, emotionally disturbed children, the use of a large room for arts and crafts yielded interesting reverses in structure: a table and chairs in the center of the room created a convening place surrounded by open space and some additional tables and chairs, such that the structure was in front of us, in the form of the activity at the table, rather than behind or around, so that the participants were not closed in and had the freedom to move into the open space as needed. Structuring the activity in the center invited engagement and focus in a voluntary way and supported both proximity and distancing.

Structure is also inherent in various forms of activity employed in social work practice with groups, offering a wide variety of features that can be matched to the needs of socially unskilled persons. As well, activities can generate and support participation and togetherness and structure opportunities for such experiences as role-taking, turn-taking, cooperating, and sharing—experiential examples of acting in concert.

Wide-area games such as baseball contain a particular mix of ingredients, both highly structured and inherently distancing. In the author's practice experience, emotionally disturbed children who played social games in their small group with considerable difficulty were observed playing baseball successfully without an adult present. This seemingly impossible feat was analyzed in terms of the play form itself. Not only is baseball highly visible, acceptable, and identified with in the culture, but it contains particular attributes that make it workable even with aggressive, impulsive, acting-out children. First, it covers a wide area, thereby distancing the players from one another. It is a highly structured play form with a known pattern for plays. It contains a set of roles, each with its own assigned activities. Its rules are well defined and well-known. The possibility of advancing to the most salient roles sustains interest. Performance is individual but has collective outcomes. It is not relationally interactive.

Many structured game forms contain a two-step start-stop pattern, consisting of action followed by cessation of action, while the action is reacted to, replayed, or scrutinized. This patterning of interaction into small contained units is comparable to interactional exchanges among socially unskilled persons, as the interaction deteriorates and is stopped, sorted out, resolved, and restored, ready for ongoing interaction to proceed.

CONCERTING

To concert is defined by *Webster's* as "to act in harmony or conjunction." It is used here to identify program forms that involve individual participation in a congregate activity, and that generate a collective product achievable only through the contribution of individuals rendered in concert.

Group singing is an example: a low-demand activity involving the concerting of individual participation into a collective product and supporting a sense of being a part as an individual contributor. The collective product is achievable only through the concerting of individual contributions.

In another activity medium, a craft is done individually with the individual products contributed to a collective outcome in which the individual parts are visible within the whole. Panels that contain multiple individual paintings, or murals that are generated through individual contributions, are examples.

Some small-group games that involve individual performance in role, in a turn-taking sequence, and practice in performing both as a specific role-taker and as a nonrole coparticipant might be seen as a form of concerting: each player in turn makes an individual contribution to the collective play.

INSTRUCTIONAL/DEFINITIONAL

Circumstances arising in the entity may require a special behavioral performance not usually present in the functioning of the participants, or invite reflection on dysfunctional behavior. The social worker may express the requirements as a cautionary instruction, evoking behaviors needed in a special situation. This instruction may generate a collective response, produced individually.

> In the craft of painting on glass, there comes a moment when the pictures produced are ready to be framed. Anticipating the potential for disorder in the collective, inherent in the situation of framing the paintings one by one, the social worker said "You will all need to be patient as you wait for help in the framing of each person's picture." Unaccustomed waiting behaviors resulted, as the participants stretched their capacity to delay gratification. The directive also implied behaviors that will remain in control. One boy stated, "I'm going to look through this book while I wait, so I won't get into trouble." Others busied themselves in various ways, principally in making improvements to their paintings while they waited. The instruction puts into

place a new order of behavior that is manifest at both the individual and the collective levels.

When Gold and Kolodny (1978:152) observed their almost adult group members placing a pornographic picture in the rear window of the van for other motorists to see, they commented, "What do you think seeing that picture will tell people about us?"

EXTENDING ENVIRONMENTS

A deliberate staging of excursions into the community can heighten the awareness of "us" from "not us," collectively experienced through transplanting to unfamiliar alternate milieus. Out-trips may define experientially the entity and its participants as intimates, familiars, in an environment of strangers. They need to be timed appropriately, following sufficient time to establish first some sense of the entity in the habitual meeting space.

PROGRAMMATIC

Activities of various kinds are an extraordinary resource for all practitioners of social work with groups and offer specialized uses for practice with socially unskilled persons and entities. The focus is on *simulations of groupness* made possible by and experienced in various activity forms.

In practice with beginning groups, social workers frequently use activities to foster and support interaction and to initiate sociality among the members. The capability of activities serves to engage the members and advance them interactionally toward achievement of groupness, mobilizing and enhancing the natural interactional capabilities of participants.

With socially unskilled populations, whose natural, interactional capabilities may be partially absent or wholly impaired, activity becomes a primary means to deliver samples of what it is like to be part of a group and an essential route to getting there. Activities offer opportunities to create simulations of groupness through particular features inherent in each activity form.

A precise simulation of groupness is experienced in small social group games that generate interaction and collective behaviors specific to each game. In play, game-related interaction arises, creating an experienced equivalent to groupness. As well, group games are recognized as providing opportunities to learn and to practice, in miniature, behaviors functional to living successfully in society: the game form is viewed as a small analog of society, delivering opportunities to learn roles, to subscribe to rules, to adapt behavior to the requirements of the situation, and to experience in a brief time frame the outcomes of one's behavior (Boyd in Simon 1971). Boyd identified group games as containing the inherent capacity to enable and sustain sociality through activity means and recognized this particular activity as providing basic training in participating, role-taking, contributing—as the "training wheels" for group membership, serving as the forerunners of groupness by placing participants in a collective interactional situation for a limited time period with a contained demand.

Each of the activity forms available for use by the social worker with collectivities and groups contains specific features capable of advancing individual and collective performance. Progressions in activity form matched to the developing capacity of socially unskilled persons can support, sustain, and advance social competence and foster progressions in interpersonal engagement.

There are many activities that contain the potential for exceptional collective engagement; sometimes it is not the activity form itself but rather progressions in the interpersonal functioning of the participants that propel them into a domain of sustained collective action above and beyond the individual functioning level of each constituent. Together, they may enter a realm of collective functioning capable of propelling individuals and entity to new levels.

Even socially unskilled persons may experience this phenomenon of entitative action lifting the participants into a new domain of social functioning. Brooks's group of isolated older men reflected this phenomenon in their dramatic use of swimming, which marked the moment of breakthrough as they began to talk with one another in a new, sustained way (Brooks 1978). A further breakthrough occurred when they began to assess their situation in single-room occupancy of a slum tenement, established aspirations together, identified their hopes, and began to plan an improved future for themselves.

In the author's practice with emotionally disturbed children, a comparable breakthrough is reported.

The group had progressed to using activity forms of greater complexity and longer duration. Linoleum cutting and block printing spanned two meetings late in the first year of their group life. In the first session, carving of chosen patterns on linoleum blocks was marked by individual performances not functional to the task. One boy carved his chair seat; another threw his tool at the table as if it were a game with a jackknife; one ignored safety precautions until he cut himself; one tried to carve with one hand while holding a large lollipop with the other; one was sure everyone else had a better tool than he did; one refused to use the tool to outline his design first as a safety precaution against cutting the design in error; one created a design that was not functional to the craft.

In the second session a small printing press, paper, and multicolored inks were available for block printing, and a pane of glass and a roller for use in applying ink to designs. Soon everyone was printing, with all that this entails in the preparation and cleaning of the blocks. The meeting became an endless process marked by excitement and pleasure with each successful print and was characterized to an astonishing degree by the sharing of equipment, patiently waiting turns for the printing press, cooperatively producing ink-printed pages on which to print multicolored designs, freely sharing each other's successes and giving recognition to each other. The children were quite awed by the finished products and for a good hour sustained a fully cooperative approach to the printing. The activity lifted the children above their normal level of functioning and sustained them at a new level of productivity and togetherness.

At the close of the meeting, the children lingered at the doorway, shuffling through their prints admiringly. They noticed that some of the frosted window panes in the double doors had been replaced with clear glass. Spontaneously they proposed that *their prints* could be fitted to the window frames, as a replacement for frosting, which protected the room from unwanted outside observers and distractions, actively holding the prints up to the windows to test for size and fit. This was a first collective action on the part of the members, directly arising from their shared experience with the printing press, and advancing their rising sense of groupness to proffer a *group-made solution* to an organizational problem—a first instance of the group acting in relation to the wider world.

The yield of grouplike experiences and simulations of groupness is a *representation of group* in the minds of the participants, as firsthand knowledge of the whole and of oneself as part of the constituency, and as *exemplars of the possible*. Grouplike experience may be generated by the social worker and sometimes arises as the signal that the participants are approaching groupness.

RITUALS AND CEREMONIES

Patterned ways of doing things often evolve in a functioning group, folkways reflective of elements important to the members. These sometimes generate a particular ritual or ceremony. They may be as simple as the customary habitual programmatic pattern followed in each group meeting (activity—snack—discussion).

> Whenever the group traveled somewhere on an out-trip, the social worker placed gum and candy in the glove compartment beforehand. On getting into the car, Dan sat in the front seat and opened the glove compartment, looked in, and remarked, "Yep, they are all here, gum and candy for us." His tone applauding this simple provision, he closed the compartment door and relaxed into his seat.

Folkways exist in the culture as well, as activities recognized as having a particular meaning or function for group life. Patterned doing can be found in such rituals as the forming of a circle with joined crossed hands for the singing of "Taps" at the close of a group meeting or a camp day. The purpose of such rituals appears to be one of fostering a sense of togetherness, of manifesting and highlighting the entity.

Celebratory events such as special meetings marking the ending of an entity's life can also be seen as ceremonial rituals, which give particular acknowledgment to the place and importance of the group in the experience of the participants.

The Centrality of Actional Modes

Mobilizing Effectance

The heart of the specialized practice in the pregroup period is the activation of individual engagement with objects, nonhuman and human, in the environment. The *actional mode* of *engaging with and having effects upon objects* in one's environment (White 1963) is recognized as the means by which individuals create and maintain current connection between the self and the external world and experience themselves as effective in that world.

One of the earliest competences of humans and central throughout our lives, the process of having effects, feeling a sense of effectance, of being effective, totaling through repeated cumulative experience to a sense of competence, defines the sense of self and the place and connections of self in the social world (White 1963).

The actional mode—doing—puts the individual in charge of his or her own firsthand engagement and experience of self in the wider world, with its own feedback to him or her of that engagement. It invokes self-directed functioning in which the individual is the central player and other individuals and the social worker are in ancillary positions.

Socially unskilled populations may not be exercising their effectance sufficiently to sustain and advance the sense of self; practice in the pregroup period recognizes the need to activate and support the participants in a doing mode, mobilizing the executive function of the self, opening to new experience, new tests of effectiveness in the world, with new feedback of effectiveness to the self.

How central is doing in all our lives: I ran 6 miles—I baked a cake—I built a cabinet—I wove a placemat—I wrote a paper—. In the joyful words of a developmentally delayed preschool child in a shelter, after rolling a piece of plasticene into a short snake and holding it up to be seen: "I di[d]—!" And of a young child as she propelled her kiddy car on the sidewalk: "I'm GOING!"

The actional mode formalizes an inherent skill of engagement with one's world, deliberately putting the person into action with materials or activities and assisting him or her to experience success in using these. This is a formalized version of "having effects" intended to reestablish this important connection to the outside world in ways that reflect the self favorably, contribute advances in sense of self, and open the route to social connection and social competence. Connection to self, the development of a new persona, self-view, experientially acquired as "effective" and "able," is prelude to an altered view of others as possible social relationships.

The actional mode engages right brain competences of the person (the creative, inventive, holistic) essential to the experiencing of effectance. It is the practice mode of choice with socially unskilled persons, activating individual performance in ways that "talking groups" cannot do. The actional mode also enables persons who are not yet social to be together, participating individually, and supports and sustains compresence in the absence of social skills.

At a more complex level, entering into actional modes with other individuals—doing with others—represents a progression, combining individual doing with social context and social engagement. Within actional forms that require social participation, individuals can learn, develop, and practice social skills essential to living in the social world. Actional modes used in practice with socially unskilled persons may advance both individual effectance and social connection. Thus, actional modes address both individual and collective needs and are relevant for furthering the functioning of both.

Centrality of Activities

Activities are the individual and collective *specific forms of the actional mode*, the means of activating individual and collective experiences of effectance.

They are essential to all social work practice with groups but have additional potency with socially unskilled persons.

Activities, sometimes referred to as program by social group workers, include an array of actional, artful, and analogic forms, from those that preexist and are present and in use in all cultures and all times; to those that arise spontaneously and are serviceable at critical moments; to those that a social worker may improvise as precise, tailor-made forms invented and designed to meet particular, recognized needs of individuals and collective in a particular situation or circumstance. Often these are generated as inventions in response to necessity in critical moments, or when a confluence of circumstances evokes spur-of-the-moment inventiveness.

Group members were immobilized by disappointment when our planned hike and cookout were rained out. The social worker, absorbing their feelings, was pressed to think of an alternative activity. She placed a long piece of kraft paper across the floor of the meeting room and invited the group to "go for a hike on paper." Together we "walked" the route, in memory, drawing its featured attributes in a progressive sequence. When the route was laid out and colorfully illustrated, we turned it into a Snakes and Ladders game, made spinners and designated features which would prompt a missed turn, a step backwards, or an accelerated move ahead, identifying "failure to look both ways before crossing the street," "careful avoidance of stepping on a wild flower," etc., and played the game. The hike on paper became our reality, and we ate lunch sitting on the floor, gathered around our mapped route. In terms of cooperative planning and integrated working together, the activity propelled the group members in their functioning as a group in ways well beyond what would have been achieved had the actual hike taken place.

The children arrived for their group meeting, excited about fresh-fallen snow, almost unable to be contained indoors. In the corner of the meeting room stood a large cardboard packing box which had contained a new refrigerator. The social worker put together fresh snow, children's excitement, and a large box: we transformed the box into a very long toboggan with curved front, attached a pulling rope, and headed for the hill in a nearby park. The toboggan was long enough to accommodate the whole group plus worker, generating a strong sense of groupness as we rode the hill together.

Preexisting activities include play and game forms, arts and crafts, dramatics, dance, musical forms, sports, and other outdoor activities, each offering a myriad of specific activity possibilities, and each available for adaptation and use for social work purposes with individuals and groups as imports from their ordinary social/recreational deployment.

Activities provide structure and support to being together when these cannot be generated through social interaction and relationship. Activities provide the means to be engaged with nonhuman objects when engagement with human objects is not yet possible. They create a context within which persons can be and do, an arena within which to engage, a way to be with others, and a provision of shared (or collectively known, held in common) experiences. Activities thus constitute an alternative form, equivalent to the structure and process created by a set of interpersonal relationships. They are the means through which persons who are not yet socially competent are able to be together in a limited, undemanding way. They provide natural means of expression and contain their own processes, which can contribute to people's growth and development.

Activities are a practice modality that provides opportunities to experience oneself and others in action, singly and together, in an activity-generated form of effectance and sociality. They contain their own developmental and expressive processes and make their own contribution to the experiences of self as being effective. In the arena of activity processes, social competences can be learned and practiced.

Activities can be seen as a substitute for sociality not yet developed—a means of holding together the persons and processes. Most of all, activities provide routes to address directly the needs of participants to experience being effective and to find their way to socially competent behaviors.

When a craft was introduced for the first time in the Single Moms Group, most of the women engaged enthusiastically with the materials. Jane hung back and was clearly uncomfortable. She said, "I was never any good in art at school." The worker replied that she was a child then, and now she was a different person—an adult, competent in child-raising and in her employment. This wasn't school, and no one would be judging or rating what Jane produced in the craft. It was for fun. Hesitantly Jane began, and soon she was fully absorbed in what she was doing. At the close of the session, she was pleased and excited with what she had made, and with the discovery that she had talents unknown to herself.

Dramatically, she was revisiting her self-view, defining herself as able, almost unable to contain her joy. Other group members engaged admiringly with her around her evident talent and the object she had made.

Activities each contain their own inherent developmental processes, capable of influencing and socializing both individual participants and the collective whole. They take the pressure off premature relational demands and offer their own ways of being and doing together.

This is an *analogic practice* where interesting, pleasurable, and appropriate activities serve to activate individual effectance and social engagement. In themselves the activities offer their own valuable experiences, and in the process of engaging with them, that which is problematic in personal and social functioning is displayed, becoming accessible to professional assists. Analogic practices play out as "life," and in so doing they produce small analogs of problem solving that apply to other parts of people's lives in ways that advance the person. The practice plays out as life joined by the social worker for purposes of enhancing it.

John was an extremely dysfunctional participant, loudly demanding all of the worker's attention and making it difficult to assist others with their craft work. He attempted to bribe others to stay way from the group meetings, proclaiming that he liked it best "when just me and George are here." In his own participation, he tried each activity briefly, without succeeding, then backed away in frustration and defeat, loudly decrying, "I can't do this."

The worker had chosen a craft with a particular process and outcome, having a good potential for successful use, with little skill involved. John was obviously impressed by the clear outline of his first pattern made by spattered paint but marred by some big blobs of paint. He moved quickly to use a stencil instead.

Worker: John, I'd like you to try a second spatter painting now.
JOHN: I can't do it any good.
WORKER: I think you could do a very good one now. You know how to do it, and I'll help you do it without blobs.
JOHN: It'll be lousy. It'll be my worst work yet. It'll be no good.
WORKER: John, I don't want you to leave today thinking you can't do it. Come on, let's try. I have a feeling you can make a good one.

John accepted fine quality drawing paper for his best opus with a grand air of doing it only to please the worker. All the time we were pinning the patterns down, he kept up a running commentary about his impending worst work. "What cheap pins," he remarked, "what crummy patterns. The paints are lousy. The Centre is cheap, buying such lousy paints." His tone was scathing. "It won't work," he said.

Worker showed him again what made big blobs, how to use less paint, a good grip on his screen, and a gentle motion with the brush. He began very carefully and continued to work with controlled, careful motions, while commenting, "It'll be awful."

When the patterns came off, he said jubilantly, "I knew it would come out right. I had a special feeling. . . . This is the first good thing I've done in eleven years, 'cause that's how old I am. I had a feeling, all the time I was working, that it would be good, and it is!" Then, thoughtfully, he said, "Maybe if I stood up to do art in school, it would work there too."

Later, Worker asked if the boys wanted to have any of their work on the display board, or keep them all. John replied, "I'd like mine hung up. I've never had anything hung up, ever before. Not one thing in my whole life!"

Some socially unskilled populations may need to begin in activity forms that involve them individually and/or in one-by-one, turn-taking, "parallel play" forms, which can mobilize individual effectance and an improving sense of self. Examples are the author's use of arts and crafts with emotionally disturbed children whose collective life was chaotic and whose sense of self was poorly developed; Brooks's (1978) use of an exercise program to engage reclusive older men; Weissman and Schwartz's (1989:52–53) "use of [s]tructured program such as exercises, sing-alongs, poetry writing, simple crafts and guided group discussion"; and perhaps the reminiscence activity often employed with disengaged, frail older people, resonating on their prior life experiences to activate current participation and involvement.

A much more challenging practice is reflected in the work of Gold and Kolodny (1978) with "socially dispossessed" teenagers. Their preferred activity of team sports placed an exceptional demand on the workers to enable functional individual participation and at the same time to mediate conflictual interaction that continually interrupted the playing out of the game, in effect concurrently dealing with the two central tasks of practice with socially unskilled persons.

Activities are both context and means (Vinter 1985) through which socially unskilled persons can advance their social competence.

The tasks of the social worker in initiating this Specialized Methodology begin with the establishment of activities as the content "norm" for the entity. This may occur gradually in the early life of the entity, requiring time and pleasurable experiences, and becoming ensconced as activity use is serviceable in meeting needs. The practitioner needs conviction that activities are a necessary part of the practice. Some attempts at activity use may be unsuccessful, requiring analysis of the circumstances contributing to their failure and readiness to try again. Caution is needed in recognizing unreadiness to use a particular activity at a particular time, rather than viewing the activity itself as lacking. The task for the practitioner is to determine which activities are suitable, appropriate, and timely and to match the chosen activity to where the participants are in their individual and collective functioning. Some of the chaotic behaviors experienced in beginning work with socially unskilled persons will modify as norms and expectations, routines, and patterns of activity are established and individuals begin to respond to the provisions of a grouplike experience.

Major tasks of the practitioner include selecting and adapting media to make them usable for a socially unskilled population; inventing activity forms with items at hand, in the pressure of the moment; and using activities progressively, from simple to complex, from short-term to extended, from individually used to interactive and collectively engaging. In response to the developing capacity of the participants to sustain interest and involvement for a longer duration and to engage in activities that evoke and provide for the evolution of growing competence in participation and performance, activity selection and use must parallel and match such progressions.

Beyond the selection and staging of appropriate activity forms, the social worker must view the individual and interactional processes arising within each activity use as the locus where that which is problematic, unresolved, or merely inept can be addressed and influenced with the addition of worker intervention. Connecting with the interactional process that flows jointly out of activity use and interpersonal engagement opens opportunities for contributing professional influence—to the individual's own participation and process, to the interpersonal interactional process arising as the activity plays out, and to the activity's own process as it thrusts the participants into new levels of engagement together.

Engagement of the social worker with participants in activities that create their own analogs, as real-life experience, gives the opportunity to influence social functioning of individuals and entity at a deeper, characterological level.

The process of intervening is partialized, distributed, and piecemeal and requires an adequate time frame for the interventive task. The social worker sustains awareness of each participant's functioning within the whole, contributing professional inputs as needed. These cumulate, culminating in significant change and advancement in individual and collective functioning.

Functional behaviors, achieved within the predominant activity form used, may not be transferable immediately to another activity new to the participants. In new circumstances, dysfunctional behaviors may recur, and appropriate behaviors may need to be relearned, before they can become dependable, consolidated, and transferable.

Activities can be seen as offering options and progressions in engagement and interaction. Activities precisely selected and adapted to the needs of the socially unskilled population to be addressed are critical in this practice.

Grouplike Experiences—Camps and Campuses

In many new social situations, programmatic means are employed to generate rapidly some initial group feeling, some early attachment to and identification with persons who will form an entity together. Program activities to accelerate a sense of groupness may be used when the time frame is brief, as in summer camps, or when a need for rapid bonding seems urgent, as with incoming new students at university, in order that strangers can find connections so necessary to their survival and social functioning in a new context, and that their beginnings together will lead to well-functioning, sustaining groups.

Activities also figure prominently in children's groups, providing structured and supportive means of being and doing together, while social competences are being developed, and preceding those age-stages where verbal interaction becomes the primary mode of group life.

Programmatic means must be recognized for their capability for initiating those social interactional processes that lead to relationship and group formation, and for providing vehicles through which relationships can develop and be sustained.

To a much greater degree, activities are the primary means through which socially unskilled populations can be enabled to enter social worlds in limited ways. While persons who possess normal social competences will use activities to identify, to relate, to activate group belonging, and to form and use groups, socially unskilled populations may make distinctive uses of program activities.

The principle difference in activity use between socially competent and socially unskilled populations can be seen in what is generated through participation in activities: socially competent populations take off together, activating and using their social interactional capacities in collective group endeavors. Socially unskilled populations, in their program use, are akin to young children in their collective functioning because those central social competences are not yet developed and in place. Thus, the program activity serves as a learning modality, providing ways of being engaged with others and offering teachings, directives on how to be together functionally, emotionally incorporated as social learnings.

Activities act as stand-ins for what members are able to generate together relationally. Grouplike experiences are produced by and through the activity form, through its innate requirements for participation and performance in particular ways and through the ways in which the activity plays out. In this sense, grouplike experience is externally generated by the program form, rather than arising in the feelings of the participants as they relate and interact.

Activities create an aura, an ambience akin to groupness, providing moments that lift the individual participants out of themselves into a collective domain where they can sample what it is like to be a group, to draw close, to work together, to share emotion, to cooperate. Such moments permit glimpses of group life that become examples of group in the minds of the participants. Activities make it possible to be together and engaged productively on an individual level.

14

The Route to an Achievable Entity

How the Specialized Practice Evolves

In this chapter the elements, processes, and interventions leading to an effective experience in the pregroup period are examined. The materials address the *route and processes* leading to an entity serviceable to the tasks of enabling competent social functioning, and they identify a practice modality evolving in three steps or stages. Steps in the transformation from presocial to social are described.

The capability of *collectivity* is explored as an achievable social form, functional to the task of working with socially unskilled persons, when elements of group life are not attainable. The chapter explores how social competence evolves within the group experience and details the domains of intervention.

The Route

The route to the formation of an entity with socially unskilled persons is indirect and roundabout. Because normal social interactional processes are not available, the social worker must take responsibility for establishing elements that together will create an entity sufficiently functional to enable growth and change in individuals and in the collective whole. The task is one of surrogation in group processes, as identified in chapter 7.

The elements may be initiated in a piecemeal fashion, each opening a component essential to the practice and gradually taking hold and becoming established. Together, the elements, which are purposive, relational, normative, procedural, and substantive, define the nature and boundaries of the experience to be had in the entity and how it will play out.

Evolution of the entity occurs in a *stepped pattern*, each step in turn opening the gateway to the next step. This pattern gives the practice a phased appearance, marking off each step as having features different from its predecessors. A growing complexity also characterizes the sequential steps. The steps are identified as an initial stage that is Prerelational, an intermediate stage that is Part-relational, and a final stage that is Relational-preparatory.

The steps in the pregroup period must be seen as preceding and preliminary to the formation and phases of group development experienced in the progression of normally developing groups (Garland, Jones, and Kolodny, 1965, 1973; Sarri and Galinsky 1974, 1985; Northen 1969, 1988). The pattern and developmental progression in the Specialized Methodology in the pregroup period are illustrated in table 14.1.

TABLE 14.1

Route to and Evolution of an Achievable Entity in the Pregroup Period

	INITIAL STAGE—PRERELATIONAL	INTERMEDIATE STAGE—PART-RELATIONAL	FINAL STAGE—RELATIONAL-PREPARATORY
Content	Establishing activity as content mode Use of activities with successful outcomes	Extending the forms of activity used, re duration, complexity, intervention and skill required	Employing activity forms that enable interpersonal engagement and connection
	Use of activities not requiring interaction	Fostering interaction within activities	Selecting activities that employ interaction
	Engaging individuals in activity, assisting in effective use Enabling experiencing of effectance	Encouraging experimentation in activity use, to activate effectance	Enabling increasing involvement, commitment, productivity, and competence in use of activities

(continued)

TABLE 14.1
Route to and Evolution of an Achievable Entity in the Pregroup Period (*continued*)

	INITIAL STAGE—PRERELATIONAL	INTERMEDIATE STAGE—PART-RELATIONAL	FINAL STAGE—RELATIONAL-PREPARATORY
Relationship	Establishing worker presence, involvement, and participation	Establishing worker role	Extending sphere of influence in worker role
	Initiating relationship between worker and each participant	Relationship between worker and each participant becomes well established and used	Relationship between worker and each participant, deepens, expands
	Establishing a visible helping role through assistance with activity	Helping role of worker expands beyond activity	Helping role of worker established, more general and enlarged
	Individualizing each person Enabling tolerance of compresence	Tolerance of individual idiosyncrasies evolves from worker's individualizing of each person	Peer relationships are initiated and fostered
	Sustaining the whole	Prerelational awareness of one another as part of activity	Beginning awareness of entity
Entity	Orienting to nature of entity Establishing boundaries, requirements, routines, patterns	Elements of entity are becoming established	Learning how to go in peer relationships Learning to function together
	Establishing norms for individual and entity functioning	Norms become effective dysfunctional behaviors adapting	Interactive moments assisted by worker
	Managing interactive process	Interactional arena becomes functional	Practice at being in social interaction
	Providing limits, controls	Limits become effective	Mastering the skills of being related

Stages in the Pregroup Period

Initial Stage: Prerelational and Orienting

The first stage in the pregroup period is characterized as both *prerelational and orienting*. Prerelational characterizes the presocial nature of individual functioning, personally and interpersonally. Orienting identifies the major task of setting the stage for a collective experience designed to advance social competence of the participants. While orienting as participants to the nature of a new group experience is a common task facing all people in forming new groups, orienting here defines tasks of the worker unique to practice with socially unskilled populations in the initial stage. In fact, because the social elements expectable in socially competent persons in the initiating phase of a forming new group are not present and available, the tasks of creating a serviceable entity with socially unskilled populations rest with the social worker.

The initial stage is amorphous and anomic, as participants "simply behave" (Mills 1967) in ways that do not lead to social interchange, relationships, and formation as group. The task of orienting is major. Rosenthal (1970) identifies anomie as the beginning experience felt by participants, preformation as a group, an uncomfortable social condition that propels social connection and efforts to achieve social orientation (to this group with these persons and these goals). In contrast, socially unskilled persons may simply generate more anomie when convened, their behaviors unpropelled by a sense of social appropriateness.

The *Oxford English Dictionary* defines "to orient" as "to bring into clearly understood relations" and "to ascertain one's 'bearings', find out 'where one is.' " The *New College Standard Dictionary* defines "to be oriented" as achieving "awareness of one's own temporal, spatial and personal relationships." To orient has the general meaning of becoming attuned to and adapting to specific circumstances within a social situation here and now, with an assumption that social skills are in place to accomplish this.

Orienting has a distinct and extended meaning in work with socially unskilled persons: it involves establishing elements of a social entity at the same time as one assists the participants in learning how to be together socially within it. The two tasks occur together gradually, with participants learning experientially and episodically both how a social context is created and how to function socially within it. The shift is in the source of action, from participants capable of orienting to and generating a new social entity to the social worker carrying the task of establishing elements of a social situation while at the same time guiding the participants to ways of functional social response within it.

Elements essential to the creation of a sufficient and appropriate social entity for work with socially unskilled persons include

- delineation of the *nature of the experience* to be had in this social entity
- establishment of *boundaries* on what will be relevant in the functioning of this entity, the requirements of the situation
- establishment of *norms* for appropriate interpersonal behavior, especially the norms that generate the Social Work Group
- establishment of *activity* as the enduring content mode, in forms appropriate to the needs, interests, and functioning capabilities of the participants
- establishment of *attunement* in the response of the social worker to each individual and to the collective whole
- development of a *relationship* between the social worker and each participant, and between worker and entity
- establishment of a *helping role* for the social worker, boundaried initially as assistance in the use of activities
- establishment of a *pattern for dealing with critical moments*, with the social worker playing a central role in resolving difficulties, demonstrating how social interchange will be handled and facilitated
- the use of *limits and controls* in the management of interaction that is nonfunctional to the purposes of the collective experience
- evolution of an implicit, unarticulated *purpose*, comprehended and evolved gradually through experiences together that are satisfying, and that have the social worker's help to play out well
- evolution of *folkways* reflective of how things are done in this entity

These several elements are essential to the creation of an enduring social entity within which social learnings can take place. They may be accomplished gradually, noncognitively, experientially, actionally, and relationally, in a pattern of resolving critical incidents that arise as interruptions in the playing out of experiences together in the entity. Note that purpose and relationship emerge out of the experiences together in the entity, rather than shaping the entity initially.

From the standpoint of the practitioner, the initial stage of the pregroup period is focused on engaging the participants, fostering their relationship to activities, enabling them to experience effectance in their use of activity, individualizing each participant, and establishing a limited helping role of the worker in relation to activity use and to the management of togetherness. This is essentially a pre-relationship period, opening the possibility of relationship development and setting the stage for engagement together.

Activities are central in the initial stage of the pregroup period, engaging the participants, sustaining the collective whole, providing opportunities for individuals to experience effectance, and generating a limited, activity-related helping role for the social worker. Within the context of activities, the boundaries, routines, patterns, and norms of the pregroup experience are established. The stage can be characterized as one in which some elements of a potential group life are gradually put in place, and the parts essential to a supportive collective experience are evolved. The actions of the worker are critical in establishing the elements of an intended group, the participants being unable to contribute to this process initially.

Activities capable of generating a sense of being effective and allowing a limited engagement with the social worker through activity-related assistance together create an opening to relationship possibilities. The achievement of worker–participant relationships propels the entity into a second stage. Dysfunctional behaviors are gradually replaced as participants learn how to go together.

In total, the initial stage is focused on initiating and activating the elements leading to the establishment of a functional entity for helping purposes, and a visible professional role. The stage spans the period from nothing in place but dysfunctional and presocial behaviors to the point where essential elements for a collective life are in place and the first set of relationships, those developing between the worker and each individual constituent, are being established. These tasks may require an extended time frame to accomplish, depending on whether social skills, atrophied or disused, are being reactivated or being acquired for the first time.

In the initial period, the social worker must be active in establishing each of the several initiatives that will shape the nature of the practice. They are put in place in partial, piecemeal fashion, in response to specific, concrete moments that evoke each of them, and as initiatives that will define the boundaries of the collective experience.

During this pregroup state, when the worker is establishing actional modalities, special norms, relationships, socialization elements, and mediation in interaction in critical moments, there is a sense that the collective is not yet able to give back anything functional to the enterprise. The worker deals with dysfunctional behaviors through the several initiatives that define the practice. At the same time, the worker may experience a sense of *bleakness* in the interval before the practice initiatives begin to take hold, and while the participants are becoming oriented to the nature of the experience to be had in this entity. There is not yet a sense that the participants are connecting in ways that would be expected with socially competent persons engaged in group formation.

Weissman and Schwartz (1989) document well the frustration and despair experienced by group workers when the population with whom they work cannot generate group, and whose behaviors cannot advance toward group formation. It is a lack of relevant social response on the part of the participants that creates a sense of bleakness for the worker. In the initial stage, when dysfunctional nonsocial behaviors prevail, the practitioner experiences a sense of loss of expectable social response normally mobilizing in new groups composed of socially competent persons. The absence of normal social response and the presence of nonsocial behaviors challenge the professional expectations for practice with groups and create a sense of uneasiness for the practitioner.

This is the gift of the socially unskilled participants to the practitioner— letting him or her know the nature of their interpersonal dilemma, and conveying experientially how it feels to be with others without the social skills necessary to being together. In effect, the worker is given a clear sense of feeling like the participants do in social situations and needs to understand this and not be professionally disabled by it.

The initial stage of the pregroup period may require an *extended duration* during which the preliminary elements of norms, routines, boundaries, activity modes, folkways, and beginnings of the relationship to the worker evolve and are established gradually. The progression in the establishment of these essential elements is reflected in an emerging ambience, a reliability in initial functional participation and response, with some variability. There may need to be a period of consolidation of these initial features of pregroup life, with repeated experience of successful use of activity and of the worker's assistance, and of successful compresence.

With the establishment of worker–constituent relationships, the beginnings of entity and a collective arena emerge.

The absence of social response and the presence and manifestation of dysfunctional behaviors create the necessity for the worker initiatives. These are directed to creating a functional interactional arena sufficient for the collectivity to develop and proceed. Although the worker deals at a subentitative level, establishing behavioral and interactional boundaries primarily with individuals, dyads, and triads, he or she must also address the potential whole that will enable entitative functioning to be achieved, and forge a relationship with the entity as well as with the individual constituents. This reflects the dual task of dealing with individuals and their interaction while working toward the functioning of the whole.

Intermediate Stage: Part-Relational

As relationships between the worker and each participant and the several elements that generate collective life are established and operational, a second stage in the pregroup period is manifest, approximating some early, preliminary characteristics of beginning groups, in variant form. A limited formation occurs as the relationships between the worker and each constituent take hold. The entity emergent in the second stage is likely to be a collectivity, that lesser small social form that contains some features of groups but is lacking noticeably in others (Theodorson and Theodorson 1969; Gould and Kolb 1964; Borgotta and Cottrell 1955; Lang 1987).

Peer ties appear to be the essential element that enables group formation to occur. Only collectivity seems achievable when the principal relationships in place are between the worker and each individual. The absence of peer ties, and the shared purpose arising from these, limits the entity to the less developed social form—collectivity.

The particular type of collectivity achieved initially with socially unskilled participants is constitutionally limited by the activation of only one relational-interactional subsystem, achieving connections between the social worker and individuals, subunits and the entity as a whole, but lacking peer relationships and those group-relevant elements emergent as peer ties develop.

Collectivities created by socially unskilled populations have the characteristics of a disparate type collectivity (Lang 1987:20–24) because the relationships between worker and each constituent are relationships between disparates rather than between peers (Shapiro 1977). Further, of the twelve possible relational-interactional subsystems to be activated, portrayed in figure 14.1, only two or three may be activated, as represented in figure 14.2 (Lang 1987:23–25).

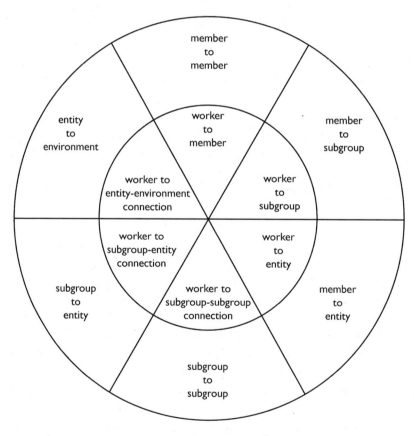

Figure 14.1 Twelve Relational–Interactional Subsystems Contained in Group with Worker: Disparate Type Pattern

The limitations in subsystems activated in constitutionally limited collectivities (Lang 1987:25) portrayed in figure 14.2 can be expected to advance from A to B as socially unskilled participants acquire social skill and advance to stage 3 of the pregroup period. The particular form of collectivity achieved through the establishment of worker–individual relationships—disparate type—creates a worker centrality essential to the task of advancing the social functioning of the constituents.

Note the terminology, which refers to participants, persons, individuals, and constituents rather than to members because belonging exists initially only in the worker–constituent dyads rather than in the entity as a whole. The terms "entity" and "collectivity" are used to differentiate a whole that lacks elements essential to group and has a more limited life experience.

Nevertheless, the collectivity achievable with socially unskilled persons as participants is a significant, useful social form, within which advances can be made in the achievement of social competence. The centrality of the social worker, arising out of a set of worker–participant dyads, empowers the efforts to enable social learnings within a significant grouplike experience. Such progressions may enable the participants to form peer relationships and achieve advancement to groupness. The dominant relationships

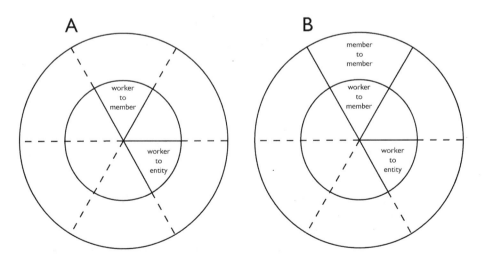

Figure 14.2 Relational–Interactional Subsystem Patterns Activated in Constitutionally Limited Collectivities

in disparate-type collectivities appear to replicate a stage in familial life and development in which the relationships to parents are more prominent and important than the relationships between siblings, and parental influence is major. This is seen as an important stage of socialization in family life. Perhaps an equivalent experience in collectivities composed of socially unskilled persons is required when that stage in prior family life has not been effective or completed and needs revisiting in a subsequent entity.

Within the less developed social form collectivity, conditions are sufficient for a socializing experience to take place. The worker has the opportunity to guide the collective experience toward functional participation, and to assist individuals in adapting dysfunctional behaviors. Worker initiatives reshape the dysfunctional, showing the way to appropriate entitative functioning, and creating a functional interactional arena.

The social worker must be able to recognize in here-and-now interactional exchanges the import these will have for the creation of a functional group, and the need to establish what is functional to the life of the entity—helping participants to learn adaptations to behaviors that would work against group forming and functioning. Some socially unskilled populations seem to require a prolonged time period in such socializing collectivities, and a few may have their entire experience together in this social form, that is, in stage 2 of the pregroup period.

The second stage is characterized by a growing capacity to use activities well, with increasing and regulated involvement, commitment, productivity, satisfaction, and competence, and by an extensive engagement in and testing of the relationship with the worker.

The entity achieves an ambience missing in the initial stage, with some beginning sense of compresence, of being and participating together in activities, of sharing a common experience. While there are major elements of group life missing and unconstructed, the degree of achieved ambience reflects elements, introduced by the worker, taking hold and becoming operational; in particular, relationships to the worker, special norms, activities becoming habituated, and interventions to assist interaction and to socialize participants each becoming effective. The entity acquires functional characteristics as participants are helped to learn social interactional repertoire in critical moments.

The central relationships that are emergent at this stage are between the worker and each constituent. The worker–individual ties represent the initial experience of belonging—not yet group. The stage is one of consolidating experiences of engagement with activity and with the worker. The ambience of this stage is pleasing, relaxed, becoming more reliable, and less traumatic for the worker. As the worker individualizes each participant, *prerelational awareness* of one another develops, a process of recognizing and individualizing one another that precedes the establishment of peer ties. The sense of being heard, understood, responded to, and cared about creates the circumstance for being able to hear, see, and respond to one another. With the development of interpersonal awareness, communication emerges, the forerunner of peer relationship. Interpersonal exchange is merely benign but prerelational.

The pattern of relating to the worker prior to forming peer ties is a clear reflection of a step in the normal age-stage relational progression identified in chapter 2. It suggests that the tasks in that relational evolution are incomplete or arrested for socially unskilled populations, requiring relationship with the worker as the means to advance. The avenue to peer relationships appears to be through the relationship of each individual to the worker. This relationship, replicated between the worker and each constituent, creates an initial form of collectivity, rendering the entity operational in a form limited by missing relational elements. It appears essential that this relationship be formed first in order to create conditions allowing for advancement to other elements capable of achieving groupness.

Both the prerelational initial stage and the part-relational stage may require an ample time frame of multiple sessions to be accomplished and consolidated. Consolidation of gains in both steps requires time and repetition of rewarding experiences, both personal and interpersonal. From the progression to recognizing one another as persons comes the beginnings of peer relationships, fostered by the worker's assistance in interacting functionally and by a growing sense of satisfaction and pleasure in being and doing together.

ACHIEVING NORMALCY

The cumulative effect of this Specialized practice tailored to the needs of socially unskilled populations is the arrival at "suddenly normal" social interaction; "the achievement of a conventional level of interaction" (Gold and Kolodny 1978:146), which "in its very ordinariness, represents an achievement" (145). "The interchanges themselves . . . seem almost incon-sequential. None of the behavior would cause raised eyebrows or perhaps even arouse interest on the part of an observer, whether lay or professional. But it is precisely this of which the group's accomplishment consists" (146).

Brooks (1978:61) also highlights this phenomenon in her description of the moment when her group of isolated, reclusive men achieved "conver-sations . . . loosened into a stream of mutuality—not witnessed before" in the swimming pool, precipitating full communication beyond the group meetings for the first time, and activating discussion intended to address the dilemmas of their living situation.

In the author's practice with emotionally disturbed children, a "sud-denly normal" meeting is recorded, acknowledging that in thirteen ses-sions, six boys have progressed from infantile, highly impulsive, chaotic, uncontrolled, hostile, and unrelated behaviors to a functioning level com-parable to that of normal children. The worker records "counting heads, thinking things were too calm for everyone to be present."

Six boys sit quietly around the table, six heads bent intently over their work. It is peaceful, quiet, comfortable and relaxed. Their work has meaning to them; they work with loving care, with pride and with assur-ance. . . . Although they are absorbed in their work, they no longer work in isolation. They are aware of each other, in tune with one another. There is much communication, much interaction of a mutually accepting kind. There is room for humor, enjoyment, appreciation. They are control-ling themselves better, and responding more quickly to worker's limit-setting. . . . They are learning to trust, to know that worker cares about them and about what they are doing. With trust comes a new capacity to wait for help and attention. They wait with a patience that speaks of their assurance that help will come. They are beginning to express themselves more fully, to reveal themselves and their needs in words and actions which speak of their vulnerability.

In practice with socially unskilled populations, one can expect small, imperceptible increments rather than large, significant advances. The rewards for the practitioner may seem few, through multiple meetings. To arrive at a point where "suddenly normal" social interaction pervades is especially rewarding after weeks of struggle, conflict, disjuncture, and miniscule signs of progress.

In the multiple sessions preceding the breakthrough of "suddenly normal," the participants are engaged in in-depth learning and incorporation of social learnings about how to be and do together in the entity. In effect, the practice is about learning functional behaviors, which require time and repeated experiences to accomplish.

> When you put your hands around his neck, that hurts him . . . .
> When someone does something well, it is customary to compliment him on his achievement . . . .
> This is the kind of behavior that always ends up getting you into trouble . . . .
> When things go wrong, blaming others doesn't help. We all have a part in it, we all contribute, we are all responsible . . . .

Incorporated social learnings may be manifest in new performances of both individual and entity. Some of these result from the patterned, routine ways of being and doing in the entity and emerge as civilized behaviors arising from a kind of unconscious socializing on the part of the social worker, through the establishment of customary procedures, processes, and ways of doing. Others result from interventions contributed by the social worker in the process of maintaining a functional interaction process. In the thirteenth session of practice with emotionally disturbed children, the author observed interactional exchange playing out favorably, which previously required her intervention as a mediary and now took place successfully without the need for intervention. These behaviors were highly visible in the small interchanges of sharing paint colors, soliciting knowledge about mixing an additional color, locating needed materials already in use, and discussion of paintings in process. They could have been overlooked easily as normal, functional interaction, except that they were behaviors newly in place: they reflect a learning process occurring in small, concrete, everyday moments and incorporated as new behaviors.

The phenomenon of "suddenly normal" may be manifested first within the most constantly employed and comfortable content form. It may not carry over initially when new forms of content are introduced. This suggests that the social learnings mirrored in "suddenly normal" are contextualized in familiar and known activity forms: the shift to a new content form may precipitate the need to relearn functional social behaviors in a new context. Progression is from context-specific social learnings to the circumstance of normal social interaction being sustained in activity forms additional to those in which "suddenly normal" interaction first was manifest. In effect, "suddenly normal" behaviors need to become stable regardless of what context is being employed; their emergence in one content form can indicate the likelihood that ultimately they will become accomplished pervasively.

"Suddenly normal" social interaction represents not an end, but a beginning, opening avenues to group formation and to significant group experience. It may be the defining moment when socially unskilled persons progress to the relational phase of the pregroup period and a social experience can be realized.

INTERACTIVE PATTERN IN GROUPS AND COLLECTIVITIES OF SOCIALLY UNSKILLED PERSONS

The pattern of interaction with socially unskilled persons in the pregroup period is likely to be short-term, brief, and episodically boundaried, terminating abruptly with the rise of conflict, breakdown in response, or the failure to resolve something well. This gives the interaction a start-stop-restart pattern, as the social worker assists in resolving difficulties and sets the interaction back on course with a fresh start. As the participants learn to resolve interactive exchanges favorably, the interactive pattern will smooth out and begin to flow more reliably and continuously. It will resemble normal social interaction over time as the participants incorporate learnings about how to manage interactively, and as they achieve the phenomenon of "suddenly normal."

It is notable that as brief a time frame as a group meeting once a week for ninety minutes can be quite effective in fostering the advancement of individuals and entity to normal social functioning and to the achievement of group formation. If circumstances elsewhere in the participants' lives perpetuate dynamics responsible for creating social noncompetence, the time frame for advancing social competence may be of longer duration.

Final Stage: Relational-Preparatory

In the previous two stages, participants have learned to modify dysfunctional behaviors, to be together successfully, to achieve beginning relationship with the worker, to develop prerelational awareness of one another, and to own their experienced individual competence. Depending on the extent of social noncompetence, the third stage may be characterized as one in which peer relationships are initiated, and relating to peers is learned and practiced. The tasks of recognizing, individualizing, and relating to one another and of learning functional social response predominate.

The experience of being and doing together elaborates and stabilizes, but the stage is still a forerunner of group experience, still pregroup. *Learning how to be related* precedes the generating of group-relevant functioning, hence the collective manifestations of groupness may not yet be present. Learning to be related has its own requirements. The special quality of this stage arises from learning how to go, in peer relationships, which may be a new experience, or from reestablishing peer relational capacity once possessed and then atrophied.

The achievement of readiness to relate to peers poses new dilemmas for socially unskilled persons: they may lack a *social repertoire* of appropriate ways to engage, interact, relate, and build and sustain relationship. Interactive moments require assistance of the social worker to make them good, to provide guidance in how to go relationally. The process of tutoring the unsocial response continues in this stage as participants gradually acquire, in interactional exchanges, a functional social interactional repertoire. The third stage provides opportunity to learn and to practice being in social interaction and to experience relatedness. Participants use this stage to master the skills of being related, preliminary to being able to function in relationship sufficiently to form group.

This stage in the pregroup period is a rehearsal for the condition of being related, a preparatory stage that enables social competence sufficient for constructing relationships to be acquired. In this period, relationship is being learned, opening an interactional arena that evolves as the relationships develop. Dysfunctional patterns of relating may be replaced with newly learned, functional interactional patterns.

When functional interchange and interaction are achieved, the possibility of achieving groupness is opened. At the same time that peer relationship is being explored, the relationship of each participant with the social worker is expanding and deepening. The helping role extends beyond assistance with one's performance in activity, encompassing the life experiences of the entity and its participants, and enabling major socialization to be contributed. Elements of socialization may be reflected back several sessions later, often in the same words used initially, indicating the importance of social learnings acquired in situ, in the context of a significant relationship.

During this phase, the social worker is actively encouraging interpersonal connection, through comments that heighten awareness of commonalities between individuals; intentional subgrouping of individuals to work together or to assist one another; and employing activity forms of greater complexity that involve joint participation or even integrated performance.

In addition to learning how to go in relationships, there are learnings to be accomplished about how groups function. If learning in relationship is achieved, the participants may be ready to progress to entering groupness and learning how to function together in group and as group. This progression may be accessed more easily by populations who possessed past social competence and for whom participation in the current entity may reactivate disused or atrophied social competence; and for persons who possess some partial but not yet complete social competence. The biggest challenge in enabling the progression to socially competent interpersonal functioning is with populations who are acquiring social competence for the first time.

Hence, some populations served by the Specialized Methodology may progress through the three stages in the pregroup period and be ready and able to form group. Other populations may not progress beyond collectivity, achieved in stage 2, and may have their whole experience together therein.

For populations whose restored or acquired social competence enables entry into groupness and the emergent ability to generate group, the group form achievable is likely to be an allonomous group (chapter 7). This reflects the structure of worker–participant relationships, with worker centrality characteristic of stage 2 now advancing to the establishment of peer relationships. For some becoming groups, the centrality of the worker will be modified as the members are able to evolve normative group processes and the entity progresses to transitional or even to autonomous group form (chapter 7). For others, the whole entitative experience may take place in the less developed social form, collectivity, where social competence can be acquired and practiced.

At the interface between the three pregroup stages and the normal pattern of group formation and development usually conceptualized as phases of group development (Garland, Jones, and Kolodny 1965, 1973; Sarri and Galinsky 1964, 1974; Northen 1988, Northen and Kurland 2001), readiness to form group may be reflected in the transition from pregroup stages to group-forming phases. At best, then, the acquisition of social competence in the pregroup period will enable the progression to membership, belonging, and formation of a group. The pregroup period and the phases of group development can be viewed as a continuum, not needed for persons possessing normal social competence and capable of forming group

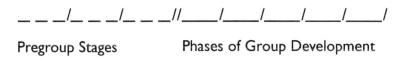

Pregroup Stages   **Phases of Group Development**

Figure 14.3 Continuum of Pregroup Stages and Phases of Group Development

together, but essential as preliminary steps for those requiring help to achieve social competence (fig. 14.3).

Socially unskilled persons in this specialized practice may progress through the first and second pregroup stages, having the preponderance of their experience in the second stage as a collectivity.

In the progression from the pregroup period to the normative pattern of phase 3 of group development in group formation, developments within the prerelational, part-relational, and relational-preparatory stages will bring alterations to the tasks identified in phase theory (Garland, Jones and Kolodny 1973). Elements in the approach-avoidance, power and control, and relational phases will be altered by prior experience in the pregroup period.

In particular, norms and relationships are already established at the transition from the pregroup period to the group formation period, such that the preaffiliation and power-control phases may be bypassed, and entry into the relational, group functional, and productive work phases are more immediate.

The progression from the pregroup stages to the later developmental phases of group formation may occur as a smooth, imperceptible transition with populations able to move beyond social noncompetence to normative social functioning.

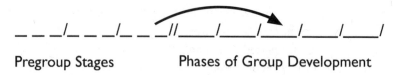

Pregroup Stages   **Phases of Group Development**

Figure 14.4 Progression from Pregroup Period to Relational Phase of Group Development

How Social Competence Evolves within the Group Experience

In the author's experience of group work with emotionally disturbed children, a pattern is discernable, indicative of the process of acquiring social competence. It may be more apparent in work with these vulnerable and damaged children than with some other socially unskilled populations, or it may be a constant in all practice with socially unskilled populations focused on the advancement of social competence.

The pattern is one in which something experienced in one time period is recapitulated at a subsequent time. That which is experienced is incorporated and is replayed later, sometimes using the same language that characterized the original. The process of taking in, incorporating, and adopting appears to be unselective and total, that is, it may be reflected back in the initial language, even from incidents that were of little consequence in the first place. This is the evidence that the participants are monitoring closely everything that happens in the group experience. The process of incorporating the experience is unseen but is clearly reflected in their replay.

The pattern reflects a combination of interactional steps, observational, incorporative, and replayed in a subsequent time period as a learned skill now being practiced in new episodes. It appears to contain the following elements and steps, flowing out of the interaction process:

THE CONTEXT

1a. A caring relationship with a worker who manages the group experience for the benefit of all, and who socializes the participants to rewarding forms of social interaction

1b. Engaged, involved participants

THE EVENT

2. An incident arising in interaction requires some resolution other than what the participants are able to generate, to make it consonant with the ongoing group experience.

THE RESOLUTION

3. The worker may guide the resolution of the incident in the present moment.

THE OUTCOME

4. Participants may witness not only the manner in which the incident is resolved, but also the effect its resolution has in the resultant smoothed progression in ongoing interaction.
5. (not visible) Both the specific resolution of the incident and its outcome in smoothing and making ongoing interactions possible are incorporated by the participants, who are both engaged in and monitoring the group interaction. The resolution—a worker action or the action of a participant guided by the worker— becomes a *miniature model* of how to go with successful social process and outcome.
6. The resolution may be played back in an unanticipated subsequent time period, as a learning now being reflected in a new time frame, or as a learned skill being tried out, practiced in a new episode. Participants appear to monitor closely events as they happen in interaction.

The members, monitoring closely the interaction in a rewarding and pleasurable group experience, may be as fully aware of the process of interaction as is the social worker. Negative past experience puts them on guard, wary of possible harm or damage to themselves, but also attuned, therefore, to good resolutions of incidents.

In this sense, whether a participant is involved directly or indirectly in an incident in interaction with another participant, he or she may be learning vicariously through observing the incident, its resolution, and its effect on the ongoing group process. There is a sense that each episode in group life may be incorporated collectively by the observing, monitoring participants.

The pattern of replay may be comparable to the process through which very young children give back what they hear and experience in their family, mirroring what has been said to them as evidence of their learning in concrete preconceptual moments. But here, in the nonfamilial socialization group, replaying of words said at a prior time are an indicator that the group has become important, meaningful, and valued, such that the experience together is being incorporated fully and collectively and replayed at a moment when dynamics are recognized as relevant here too. The small learnings gleaned from the resolution of difficult moments act as a variant on the usual pattern of norms, established and articulated, influencing behavior of members. Here, normatively the flow is upward from specific concrete incidents to the level of modifying behaviors, rather than from the conceptual level downward. They are not expressed as group norms but evolve out of the way in which difficulties and conflicts are resolved, and they stand as small signposts for how to go together successfully. These small experiential moments accumulate as repertoire in the minds of the participants, eventually emerging at moments when they replay as incorporated new repertoire for effective interaction, and as new social competence for participation.

The phenomenon of "suddenly normal" behaviors seems to arise from the accumulation of new repertoire, learned in the handling of multiple incidents, and manifest fully when the cumulative entitative experience yields to a new way of going, at a time in the life of the entity when the ambience of the entity's functioning permits. There is a sense of a progression toward sociality, imperceptively mobilizing session by session until it can emerge as a newly acquired set of social behaviors. This is not to say that once achieved, it totally replaces all the dysfunctional behaviors of previous group sessions forever after. Rather, it marks a significant progression in the social functioning of the participants, variably manifest, as members go back and forth between less social and more social.

It stands as an outstanding marker of the progression from presocial to social interaction. It is particularly rewarding for the practitioner, arising as it does after extensive efforts to assist the group members in finding their way to effective communication and interaction.

It is possible that some populations may hold in their minds repertoire for normative functional interaction before they are able to deploy it, that is, that normative social behaviors are known but inaccessible for use.

Other group conditions may be essential in order for the evolution to social behaviors to occur. In the author's experience, the combination of necessary conditions included a strong engagement with the experience of effectance, which created the circumstance in which the participants were actively involved in the craft; in that context, they began talking with one another in a new way, and they displayed awareness and attunement to one another, a willingness to share, and responsiveness to one another's needs. Their new behaviors were astonishing to, and unexpected by, the social worker, reflecting the arrival of "suddenly normal" social functioning. Incorporation of the total group experience occurs when elements of caring and interactional management are present and may be fed back in the same words or paraphrased and reapplied to new but comparable circumstances. Such moments may reflect a learned competence being practiced in new episodes and are clear evidence to the social worker of the effectiveness of the practice.

Some Reflections of Incorporated Group Experience and Replay

Instead of the usual disruptive behavior, Danny and Bruce began spinning around in circles, ostensibly to dry the paint on their puppet heads faster. Worker pointed out how this made the paint run. They put their puppet heads down and resumed their spinning. Worker cautioned them about making themselves dizzy and, hoping to stop them, without limits, made a game of setting them in countermotion "to unwind" them. Their need for this kind of attention was such that they continued to spin, winding up to be unwound. Danny stopped when his puppet head was dry, but Bruce went on until he was staggering. Worker helped him to a chair and remarked, "Well, I guess you won't want to try that again!" He agreed. [Session 5]

✳ ✳ ✳

Before leaving, Danny said, "Hey, let's twirl!" Bruce replied staunchly, "Oh no, I'll never do that again." [Session 14]

RAY: There! my painting is done! How do you like it? It's a boy swimming.

Worker: And the diving board is still going "boing" from his dive. I know someone who's looking forward to summer! . . . Perhaps his clothes would be under the tree; and if it's warm enough to swim, that tree would be growing some bright green leaves, don't you think?

Ray: Yeah! and I'll hang his clothes on the tree.

He completes the painting, moves the easel into a prominent display position, attaches the painting. [Session 13]

* * *

By this time, the others were asking for help, and Worker left John on his own. When Worker returned John was building a clay swimming pool, with animated comments about its size and depths. The boys listened with interest, Ray remarking, "I know who's looking forward to summer!" [Session 14]

Sam arrived, going directly to his clay models and inquiring anxiously, "How did they turn out?" Worker said they had come out beautifully. He inspected the others' modeling, asked Worker a second time how his came out, and was again assured by her that they came out beautifully.

As George entered the room, Sam ran to meet him, saying, "Oh George, come and see our clay. Look! (picking up one of George's models) It came out beautifully!" [Session 15]

At the sink, everyone crowded together in a simultaneous hand-washing. John and Danny exchanged words, then mild blows under the pressures of too close proximity and too little room.

John said, "Gee, what's he have to be in our group for? He swears all the time. Even though I swear sometimes, I don't swear like he does. All in favor of Danny moving to Ted's group, say 'Aye.' "

George said "Aye," and coming up behind them, Worker said, "Nay, Nay!" John and Dan turned, smiling, as Worker said, "Danny belongs in this group, and John belongs in this group." [Session 14]

* * *

The reference to getting Bruce out of the group seemed to reflect a prior discussion because Bruce looked up and said calmly, "You mean getting me out of the group? Oh yeah" and continued to work, quite unperturbed. John commented (as though Worker weren't right beside him), "Only Miss Rory would say 'Bruce belongs in this group,' " spoken with great assurance and acceptance. [Session 15]

Domain for Worker Intervention

This section identifies the central components in the worker methodology for practice with socially unskilled persons and indicates a range in their deployment, shaped by characteristics of various populations having social noncompetence.

To begin, the central feature of this adapted methodology is reflected in the domain for worker intervention. Socially able populations can be said to define boundaries and limits to worker intervention, established by the capabilities for effective interaction held by the members. In effect, there is little need for intervention when the members of a normal group can manage their interactional sphere well and can evolve elements of group life effectively. Interactional effectiveness sets limits on what the worker needs to do, *defining the interventive domain* for the worker. With constituents in a collectivity composed of socially unskilled persons, the domains of intervention are not different from those addressed in practice with groups composed of socially able populations, but the spheres and extent of intervention are greater. The need for help in being and doing together defines an enlarged domain of intervention requiring a greater speed and frequency of intervention, and involvement in and response to more items.

The social worker must be able to enter into a wider interventive domain, extended by the necessity of assisting constituents' efforts to function socially together, and to contribute effectively toward the evolution of an entity serviceable to the special needs of socially unskilled persons. The interventions may not differ in quality or content but will be much more substantial with socially unskilled participants.

The difference in interventions with normal groups and those more limited collectivities composed of socially unskilled persons is defined in the personal and interpersonal domains: socially able group members may require limited interventions in these areas, while socially unskilled constituents require major assistance in becoming socially functional. This difference is portrayed in figure 14.5.

In effect, with the socially noncompetent collectivity, the social worker crosses a boundary, in place with normally functioning groups, entering into the personal and interpersonal domain to assist in achieving conditions and competences that can lead to the construction of group. The worker must function in realms unneeded by socially competent group members in order to foster socially effective functioning and the achievement

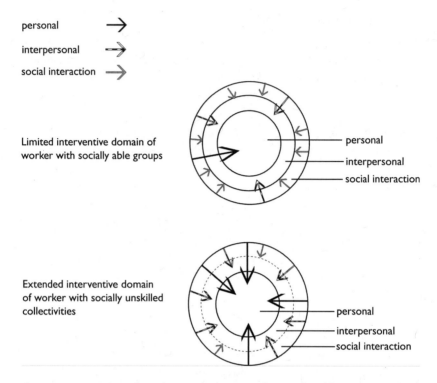

Figure 14.5 Domains of Worker Intervention with Socially Able Groups and Socially Unskilled Collectivities

of social competence. The worker becomes an effecting member of the entity, influencing interactional functioning and performance sufficient to enable collectivity to be achieved or group formation to begin.

Components in the Interventive Domain

The interventive domain with socially unskilled persons consists of those elements of personal and interpersonal interaction that require help in becoming socially functional. The worker is active in a large way with dysfunctional interaction that would have a limited manifestation and much more limited involvement of worker action with socially competent groups. Interventions are of several kinds and are directed to enabling collectivity or group to operate functionally in all their parts and as a whole.

INTERVENTIONS WITH INDIVIDUALS

- to assist in dealing with personal behaviors that impede social functioning
- to enable advancement from presocial behaviors that limit social connection
- to enable individuals to experience effectance and to recognize their own capabilities and those of others
- to enable the individual to learn to manage interactive social behaviors and to achieve functional participation

INTERVENTIONS WITH INTERPERSONAL INTERACTION

- to enable interchange that resolves differences and conflicts
- to enable interchange that is functional to building relational ties and to forming entity
- to enable learning how to interact socially

INTERVENTIONS WITH ENTITY

- to enable collective functioning
- to make the entity visible to the participants
- to enable forerunners and equivalents of group to be experienced
- to foster entitative development and advancement
- to provide grouplike experiences

INTERVENTIONS WITH CONTENT

- to provide appropriate activities with advancing complexity
- to enable activity to play out well
- to enable constituents to engage in activity, use it, process it sucessfully
- to match activity forms to progressions in individual and collective functioning

With What to Intervene: That Which Is Dysfunctional

- to the individual's functioning in the entity
- to the interpersonal connections
- to the entity
- to the content

The purposes of intervention in this Specialized practice are to enable individual social functioning; to foster functional social interaction; to enable interpersonal relationships; and to enable functioning as an entity, to enable group to form. These classes of intervention are intended to advance individual social functioning to the point where the entity can become effective. These interventions are not different from those employed with socially able groups: but the frequency of use and the focus on the elements to be addressed in order for group formation to be achievable mark this as a special methodology designed to enable group to become.

An essential component in this practice is the social worker's entry into and participation in the life of the entity—as a participant with a differentiated role, but engaged as part of the collective experience. The nature of the entity's life must be authentic, meaningful, and significant to the social worker through the lens of its impact on individuals and entity, viewed through the differentiated role of worker, but also having primary significance for the worker as a key element in professional practice.

The experience of the entity must resonate for the worker as well as for the constituents. It is only as the collective experience achieves reality, and importance to the constituents and to the worker, that the (re)socialization of individuals can be achieved.

Observing the progress of individual constituents and the entity endows the experience together with special meaning for the practitioner and confirms the huge investment of interventive action and energy as viable in work with socially unskilled persons.

15

Portrait of a Practice
with a Socially Unskilled Population

The chapter presents in brief an illustrative portrait of practice with one group of socially dysfunctional persons. The portrait contains a narrative summary of the practice, with illustrative episodes selected from the process recording of the practice.

This example of a practice with a socially unskilled population presents work with emotionally disturbed children in a residential treatment setting. The materials are presented in three pregroup stages: initial—prerelational; intermediate—part-relational; and final—relational-preparatory.

The Participants

The children are in the chronological 10–11-year-old age-stage but do not possess the capabilities expectable for their age group. Emotionally, they display arrested behaviors typical of much younger children, as well as devious and incomplete socialization. They have acquired a number of dysfunctional "street" behaviors for defending themselves in a hostile world. The participants reflect an array of symptomatic behaviors, ranging from extreme aggressiveness; excessive need for attention; acting-out; a variable hold on reality; high impulsivity; violent tantrums; resistance, contrariness and withholding; volatility; tremendous fears; suppressed rage; delinquent activities; threatening behaviors; negativity; to high vulnerability to contagion. Aggressiveness, impulsivity, and contagion are shared characteristics; the others are individually owned.

The children are of normal to superior intelligence, and all but two are able to attend public schools. Their grade range is from 2 to 5, this variance reflecting such things as school phobia, unmanageable behaviors in school, multiple moves through foster home placements, and unstable family units.

The children are bright, loveable, engaging, inventive, and creative and have many capabilities and competences in place or waiting to be mobilized and advanced. How fascinating these children are to work with—emotionally arrested; educationally retarded; intellectually bright; in chronological age ahead of themselves; and in their knowledge of the ways of the world, saddened old men.

Early in employment in the residential treatment center the author conducted a sociometric study of relationships among the children in each living unit. The resultant portrait of friendship ties was devastating: in each unit of fourteen to sixteen children, there were at most one or two reciprocal relationships, a chainlike pattern of unreciprocated likings, and a number of isolated persons not showing any connection to a peer.

Had the study been based on dislikes, enmities, antipathies between children, the pattern might have looked quite different, but it would not have predicted any better the possibility of the residents, negatively engaged, becoming friends and forming such significant entities as group or network.

As a reflector of the limited relationships among the whole population, the study highlighted the need to deliver a group work practice that could enable peer ties to develop and predicted some of the difficulties that could be anticipated in the practice.

The Group

The entity is a formed group that brings together from several different living units seven children who either do not know each other or have had minimal interaction with one another. This is seen as an optimal provision for the creation of a treatment group having the possibility of achiev-

ing functional behaviors and relationships, and acquiring social competence. The formed group gives the opportunity to proceed without having
to counteract entrenched dysfunctional behaviors and relationships, and to
construct the worker into the developing relationships.

In precise terms, the entity is a formed collectivity (Lang 1987) for a
significant portion of its existence, until the participants become able relationally to achieve formation as a group. While there are some differences
in the process of engaging children as distinct from adolescent, adult, and
aged populations, the tasks are comparable for engaging any socially dysfunctional population. A principal difference centers on the need for limits
and controls when the participants have not achieved inner controls.

The Content of the Group Experience

The necessity of enabling connection to one's own effectance and of supporting compresence prescribed the use of activities selected for their relevance to the participants; and for their capability in supporting togetherness and mobilizing connection to a sense of competence with nonhuman
objects.

Activities employed in the practice began with crafts that had a guaran-
teed successful outcome from a simple process, advancing to crafts that
invited experimentation and creativity and which progressed in complexity,
skill required, and duration. Activities encouraged tolerance of compresence and permitted working side by side, turn-taking. Eventually interactional forms were introduced. Engagement in activities served to move the
participants from short-term, limited interest spans to deeper involvement,
extending across several sessions. Over time, interaction arose and became
stable among the participants, later involving some sharing, helping one
another, working together cooperatively.

Stages in the Pregroup Period

The Initial Stage—Prerelational

The beginnings of the "group" were a study in contrasts, reflecting a complex process of engaging positively with the activity, trying out briefly what

could be achieved with it, abandoning it, accepting worker assistance with it, and eventually elaborating it or using it as a springboard to freehand painting and experimentation with the materials. At the same time, the children's initial engagement with each other was aggressive, conflictual, self-protective and hostile, or nonexistent. There was considerable tangling with one another, with verbal threats and physical blows. As well, there were many individual tests of worker reactions, culminating in an early collective test of worker tolerance of "worst behaviors," a pattern employed by emotionally disturbed children as an efficient way to ascertain whether the proffered experience would be a worthwhile one in which to invest themselves.

In the first session with everyone present, "simply behaving" (Mills 1967), high impulsivity and swift contagion produced multiple rapid serial incidents, some involving shifting constellations of persons in combat, with verbal and physical fights, others stemming from one person's action, quickly imitated by others. Some of these unconstrained behaviors affected the activity chosen for the session, the craft of printing with potato pieces on which designs had been carved. The use of the designs applied with too much force decimated some of the prepared designs, while the impulsive action of one participant to eat a potato led immediately to others following suit, thereby diminishing the supply available for additional designs. The shift to freehand painting and experimentation was the outcome of this session, as participants settled at last and became involved in their work, initiating their own process of creating pictures of their own invention. Threaded through these many interactions, the worker worked to enable connection to and use of the craft, fostering engagement in a process that could reflect individuals' ability to themselves, assisting in successful outcomes, establishing a helping role. Setting limits and redirecting persons from negative and impulsive acts and interactions not conducive to the construction of a group experience and attempting to establish boundaries and patterns for the group experience all were a major part of the worker activity in this stage.

The early sessions in the initial stage carried a mixed portrait of readiness to engage in the activity, inability to engage with each other, while being essentially uncommitted to the whole experience. As this complex process of engaging positively with the activity continued while sidestepping into negative interactions at odds with being and doing together, the negative exchanges and digressions reached a peak of being out of control.

A particular dilemma of the social worker arose out of the necessity of engaging impulsive children quickly in activities prior to establishing any norms for the group experience, except as these were expressed as the activity played out, in relation to dysfunctional behaviors. Thus, norms were not yet in place to constrain behaviors in an overall way.

The Intermediate Stage—Part-Relational

The intermediate stage was marked by a deeper involvement and invest-ment in the varied crafts, and by repeated experiences of being effective and gaining awareness of their capabilities. The activity forms selected were of longer duration, having the effect of lengthening short interest spans. This was a period of consolidating small gains in individual functioning.

During this stage, the worker recognized the need to become engaged interpersonally, interactively, and to extend the content of the group expe-rience to include interactional play and game forms. Early ventures in interactional activities revealed the depth of the problem in being engaged interpersonally, and the long way to go in surmounting it.

The individualizing of each person through the process of engaging them in activities, assisting in their use, and of recognizing emergent capa-bilities, set the stage for a preliminary awareness and differentiating of one another in a prerelational way.

The Final Stage—Relational-Preparatory

In the third stage of the pregroup period, the members had moved beyond interpersonal combat, strengthened and owned their sense of their own abilities, and were approaching relational ties, first through linkages cre-ated by the worker in moments that evoked interpersonal assistance or temporary cooperation, and later through moments of spontaneous being and doing together.

In the third stage, participants were thoroughly engaged with productive doing, moving to more complex crafts that also brought the need to help each other and to work together cooperatively. The children were oriented to one another as constituents of the group experience and interactive, but not yet engaging together relationally. The new directives to help one another and to work together felt foreign and uncertain.

Interaction had become more positive, more functional, and a growing sense of the collective whole was emergent. Lack of competence in social interaction could be dealt with, directing the participants to more appropriate responses. Although aggressive behaviors had subsided, the children continued to present symptomatic behaviors reflective of their individual problems. They also presented their concerns, sometimes as "one-liners," sometimes as whole episodes of discussion. The group meetings achieved a benign quality, making the manifestation of individual problems more apparent, and more accessible to being addressed unobtrusively. As well, conversation became focused as the participants' concerns emerged.

During this stage, a great deal of work with individuals became possible, dealing in particular with personal behaviors that limit the possibility of relationship development; and with emotions and attitudes that interfere with participation and engagement.

Work with the Group

Evoking Commitment

In the fifth session, the social worker staged a discussion of the difficulties experienced in the previous session, with the intent of evoking some commitment to the group experience, and the better establishment of controls, norms, and boundaries.

WORKER: When you walk down a road and come to a cross road, you have a choice to make: which direction to go . . .
RAY: Forward!
BRUCE: Left!
GEORGE: Right!
RAY: Or turn around and go back.

Worker said for purposes of this discussion we would talk about forward or backward. Last week's meeting had not been a good one, not happy for either them or her. Worker asked what they thought had gone wrong last week.

RAY: Some guys goofed around and threw some paste and got into trouble and got thrown out.

The other boys added similar comments, and Worker asked if anyone was aware of any rules about behavior in this room. At first there was denial of any knowledge of rules, the consensus being, "There aren't any rules."

Bruce smiled his sick smile and said, "The rules are, you should climb up there, and up there, and fight, and swear, and throw things around and . . ."

WORKER: Bruce, you seem to be telling us that there are some rules; can you say them so we'll know what they are?

BRUCE: (with his usual single-mindedness) The rules are that you should climb, swear, open the fire door, fight . . .

Worker asked Ray to state the rules, and he did so. Worker wasn't convinced that everyone heard, since this was not a disciplined discussion, and at points everyone was talking and John was yelling. Danny made some comment which suggested the discussion was passing him by, so Worker asked him to restate them.

DANNY: (improvising wildly) You shouldn't tear pictures down off the walls, or spray water around . . . or . . . climb on the "jungle gym" (coat rack) . . . or . . . fight . . .

GEORGE: (prompting) or swear . . .

DANNY: (with the greatest reluctance) or swear . . . oh yeah, swear . . .

Bruce was still in contrary motion, stating the "do-nots" as "should do's." Worker said that this was serious, and that we were really deciding now whether this group could go forward or backward. If forward, we could have some happy times, if backward, that would be the end of the group. The boys began to chant "Forward" "Backward" "Forward" "Backward" with the "Forwards" gaining strength and Bruce upholding the "Backwards."

Worker then spelled out what she thought had gone wrong last week, highlighting that John's talk about sewers had started something. He protested innocently until Worker recalled the gist of what he had said; at this he subsided with a quick look of acknowledgment of his part in the difficulties. Up to now Worker had mentioned chiefly fights, language, paste-throwing.

BRUCE: (a faint-flush appearing on his pale face) All right—say what each of us did.

Worker replied that perhaps she really didn't need to, because they each seemed to know what part they had played in the difficulties. Bruce's flush deepened and he insisted that Worker spell it out. Worker said that if what he wanted was for her to say what he did, she didn't need to tell him, really: that when anybody did anything he shouldn't do, Bruce seemed to feel that he had to go and do it too, although he knew better.

Worker then did a quick summary of what we had said thus far, add-ing that of the new week-day groups, this was the only one which had behaved so badly, and that while children were asking to get into a new group, this group seemed to be trying to work its way out, by doing things that they would not do elsewhere. . . . The big trouble last week, Worker said, was that no one was thinking of anyone else, or thinking how they each were making things worse.

RAY: (shrewdly) Yeah, but if we all behave except one guy, he can spoil it for everyone.
WORKER: That's true, Raymond.
BRUCE: The way to act is to swear, climb, open the fire door . . . etc.
WORKER: Bruce, if you really think this, then you can put your hat and coat on and leave right now.
BRUCE: No!

John and Ray sprang from their chairs to oust him, grabbing his coat and trying to put it on him. Worker ordered them back to their chairs, stat-ing that this action highlighted one more rule, namely, that what Worker said to one kid was between her and him, and they were not to interfere in what was not their business, that Worker was the person to take care of difficulties.

Bruce apparently relieved at this protection, and responding at last to Worker's pressure, said, "O.K. here's the rules," stating them correctly.

Worker said, finally, that for the next few weeks, we would have shorter meetings, and when they had shown her that they could behave reasonably for a short time, she would begin to lengthen the meetings. This had the effect of a bombshell, and all 5 boys were subdued and serious at last, as Worker brought out paints, and puppet heads, which miraculously had been fashioned in the midst of the previous session's difficulties.

A First Attempt at an Interactional Form

The preliminary work of engaging and involving individuals in experiences that generated a sense of effectance opened the way to the more pressing need—that of becoming functional in interaction. In the eighth session, an early attempt to create and stage a puppet play, using the puppets made by the children and incorporating their ideas to be included in the play, was sabotaged at the point of interaction among the puppets, ending in disaster, the puppets attacking each other in a replication of their owners' interactional dilemmas.

Attempting to Play Together

After nine sessions in arts and crafts, the social worker introduced a first session of game-playing. The weeks in activating individual effectance and fostering self-esteem moved the members toward the need to develop functional relational-interactional competence. In an effort to learn at what level the participants could play well together, the social worker introduced a variety of games. These ranged from one with no rules or roles other than batting a balloon to see how long they could keep it in the air, to a game played in two teams that summoned a player from each team to either snatch an object centered between the two facing teams and return to his team without being tagged by the opponent; or to tag the opponent if he had snatched the object first.

The game was played with a maximum of aggressiveness and undisciplined behavior, at times all 6 boys being out of their chairs. The desire to have their numbers called was so overpowering that everyone was on the edge of his chair, looking eager. The calling of a number brought 3 or

4 boys into play, as often as the 2 specified by the number. Worker's lib-
eral praise for each successfully completed action was somewhat offset
by Ray's "Stupid, you're supposed to tag him if you can't grab the tube" or
"Hey, dope, she didn't call your number." Bruce humorously led a move
to pull his chair closer to the centre. Everyone followed. Only a tremendous amount of limit-setting made it possible to play at all. The game
deteriorated in an altercation between 2 players . . .

WORKER: (slowly) Perhaps I picked a game that is just too hard for us to
play together yet.
JOHN: (quickly) Yeah, maybe if we played something like Dog and Bone . . .

The challenge here was to move to a simple, turn-taking game form, but
to make it acceptable to children much older than those for whom it was
designed, and for whom Dog and Bone would be viewed as a "baby game."
The game involves one child creeping up behind "the dog" who is seated
with his back to the group, stealing "the bone" from beneath his chair,
and attempting to return to his seat without being detected. The game
constrains the players to be silent so that the person, whose turn it is to try
to steal the bone, can creep up undetected. If "the dog" hears any noise, he
barks, and the turn is ended. If the player reaches his chair with the "bone,"
the "dog" must guess who has it.

The social worker improvised an equivalent, camouflaged version of
the game, substituting a space ranger for the "dog," a captured alien for
the "bone," and a space cop coming to free the alien. For the players, the
sound of a fired gun replaced the bark. The need for silence during play
was retained.

The game retained its basic features and its simplicity of play but gained
a new ambience and acceptability in its recast, camouflaged version, making it accessible for play at a level the group needed as a turn-taking, one-
by-one play form, constraining disciplined behavior briefly on the part of
the players during each round of play.

The children responded with enthusiasm as we blindfolded the space
ranger, tied loosely with a scarf the feet of his captured alien. A number
of space cops crept, unbidden, to free the alien before the blindfold was
on, and Worker reminded them that we hadn't started yet. When the

game began, the boys briefly contained themselves beautifully, the space cop's silent creep-up being discernible to the blindfolded space ranger, who was firing in the direction of sound. Each time things got out of hand, which was often, Worker reminded the boys that this was what we had been talking about earlier; such reminders brought disciplined responses, if only momentarily. Throughout this game, much limit-setting had to be done, on creeping-up out of turn, on removing the alien's ties illegally, on peeking from under the blindfold, on making noises which made the space ranger's detecting-by-sound difficult, on throwing a shoe at the space ranger. The need to be "It" was very strong. Ray did a pantomime begging-on-bended-knee, periodically, to convey his need to be "It." Selection of "It" was often followed by complaining distortions of "You never pick me," "I haven't had any turns yet," or "You always pick Sammy."

With this indication that simpler game forms were appropriate, the worker introduced two additional turn-taking "It" games. The first, a game much loved by 6-year-olds, involved "It" distributing a small object by going to each person's hands in turn and depositing the item between one person's hands, then initiating a guessing sequence as to who had it.

Worker returned her attention to the group. Rueful looks greeted her. Worker commented that we seemed to be back where we were before the last game, with 2 guys hurt, and it sure was hard for us to play together. The looks of anguish deepened. Worker said, "Let's try again" and quickly launched a disguised version of King's Key, labeled Silver Arrow. Dan slid into the circle of chairs, coat off, ready to play again. This game was played for a sustained period, with continuing concern about being "It," but much more acceptance of limitations. Sammy, surprisingly, was the most chosen boy in this game, Ray and John the least. John begged often and fervently, "Give me the chance," each time another boy was about to guess who had the arrow. There were expressions of enjoyment, excitement, high interest, and anticipation on their faces. There was much smiling, catching one another's eye, good communication. Ray alone played aggressively, throwing rather than giving the arrow when someone guessed correctly that he had it.

Finally we played Guess the Leader, which Worker introduced on the basis of the usual gestures employed in playing this game, and how these could be made more active and interesting. Things went fairly well until Ray, as the hidden leader of the game, inevitably introduced the finger gesture as his motion. Instantly several boys leaped from their seats to return the gesture to him hotly.

WORKER: (rebuking) Ray!

The boys returned to their seats, still incensed.

RAY: (righteously) Well, you said we could use any motion—
WORKER: Within reason, Ray—and that's not within reason.
GEORGE: (protesting) Hey, you gave it away—I didn't guess yet.
WORKER: I had to give it away, George; Ray, I guess you spoiled this game.

The boys grumbled at Ray. Fatigue was beginning to show in their faces. Worker said she thought we'd played enough games today, and had worked hard at playing better together. Now we needed to decide about the puppet play.

At the close of the meeting, John announced his intention of washing the tables. Worker protested that they didn't need washing, but he went ahead anyway. Sammy hid behind the puppet stage, Danny left and returned five times, saying at one of his departures, "Maybe I will be in the play. I guess I really want to." On his fifth exodus: "I just came to say one more thing – goodbye!"

Bruce departed in his stocking feet, shoes left behind.

RAY AND GEORGE: We're going now, Miss Rory.

Sammy stayed behind the stage, behind the screens, and under the tables until John was finished. Frequent calling or locating him did not bring any response. Eventually Worker said, "Come Sammy, it's time for dinner, time to close up."

No response. Worker found him lying across the seats of three chairs under the table. Pleased that Worker located him, he came out. Looking about the room, he grabbed a paper from the display screen saying, "I'm going to tear this!" Worker said the boy who made it would feel badly if it were torn. He ripped it in half, looked about uncertainly, said, "I'll throw it on the floor" and did so. Worker told him to put it in the basket, and he did so.

Bruce popped out of the washroom as Worker passed, retrieving his shoes with a grin.

The worker's analysis of this session highlights the "yield" of the activity, reflected in the ambient behaviors arising during the playing of King's Key—nearly normal—and the lingering departures that reflected relationships arising between members and worker, a pattern viewed in socially competent groups at an early stage, and here manifested in the tenth session.

This session would not have been possible a few weeks ago. That it was possible today indicates that the group, its members and its Worker have taken on meaning for these children. They are responding to controls and limits; they really want to manage better, and they were trying very hard today.

Worker believes that in this meeting, we went through a highly emotional experience together. The effort it took was tremendous, and both the children and Worker were spent and exhausted at the end. For herself, Worker felt that she had spent a week's energy in this one hour-and-a-half; and the children's faces showed fatigue at the end of the games.

This meeting verified for Worker the fact that emotionally disturbed children can play with success, only those games which are appropriate for normal children of much younger ages. It is no accident that these 10–11–12-year-old boys are most at home with the much-loved game of 4–5–6 year olds, King's Key. In their emotional development, these boys are 4, 5, and 6 years old. Their behavior is strikingly similar to that of a preschool group; moreover, many of the incompletely developed characteristics of the group itself are comparable to the attributes of the preschool group.

Also running through Worker's mind today were recollections of emotionally healthy children in other groups, in other agencies, and the memorable, ingenious ways they developed for playing these same games, the delight and satisfaction they experienced in highly related play, the good things that happened in their interpersonal relationships.

Some of Worker's deep feelings for these little boys, for what they suffer, what they miss, what they hope, expressed themselves today in her first confrontation to the group. Their own deep feelings answered hers, as they tried again and again to play together. They do not want to leave, in anger; they want to try again. Their regret is deep and real.

Individually, each boy is so highly impulsive, so poorly self-controlled, that even the small success of today is remarkable. The unanswered question here is how much of their behavior is born of disturbance, how much out of inexperience with any kind of primary group constellation in which to experience the desire to be any different (because it matters to the child and to the constellation).

In today's session, the children truly felt the desire to be different, and the faintest beginnings of self-controlled behavior resulted. Most remarkable of all, we were able to have a quiet discussion at the end, something hitherto unheard of.

"Suddenly Normal"

In the thirteenth session, "suddenly normal" behaviors emerged unexpectedly and were sustained throughout the session.

Six boys sit quietly around the table, six heads bent intently over their work. It is peaceful, quiet, comfortable and relaxed. Their work has meaning to them; they work with loving care, with pride and with assurance.

RAY: I'm erasing! [See what a clever way I have figured out to clean off my mistake, with a wet paintbrush.]

GEORGE: I'm painting this part a second time, I want it to be real bright. [This picture is important to me, I am going to put a lot into it.]

JOHN: I think I'll do the outline on this sail again and make it look better. [You see, I can do well! You are right!]

BRUCE: What color should I paint the windows? [I am relating to you, and I want your advice.]

DANNY: How's this look, Miss Rory? [I think I am doing this well, and I want you to reinforce this feeling.]

SAM: Isn't my painting nice! Is there anything more I should do to mine? [I am very relieved that you are not angry at me about last week, and I cannot fight you today. I need to let myself enjoy this meeting fully; at a future time I may have to be hostile again, but not today; I came late because you might be mad at me.]

Although they are absorbed in their work, they no longer work in isolation. They are aware of each other, in tune with one another; there is much communication, much interaction of a mutually accepting kind. They share, they respond to each other's questions and comments. There is room for humor, enjoyment, appreciation.

RAY: Are you aware that I made a poster? . . . advertising Pinocchio with the foot-long nose!

BRUCE: (comfortably) I wonder if we'll ever have the puppet show.

RAY: We can't have it, without Pinocchio—at least, I mean, we can't have my Pinocchio in it; we could use another puppet for him though—

JOHN: My puppet could make a good Pinocchio—he almost has a long enough nose.

WORKER: Yes, perhaps I'll have to change the play a little bit.

DANNY: What color makes pink?

GEORGE: White and red.

John: What colors make light brown?

CHORUS: Brown and white!

WORKER: White lightens any color.

RAY: What color have I made, with red and green? I don't understand that color wheel business, I flunked it at school.

WORKER: Would you like to learn it?

RAY: Yes!

(Demonstration followed with full interest by everyone.)

JOHN: Pass the white please.

(Three pairs of hands reach out to pass it.)

RAY: Who has the black?

WORKER: John has some, and so does Bruce.

JOHN: (pushing pan towards Ray) You can use mine.

SAM: Thanks for the raisins, Danny.

WORKER: It was sure nice of you to bring a box for everyone, Danny.

DANNY: (diffuse smile)

RAY: Hey, we should each take turns bringing something to the meetings. This week, Danny, next week, me, next week, George, next week Miss Rory and so on.

GEORGE: (taken aback) Our house parents would never let us.

(We move close together to discuss this.)

DANNY: Yes they would, mine let me bring the raisins.

RAY: Mine would let me.

BRUCE: Yeah—let's!

JOHN AND GEORGE Ours wouldn't.

WORKER: Ray, do you mean bring snacks from the cottage, enough for the whole group, and have them here? Or do you mean something to eat after snacks?

RAY: I don't mean snacks here, I mean after snacks, but special things that we'd each take turns bringing. We'd buy them at the store with our allowances . . .

They are persevering with their work, in the face of difficulties. They are engaged.

JOHN: I don't want to work on the boat. It's no good—it won't turn out. I'll finish the deer instead. The boat's no good.

WORKER: Wait a minute, slow down! This boat will be a dandy with just a little touching up. Only you need a bigger brush to go over the sail. The paint goes on easier then—Watch!

JOHN: It'll be no good . . .

WORKER: (making as though to touch his nose with the paint brush, and looking down at him with affection). Let's surprise you! Let's just surprise you with how good it will be. Like this—lots of paint this time—now you try . . .

JOHN: O.K. I think I'll paint the boat's lines over, too, that would make it better.

WORKER: Yes, and remember, you usually lean hard on the brush when you first start, so go easy.

They are learning to trust. They are beginning to know that Worker cares about them, and about what they are doing. With trust, comes a new capacity to wait for help and attention. They wait with a patience that speaks of their assurance that help will come.

GEORGE: Will you help me with mine?

WORKER: Yes: Do you want to watch Bruce and I put his frame on so you'll know how? Danny, you could measure off the strips of tape for yours, and be all ready for me to help you. John, you could try your picture against different shades of construction paper, and see which goes best with your picture. Yes, Sam, that's a good color. Bruce, can you show Ray and Danny how we made the hanger?

SAM: Will you do mine next?

WORKER: Yes—we can put them together as they're ready. This part is slow, and you'll all need to be patient while you wait for help.

GEORGE: Mine's ready—I'll do a painting on paper while I wait.

DANNY: Me too!

BRUCE: I'm going to try framing my second one myself.

WORKER: Good!

SAM: If there isn't time to finish them all, you'll fix them for us, won't you?

WORKER: Yes.

SAM: Could we come back after supper if we're not done?

WORKER: I wish we could. I have to go to a meeting tonight.

SAM: Well, if I do a quick painting now, would you put it together for me after? There's one more I wanted to do.

WORKER: Sure.

They are beginning to express themselves more fully, to reveal themselves and their needs, in words and actions which speak of their vulnerability.

Everywhere Worker turns, Sam seems to be underfoot. He is at her elbow, soliciting praise; he is leaning against her as he consults her about his work; Worker moves to the framing table and he is there beside her. Softly and shyly he says, "Isn't my painting beautiful—it's my best one— will you help me frame it? Is it coming out right? Oh, it looks good—." In an unending process, he goes away and returns, coming back for reassurance that Worker is there, that she likes him.

John wears his bleak, unsmiling look. He lets himself in the door in a quiet, un-John-like motion, closing the door softly. His eyes sweep the room anxiously; they meet Worker's.

JOHN: (bitterly and unhappily) You went skating while I was away. I knew you'd do that, as soon as I went home—I wanted to go with you.
WORKER: I know, John. We missed you. We wanted you to come. But you really didn't miss very much. We didn't skate—we just got as far as the rink.

(Sam stiffens, watching Worker's face.)

WORKER: It wasn't open when we got there; we had to wait. By the time it opened, we were all cold (looking at Sam) so we came home. All you missed was a ride to the park. I'm glad you're here today.

Both boys relax visibly. Sam's face wears a look of astonishment and relief; John is assured that he was missed, but missed little in activity.

Bruce moves through this meeting like a bud just blossoming, alert, keenly interested in everything and everybody, competent and confident in his work. As we frame his picture, he engages in the process so sensitively that he perceives Worker's struggle to "unstick" the tape from her fingers and helps to put it flat on the table. He smiles at Worker over this recurring struggle. His enjoyment of this moment of undivided attention is deep, and Worker glimpses the tremendous potential in this little boy, freed of his unreasoning resistance.

Can this be the Funday group? For a full hour and a half? In the beginning, it seemed like twenty children, or at least that six of them were five too many. In the past few sessions, there has come a point at which Worker has counted heads, thinking things were too calm for everyone to be present.

And so, in thirteen sessions, we have arrived, in our experience of the therapeutic group, at the stage which Worker would expect to have reached, with normal children, in three to six meetings.

Here, then, is clear-cut, recorded evidence we have that in this setting, a residential treatment centre for emotionally disturbed children, with careful grouping, the use of the formed group, and the use of a trained and experienced group worker, the therapeutic group experience can be a powerful tool in the treatment of disturbed children.

In thirteen sessions, six boys have been brought from infantile, highly impulsive, explosive, uncontrolled, aggressive, hostile, and unrelated behavior to the base starting level of a beginning group of comparatively normal children. A tremendous gap has been closed— the gap between their beginning behavior in this group, and the level at which children of this age could normally be expected to function in a group. This is the first indication Worker has had that there can be such a closing of the gap for these children. In these thirteen sessions, we have been preparing for the possibility of a group experience which can be beneficial; now we are ready to begin, and the weeks of preparation have been beneficial.

How have we come so far? Worker's way of working with this group is no different, basically, than her methods with non-disturbed children. It has had to be adapted to the needs and operating level of this group, certainly. Adaptations have included

- an acceptance of the preschool emotional level of the boys
- the discarding of expectations as to what might be achieved with the group
- the discarding of all the enriching, relationship-fostering program media which the group was unready to handle
- the assumption of a much stronger limit-setting role than is necessary with ordinary groups
- the use of program activities of low demand and high potential for the experiencing of success
- the use of confrontation both with individuals and with the whole group
- the playing of a strong nurturing, sustaining, supporting role

Significant in this session is the absence of aggressive and hostile interaction. The ambience of this meeting is reflective of the vulnerability of the children, when defensive behaviors have become unnecessary.

Work with Individuals

As collective behaviors began to be more functional, individual behavior also reflected modification.

JOHN

In the beginning, this boy was as loud, demanding, and needful as a whole group. He even tried to oust other members, through threat or bribery, so that the group would consist of "just me and George." Beneath his flamboyant behaviors and dramatic entrances lurked a very different child, concerned about being left out, forgotten, slighted; silent, anxious, withdrawing, depressed, paranoid.

His need for attention was so overwhelming that his demands made it difficult to address the needs of the others. Not only was he loud and demanding, but he also frequently became "stuck" in his current reaction, ranting on, with increasing volume, out of contact and control, unable to hear the worker's response. The briefest of touches to his shoulder seemed sufficient to break this pattern and to get in touch with him, and to deal with his concern. Often the patterned behavior arose over matters of little consequence.

John checked first on Worker's presence, then on the activity, and vanished almost as soon as he had arrived. Worker went to the door and looked out in time to see the door to the patio swing shut. Worker returned to the group, remarking, "He'll be back!" In a moment he was, saying, "I fooled you, didn't I, Rory-Tory" and flung his coat across the room. It landed in the sink. He made as though to protest its landing place, instead dropping into a chair and objecting to clay.

JOHN: Where's my clay? O.K.—you don't want me to have any clay? Alright—I won't do anything then! Where's my clay?

Worker caught his eye, and he grinned as she placed clay in his hands.

As we walked along, John lagged farther and farther behind, and each time Worker stopped to wait for him, she found him watching her closely. Worker waited till he caught up, before climbing onto the breakwater, the other boys joining her in waiting for him. John's face relaxed and he came more quickly, greeting her with "I was afraid you would go on the rocks without me."

In the process of tacking a fresh sheet of drawing paper onto a drawing board, John said "How come you gave everybody else four tacks and you only gave me two?"

WORKER: Are you sure about that, John?

JOHN: (checking the other boards) Oh—they got two, like mine—yours has four.

WORKER: Actually, the top two are the most important, but there are more tacks if you want them.

JOHN: No, two is enough.

John still makes flamboyant, dramatic entrances to every meeting but is modifying his shouting at the top of his lungs.

BRUCE

The need to resist, and for help in circumventing his resistance and isolation, arises frequently for this boy.

Bruce said he couldn't paint his puppet head.

BRUCE: It's not finished. It hasn't got the white strips on it.

WORKER: That won't matter Bruce—you can paint it just the way it is.

BRUCE: No, I'm not gonna paint it.

Worker let him be for a minute or two, then started discussion with him centered on reminding him that he had intended it to be a cat.

WORKER: What color had you thought of making it Bruce? Brown? Gray? Black? You could paint it a light color if you wanted, and put a second coat over it to paint out the print. Or I can mix you a special color that will hide the print, or you can mix your own color.

Bruce stood before his puppet, a picture of rigid resistance, but this time his "No" had a wavering, uncertain quality. Worker left him to think about it, and moved about suggesting ideas and giving praise to the others.

DANNY: You fixed our necks!

WORKER: They don't wobble now, do they? I didn't even need to fix them, they just dried that way.

DANNY: (addressing the group) She fixed the necks!

The other boys inspected their puppets' necks approvingly.

On Worker's next return to Bruce, he was ready to accept a special color, made just for him, and had a part in the mixing.

At quitting time, Bruce became determined to make another jug. Worker said there wasn't time, pointing out the smoothing still to be done on what was made. He insisted and so did Worker. He went rigid with resistance. Worker put her hand over his and said, "No, Bruce." Worker then began working on one of his products. Quickly recovering himself, he picked up another and began smoothing. When Worker remarked, later, that the floor had some clay spots on it, Bruce quietly went to work cleaning them up.

WORKER: Aren't you nice to do that, Bruce.

BRUCE: You helped me, and now I am helping you . . . (animated). Once I helped Mom Grey, and she was going to surprise me and make my bed . . . but I already had it made. She said she wanted to do something for me because I did something for her. So:—you helped me, now I'm helping you!

Bruce managed well with help from both Ray and Worker; when he began to paint his design, Worker asked him to move back to the paint table and leave the clean spot he was on for Sam to use in starting his kite. He became angry, indignant, and highly resistant, stating flatly, "I can't work over there. It's all messed up and there's no room." Worker said he could make room, and he became more resistant. Worker went quietly to the paint table and made room in a clean dry spot, then called to him invitingly, "There's room now, Bruce, with all the colors handy." He looked as if he would continue to resist, then collected his kite and moved it acceptingly into the spot provided.

Earlier, before Bruce got started on his kite tail, he began spattering paint over his kite as Sam had done previously. Protests arose from kite-owners near him. Worker asked him to stop before he got paint on other kites, highlighting the distance the paint had traveled. A fiendish look came over his face and he continued to shake paint in every direction. Three times Worker spoke to him, each time placing her hand over his hand and brush and saying, "No, Bruce." The diabolical look deepened and, on her fourth limit, Worker did what helps most in moving Bruce beyond this—involved him in considering what colors of cloth he wished to have on the tail, and attached the tail string for him. Only then did he abandon the paint brush. Briefly, he attempted to control Worker by insisting that he could neither tear the cloth strips nor tie them, indicating Worker should do it all for him. Worker began tearing strips and noticing that he was watching how, Worker remarked on how easy it was to do this. Worker tied the first few strips, likening it to tying a shoe lace. In time Bruce was both tying and tearing his own strips, selecting his colors with care, and planning a color design for the tail.

Bruce was quite resistant to stopping, and when Worker insisted, he responded "I'll tear all the paper then."

Worker did not think he really would, but he began to destroy the supply. Worker put her arms around him to restrain him, saying gently "No, Bruce that won't help. We really have to stop now. You have a lot of very nice prints, especially the one that looks like water plants in the pond with your duck."

Bruce relaxed against Worker and said in a tone of mingled long-suffering and concession "Oh alright, I'll let you win this time!" He began to collect his prints, quite reasonable again.

SAMMY

A pattern of acting out hostility toward the social worker by Sammy alternates with his joy and appreciation of the worker's helping efforts.

En route to buy box kite frames, Worker passed Sam in the hall.

SAM: What are we gonna do today?
WORKER: I'm not sure yet, Sam.
SAM: It better be something good—(nastily) or I might go out—I might not come—What is it gonna be?

Worker: It depends on whether I can find what I'm looking for, in which case, it might be "something good."
SAM: (venomously) BAD WOMAN!

SAM: (scathingly) Stupid old Rory-Tory! How can you put a great big coat hanger on this little picture? How dumb can you get!
WORKER: (smiling) Not that kind of hanger, Sam—a picture hanger.

Sam later rummaged among the designs and suddenly, with a paroxysm of rage, screamed, "She copied them! She didn't draw them at all. (Worker had made no claim to authorship.) She copied them all out of this book! She cheated!" This was uttered in a frenzied, tight, rapid, clipped speech. His comments had an electrifying effect on the others, who sprang out of their chairs to go and look.

WORKER: (mildly) They're traced, Sam. If we had all been picking designs out of the book and painting over them, five guys would have had a long wait while one painted. This way, we could all start at the same time with the patterns we wanted.

Sam subsided as suddenly as he had exploded, and went back to his painting cheerfully. The others looked at Sam in some disgust, Ray commenting, "He's nuts," as they returned to their work.

Overcoming irrational fears was his need as well.

SAM: Miss Rory, is it true that there's anyone in the world who could go like this (hand gesture) and make someone disappear?
WORKER: No—that would only happen in comic books or make-believe stories or movies.
SAM: (echoing, as though reassured) Only in make-believe or stories. Miss Rory, what if the animals were caught in a forest fire, what would they do?
WORKER: Run to find a way out of it. Or maybe go into a stream or lake, with just their heads above water.
JOHN: (somewhat derisive) What would you do, Sam, if you were in a building that was on fire?

SAM: Go out the nearest fire escape . . .

JOHN: (more gently) What would an animal do in a forest fire?

SAM: Go out the nearest fire escape! (appreciative laughter)

WORKER: Yes, it would find the place to escape.

Before school this morning Worker met Sam in the hall. He asked when our meeting would be and what we would be doing. Worker mentioned John's suggestion to return to the shore and fish. Sam looked up at her, his eyes filled with apprehension.

SAM: (struggling for words) I don't want to do that. I don't want to catch one of those "stinger rays"! They might hurt me. Let's go to Brown Pond. We could fish there.

Worker: Yes, Sam, I know that to catch something as big as that "sting ray" could be frightening. It wasn't a sting ray, though. I looked it up in the book. What he caught was just a plain ordinary northern skate, and they can't hurt you. If it had been a sting ray, it would have hurt his hand when he held it by the tail to throw it back into the water. Perhaps we would feel safer, though, fishing in a place like Brown Pond. Maybe fishing in the ocean isn't such a good idea for us just yet.

SAM: Can we go to Brown Pond then?

WORKER: Perhaps. I'll think about it.

RAY

The management of aggressive behavior was a recurring issue for this boy.

Fights were constant between John and Ray, Ray and Danny, Ray and Bruce; threats flew between them all. When Worker broke up a fight between John and Ray, Ray said angrily, "Now let's fight my way." Worker said the fight was over. Ray: "No, it's not over. If he's gonna fight dirty, I'll show him what dirty fighting is." Worker insisted the fight was over; he insisted that it wasn't and both boys tangled again, tears following and choked anger, as Worker finally succeeded in separating them. Meanwhile paste was flying between Danny, Sam, George and Bruce. Worker ordered them to stop.

WORKER: Whoa back, Ray! This is the kind of behavior that always ends up getting you into trouble.

RAY: (stopping soberly) Yes, I know.

WORKER: Did you want to make another picture while yours dries?

RAY: No—but I could paint on paper while I wait, and make a picture to hang up on the screen. Would you hang it up if I made one?

WORKER: I sure would! Let's go get some drawing paper.

RAY: There! My painting is done! How do you like it? It's a boy swimming.

WORKER: And the diving board is still going "boing" from his dive. I know someone who's looking forward to summer! . . . Perhaps his clothes would be under the tree; and if it's warm enough to swim, that tree would be growing some bright green leaves, don't you think?

RAY: Yeah! And I'll hang his clothes on the tree.

He completes the painting, moves the easel into a prominent display position, attaches the painting. Moving around the room restlessly, he pauses to fill a raisin-box with snow from the windowsill, presents it to Danny. They tangle briefly.

WORKER: Hey, that's enough, you two!

RAY: O.K. It was only in fun. We were only fooling . . . I'm going to look through this wallpaper book and pick out the pattern I want for my living-room. [I'm going to control my restlessness till that glass painting dries!]

In the eleventh session, Danny was accidentally spraying paint on the edge of Ray's painting.

Ray said "Ma—," stopped short, struggled, and tried again. "Ma—," stopped, shook his head, and with emphasis and great effort, said "MA—MA—iss Rory—make Danny stop spattering paint on my picture."

This is the first time Ray has remained in his seat and in control, appealing for the worker's intervention, rather than tackling Danny directly with his fists. In evoking the worker's help, he slips into a mode typical of a young child requesting a parent's assistance in the resolution of a conflict, even deploying a parental designation and being unable to correct it.

The incident reflects both an individual progression and also a collective progression, in the sense that established worker assistance in conflict resolution opens the possibility of new ways of being related and of a group experience that can be rewarding.

DANNY

Maintaining a steady hold on reality is central for Danny.

Danny stands bemused across from Worker, ineptly framing his picture. He is quiet, preoccupied for a long time.

DANNY: (suddenly) I'm glad I'm not a cannibal. . . . I wouldn't like to eat people, would you?
WORKER: (very gently) No, Danny.
DANNY: But you're one, aren't you?
WORKER: No, Dan. I wouldn't like to eat people either.
DANNY: (apparently relieved) Oh . . . That's good. . . . I wouldn't want to be a cannibal.
WORKER: Danny, what made you think of cannibals just now?

He gives Worker an uncertain smile, and goes back to his work.

As we pass through Dan's familiar home territory, the past gushes up out of him uncontrollably—the past which upsets him so terribly that he cannot cope with it, remove himself from it, assess it, sort it out, place it in perspective. Only in terms of feeding himself does he retain good control, directing me to the nearest ice cream stand.

Soon Dan was producing a new joke, this one being a "bathroom joke." He roared with laughter in telling it, such that it was too incoherent for the group to grasp. Worker stopped the car again, put her hand on Dan's and said "Dan, there's something I want to say to you. Are you listening? (he struggled to focus and tune in) Dan, I think there must be a whole lot of jokes and stories and things you've heard and seen, tucked away in your head. I guess you really don't know which ones are 'good' things to tell, and which ones aren't—except by telling them, and finding out how people react. I think you really need to tell them, to help you sort them all out. But right now, I think you need to stop, because they are making you too upset. Let's just take it easy for the rest of the trip, O.K.?" A sidelong glance, a murmured "O.K.," a few more choking giggles, and he regained his tenuous control again.

Danny was also developing an intermittent connection to reality with commentary functional to the group.

Danny, before starting his kite, said, "We haven't any string! You have to have string for kites." Then, exploring a paper bag, announced jubilantly, "Hey, she's got the string! One for each of us!"

Dan was the only one who responded to discussion of bowing, bridles, and tails, by going ahead and bowing his own kite, with an assured, "I know how to bow kites!" This boy is full of surprises.

Dan shared his canteen freely and frequently throughout the trip, actively offering it to the boys from time to time. In between drinks, he stored it in the glove compartment, wherein he spied an assortment of gum and life savers.

Dan: (excitedly) Hey, guess what I found in here?
Worker: Those are for later on, for on the way back.
Dan was able readily to accept this provision for later on, and did not touch them; but each time he returned the canteen, he checked to be sure they were still there, in the manner of a very young child, then enumerating quantity and flavor for the other boys' benefit.

Dan: We've been going about 10 minutes, and we haven't had any fights yet!
Worker: We seldom do have any fights in this group anymore.
Sam: No, we're all pretty good friends now!
Worker: Yes, we have good times together.
Dan: Nobody fights or swears in our group any more!
John: The only times we have fights are when—Ray and Bruce are here (absent members). Ray starts the fights.
Worker: But Ray hasn't started any fights since away back last fall. We all get along well now, don't we?

General murmurs of assent.

George

Daring to express his anger was the need of one boy.

> From the bridge we could see large trout in the pool below. As we leaned over the railing to watch, John said "Hey, look at us down there in the water." Our mirrored images smiled and waved to each other. George spat into the water, commenting in a tone of mingled satisfaction and regret, "I spit on me."
>
> A rare moment for a boy who mostly experienced John's expressions of hostility vicariously as his too.

> Previous expression came in his art work, which began in one corner of the page and worked outwards until the page was filled with a beautiful pastoral scene. Then he added a raging forest fire to the picture.

In small, incremental incidents occurring within the activity of each session, the worker is able to deal with these several kinds of difficulties, moving the constituents toward a form of interpersonal engagement capable of enabling relationships to form. It is a time to practice being social together. Conversation flourishes and is wide-ranging. Activities become more complex, more challenging; the repeated experience of doubting one's ability initially, then confirming it as the activity plays out successfully is a particular aspect of the group experience in this stage.

Some of the time together is benign, near-social, as the participants experience practice in being engaged with others, in becoming social together. This stage in the life of the collectivity is clearly preparatory. The missing piece is relational. Relationship is not yet in place, but it has become achievable in this third stage. The absence of relationships keeps the entity at the level of collectivity. It is still activities and relationship with the worker that hold the entity together: peer relationships are essential in progressing toward group.

For these children, being in noncombative interaction with one another is prelude to friendship, requiring lots of practice and repetition. Interaction among the participants shows promise of the possible evolution of relationships, reflected in listening and response to one another.

Activities have become more advanced, and of longer duration, stretching across several sessions, extending interest, involvement, and skill of the participants. The complexity of the crafts provides opportunities to invite members to work together, to help each other, pairing them in temporary engagements together that may initiate relational connections. Some of these cooperative and helping behaviors take hold, carrying over to spontaneous moments of connection and assistance.

Kite-making represents a huge challenge both in terms of requiring unaccustomed physical distance from one another due to the size of the kite frames and through the need to overcome helplessness in the conceptual and manual tasks of selecting paper, cutting, gluing, attaching to the frame, and decorating. The demand for worker help is enormous, prompting the worker to initiate helping efforts between children who have accomplished first steps and those not yet started. This advances new connections between children, some of which continue spontaneously as the participants undertake to fly the kites.

At the end of the meeting, Bruce was still outside, flying his kite when the bell rang. Sam and Danny called Bruce to come to supper.

Bruce: (yelling from outside the door) I can't get 'er down. She won't come down.

Sam and Danny ran to help, returning with Bruce and his kite.

Kite-making and flying were the springboard to lino cutting and block printing, a craft that required working together cooperatively in the producing of prints. The children evolved their own cooperative procedures and worked together for a prolonged period, cheering each other's prints as well as their own, as these came off the printing press. In both of these complex crafts, interactional assistance began to approximate patterns characteristic of normal children's group life. In both kite-making and block printing, the activity itself generated behaviors akin to relational.

Wide-ranging activities followed, culminating the year together in a breakfast cookout in a park, a trip to the shore, both involving extended time periods together, preceding summer program in which the children were in other groups.

The Group – Year II

In the following autumn, on what had been previously their meeting day and time, although memos had not reached the house parents about the group resuming, the boys appeared at the doors and windows, asking "Is it us? Is it us today?"

The meeting seemed to be a culmination of the previous year together, with several characteristics not typical of emotionally disturbed children: the tenor of the meeting was of unmitigated joy at being together again and with the same people; their positive expressions of this were markedly different from the normally negative comments that typified children's reactions in that setting; and the quality of "picking up where we left off" seemed more like a normal group. The children gave clear evidence that the group had been a meaningful experience in their lives, as they looked back at many of the things they had done in their first year together and linked remembered activities to items of their work on display around them.

> The activity for this session was to experiment with techniques for float-ing paint onto a moistened page: the paint flows along the wet place but can be directed somewhat by tilting the page to enable the paint to flow into the water along a particular route or direction, with abstract out-comes. Ray remarked that all three of his pages looked alike, even though he had tried to vary them. Worker replied that each person had a style that was characteristic of his or her work and suggested looking at the works of the others. There was intense interest as the children inspected one another's work and identified what seemed to be the style of each one. This activity seemed to be a form of individualizing one another, highlighted through acknowledging what was distinctive or unique in the artwork of each person.
>
> Toward the end of the meeting, Sammy picked up the brush broom and began a rhythmical march around the room, pushing the broom ahead of him, and chanting:

I want a Funday group
Ev'ry day
I want a Funday group
Ev'ry day
Monday, Tuesday, Wednesday
Thursday, Friday, Saturday, Sunday . . .

The others joined in with amusement and delight, marching behind him in a row and chanting

We want a Funday group
Ev'ry day . . .

In this incident, the grouplike element was spontaneous, not activity-generated, but arose out of positive emotion: it predicted well for the second year, for evolving the relational element and becoming a group.

References

Alissi, Albert S. (ed.) (1980). *Perspectives on Social Group Work Practice*. New York: Free Press.

——— (2001). "The Social Group Work Tradition: Toward Social Justice in a Free Society." Hartford, Conn.: Social Group Work Foundation Occasional Paper, first series, no. 1.

Axelrod, Charles D. (1979). *Studies in Intellectual Breakthrough*. Amherst: University of Massachusetts Press.

Barker, Robert L. (1987). *The Social Work Dictionary*. Silver Spring, Md. NASW.

Baxter, L. A. (1995). A Dialogue Approach to Relationship Maintenance. In *Communication and Relational Maintenance*, ed. D. Canary and L. Stafford, , 233–54. New York: Academic Press.

Baxter, L. A., and B. M. Montgomery (1996). *Relating: Dialogues and Dialectics*. New York: Guilford.

Beavers, Robert W. (1977). *Psychotherapy and Growth: A Family Systems Perspective*. New York: Brunner/Mazel.

Berman-Rossi, Toby (2002). My Love Affair with Stages of Group Development. *Social Work with Groups* 25, no. 1/2: 151–58.

Bernstein, Saul (ed.) (1970). *Further Explorations in Group Work*. Boston: Boston University School of Social Work.

——— (1973). *Explorations in Group Work*. Boston: Milford House.

Bertcher, Harvey, Linda Farris Kurtz, and Alice Lamont (eds.) (1999). *Rebuilding Communities: Challenges for Group Work*. New York: Haworth Press.

Blanck, G., and R. Blanck (1974). *Ego Psychology: Theory and Practice*. New York: Columbia University Press.

Blitsten, Dorothy (1955). Forms of Social Organization. *Autonomous Groups Bulletin* 11, no. 1: 1–8.

Bloom, Martin (1975). *The Paradox of Helping: Introduction to the Philosophy of Scientific Practice*. New York: Wiley.

Borgotta, E. F., and L. S. Cottrell (1955). On the Classification of Groups. *Sociometry* 18: 409–22.

Breton, Margot (1979). Nurturing Abusive Mothers: The Hairdressing Group. *Social Work with Groups* 2, no. 2: 161–74.

——— (1985). Reaching and Engaging People: Issues and Practice Principles. *Social Work with Groups* 8, no. 3: 7–21.

——— (1988). The Need for Mutual Aid Groups in a Drop-In for Homeless Women: The *Sistering* Case. *Social Work with Groups* 11, no. 4: 47–62.

Brim, Orville G., and Stanton Wheeler (1966). *Socialization After Childhood*. New York: John Wiley.

Brooks, Anne (1978). Group Work on the "Bowery." *Social Work with Groups* 1, no. 1: 53–64.

Brown, Leonard. (1991). *Groups for Growth and Change*. White Plains, N.Y.: Longman.

Brownell, Colin A., and Earnestina Brown (1992). Peer and Play in Infants and Toddlers. In *Handbook of Social Development: A Lifespan Perspective*, ed. V. B. Van Hasselt and Michel Herson, 82–100. New York: Plenum.

Bruner, J. S. (1962). *On Knowing: Essays for the Left Hand*. New York: Atheneum.

Bundy, R. W., N. C. Lang, and A. F. Klein (1954). "The York Community House Project: A Report of an Innovative Group Services Project in a Family Service Agency." Paper presented at National Conference on Social Welfare, Atlantic City, N.J.

Caplan, G., and M. Killalea (eds.) (1976). *Support Systems and Mutual Help*. New York: Grune and Stratton.

Cartwright, D., and H. Zander (1968). *Group Dynamics*. 3rd ed. New York: Harper and Row.

Cavell, T., and M. L. Kelley (1994). The Checklist of Adolescent Problem Situations. *Journal of Clinical Child Psychology* 23: 226–38.

Chatterjee, Pranab, and Mandy Fauble (2008). Toward a Mission–Based Model for Social Work: A Foundation for Practice. *Social Work with Groups* 31, no. 1: 5–23.

Chovanec, Michael (2006). "Transforming Men Who Batter into Men Who Matter." Paper presented at 28th Symposium of the Association for the Advancement of Social Work with Groups, San Diego.

Ciardiello, Susan (2000). *Twenty Activities for Group Work with Latency Age Children.* New York: S. Ciardiello.

———— (2003a). *Activities for Group Work with School-Aged Children.* Warminster, Pa.: Marco Products.

———— (2003b). Meet Them in "the Lab": Using Hip Hop Music Therapy Groups with Adolescents in Residential Settings. In *Social Work with Groups: Social Justice Through Personal, Community and Societal Change,* ed. N. E. Sullivan et al., 103–18. New York: Haworth Press.

Clark, F. W., and M. Arkavan (eds.) (1979). *The Pursuit of Competence in Social Work.* San Francisco: Jossey-Bass.

Clausen, J. A. (ed.) (1968). *Socialization and Society.* Boston: Little, Brown.

Coelho, George, David A. Hamburg, and John E. Adams (1974). *Coping and Adaptation.* New York: Basic Books.

Collins, A. H., and D. L. Pancoast (1976). *Natural Helping Networks.* New York: NASW.

Collins, Lainey (1998). How Do You Spell Hippopatamus? The Use of Groupwork in After-School Tutoring Programs. *Social Work with Groups* 21, no. 1/2: 61–76.

———— (2003). The Lost Art of Group Work in Camping. *Social Work with Groups* 26, no. 4: 21–41.

Cooley, Charles (1909). *Social Organization.* New York: Scribner's.

———— (1918). *Social Process.* New York: Scribner's.

Coyle, Grace L. (1930). *Social Process in Organized Groups.* New York: R. R. Smith.

———— (1937a). Social Group Work. *Social Work Year Book.* 4th ed. New York: Russell Sage Foundation.

———— (1937b). *Studies in Group Behaviour.* New York: Harper and Brothers.

———— (1947). *Group Experience and Democratic Values.* New York: Woman's Press.

———— (1948). *Group Work with American Youth.* New York: Harper and Brothers.

———— (1959). Some Basic Assumptions about Social Group Work. In *The Social Group Work Method in Social Work Education,* vol. 11: *A Project Report of the Curriculum Study,* ed. Marjorie Murphy, 89–105. New York: Council on Social Work Education.

Crammond, Ruth (1989). Social Group Work and Community Development Practice: Complimentary Methods of Social Work Practice with Homeless and Isolated Adults. In *Proceedings of the 11th Symposium of the Association for the Advancement of Social Work with Groups,* vol. 1: 119–44. Montreal.

DeCarlo, Alonzo, and Elaine Hockman (2003). RAP Therapy: A Group Work Intervention Method for Urban Adolescents. *Social Work with Groups* 26, no. 3: 45–59.

Delamater, J. (1974). A Definition of "Group." *Small Group Behaviour* 1, no. 1: 30–44.

Delamater, John, Charles McClintock, and Gordon Becker (1965). Conceptual Orientations of Contemporary Small Group Theory. *Psychological Bulletin* 64: 402–12.

Denham, S. A., et al. (2003). Pre-School Emotional Competence: Pathway to Social Competence? *Child Development* 74, no. 1: 238–56.

Dodge, K. A., D. G. Schlendt, I. Secbocken, and J. D. Delvagh (1983). Social Competence and Children's Social Status: The Role of Peer Group Entry Strategies. *Merrill-Palmer Quarterly* 29: 309–36.

Dossick, Jane, and Eugene Shea (2006). *Creative Therapy: 52 Exercises for Individuals and Groups.* Sarasota, Fla.: Professional Resource Press.

Douglas, Tom (1979). *Group Processes in Social Work*: A Theoretical Synthesis. New York: Wiley.

Duck, Stephen (1988). Socially Competent Communication and Relationship Development. In *Social Competence in Developmental Perspective*, ed. B. Schneider, G. Attilt, I. Nadel, and R. Weissburg, 91–106. London: Kluwer Academic Publishers.

Duffy, Trudy K. (2005). White Gloves and Cracked Vases: How Metaphors Help Group Workers Construct New Perspectives and Responses. *Social Work with Groups* 28, no. 3/4, 247–57.

Durkheim, E. (1951). *Suicide.* Translated by J. A. Spaulding and G. Simpson. New York: Free Press.

Eckerman, C., and M. Stein (1982). The Toddler's Emerging Interactive Skills. In *Peer Relationships and Social Skills in Childhood*, ed. K. Rubin and H. Ross, 41–72. New York: Springer-Verlag.

Eidse, Faith, and Nian Sichel (eds.) (2004). *Unrooted Childhoods: Memoirs of Growing Up Global.* Yarmouth, Me.: Intercultural Press.

Eisler, Richard M., and Lee W. Frederiksen (1980). *Perfecting Social Skills: A Guide To Interpersonal Behaviour Development.* New York: Plenum.

Elkin, F. (1960). *The Child and Society: The Process of Socialization.* New York: Random House.

Erikson, E. (1959). Identity and the Life Cycle. *Psychological Issues* 1, no. 1, Monograph 1. New York: International Universities Press.

——— (1963). *Childhood and Society.* 2nd ed. New York: Norton.

Evans, Douglas, and Wendy Shaw (1993). A Social Group Work Model for Latency-Aged Children from Violent Homes. In *Social Work with Groups: Expanding Horizons. Proceedings, 10th Symposium of AASWG*, ed. Stanley Wenocur et al., 97–116. New York: Haworth Press.

Falck, Hans (1988). *Social Work: The Membership Perspective.* New York: Springer.

Fatout, Marion F. (1987). Group Work with Severely Abused and Neglected Latency Age Children: Special Needs and Problems. *Social Work with Groups* 10, no. 4: 5–19.

Fischer, Constance T. (1992). A Humanistic Approach to Lifespan Development. In *Handbook of Social Development: A Lifespan Perspective*, ed. V. B. Van Hasselt and M. Herson, 113–30. New York: Plenum.

Foote, Nelson N., and Leonard S. Cottrell (1955). *Identity and Interpersonal Competence*. Chicago: University of Chicago Press.

Fowler, H. W., and F. G. Fowler (eds.) (1961). *The Concise Oxford Dictionary of Current English*. 4th ed. London: Oxford University Press.

Fulghum, Robert (1986). *All I Really Need to Know I Learned in Kindergarten*. New York: Ivy Books.

Funk, Charles E. (ed.) (1947). *New College Standard Dictionary*. New York: Funk and Wagnalls.

Gagné, Elise (1991). "Processes of Affirmation and Isolation in a Collectivity of Psychiatric Outpatients: A Qualitative Study." Unpublished paper, University of Toronto.

Galinsky, Maeda J., Mary Terzian and Mark W. Fraser (2006). The Art of Group Work Practice with Manualized Curricula. *Social Work with Groups* 29, no. 1: 11–26.

Garland, James, Hubert Jones, and Ralph Kolodny (1965). "A Model for Stages of Development in Social Work Groups." Unpublished paper, School of Social Work, Boston University.

—— (1973). A Model for Stages of Development in Social Work Groups. In *Explorations in Group Work*, ed. Saul Bernstein. Boston: Milford House.

Garvin, Charles D. (1981). *Contemporary Group Work*. Englewood Cliffs, N.J.: Prentice Hall.

—— (1985). Group Process: Usage and Uses in Social Work Practice. In *Individual Change Through Small Groups*, ed. M. Sundel, P. Glasser, R. Sarri, R. Vinter, 203–25. New York: Free Press.

—— (2005). Group Work with Seriously Mentally Ill People. In *Group Work with Populations at Risk*, ed. Geoffrey Greif and Paul Ephross. 2nd ed. New York: Oxford University Press.

Garvin, Charles, and Paul H. Glasser (1971). Social Group Work: The Preventive and Rehabilitative Approach. In *Encyclopedia of Social Work*, 16, vol. 2, ed. Robert Morris, 1262–76. New York: NASW.

Garvin, Charles D., Lorraine M. Gutierrez, and Maeda J. Galinsky (eds.) (2004). *Handbook of Social Work with Groups*. New York: Guilford Press.

Gitterman, Alex (ed.) (1991). *Handbook of Social Work Practice with Vulnerable and Resilient Populations*. New York: Columbia University Press.

—— (2001). Vulnerability, Resilience, and Social Work with Groups. In *Group Work: Strategies for Strengthening Resiliency. Proceedings, 20th Symposium of the AASWG.*, ed. Timothy B. Kelly, Toby Berman-Rossi, and Susanne Palumbo, 19–34. New York: Haworth Press.

Gitterman, Alex, and Robert Salmon (eds.) (2009). *Encyclopedia of Social Work with Groups*, New York: Routledge.

Gitterman, Alex, and Larry Shulman (eds.) (1986). *Mutual Aid Groups and the Life Cycle*. Itasca, Ill.: F. E. Peacock.

Gladwin, Thomas (1967). Social Competence and Clinical Practice. *Psychiatry* 30: 30–43.

Glasser, P., R. Sarri, and R. Vinter (eds.) (1974). *Individual Change Through Small Groups*. New York: Free Press.

Glasser, Paul H., and Charles D. Garvin (1977). Social Group Work: The Organizational and Environmental Approach. In *Encyclopedia of Social Work* 17, vol. 2, ed. John B. Turner, 1328–50. Washington, D.C.: NASW.

Gold, Jeffrey A., and Ralph L. Kolodny (1978). Group Treatment of Socially Dispossessed Youth: An Activity/Discussion Approach. *Social Work with Groups* 1, no. 2: 145–60.

Goodman, Harriet, and Manny Munoz (2004). Developing Social Group Work Skills for Contemporary Agency Practice. *Social Work with Groups* 27, no. 1: 17–33.

Gould, J., and W. Kolb (eds.) (1964). *A Dictionary of the Social Sciences*. New York: Free Press.

Greene, John O. (2003), Models of Adult Communication Skill Acquisition: Practice and the Course of Performance Improvement. In Greene, John O. and Brant Burleson (eds.) *Handbook of Communication and Social Interactional Skills*, 51–58. London: Erlbaum.

Greene, John O., and Brant Burleson (eds.) (2003). *Handbook of Communication and Social Interaction Skills*. London: Erlbaum.

Greenfield, Wilma L., and Beulah Rothman (1987). Termination or Transformation? Evolving Beyond Termination in Groups. In *Social Group Work: Competence and Values in Practice. Selected Proceedings, 6th Symposium of the Association for the Advancement of Social Work with Groups*, ed. J. Lassner, K. Powell, and E. Finnegan, 51–65. New York: Haworth Press.

Greif, Geoffrey L., and Paul H. Ephross (eds.) (2005). *Group Work with Populations at Risk*. 2nd ed. New York: Oxford University Press.

Hallas, Vicki (2006). You Don't Always Have to Pick Up Your Mess Right Away: How Being Messy Can Be Really Neat. *Social Work with Groups* 29, no. 2/3: 175–94.

Hare, A. P. (1976). *Handbook of Small Group Research*. 2nd ed. New York: Free Press.

Harter, Susan (1978). Effectance Motivation Reconsidered: Toward a Developmental Model. *Human Development* 21: 34–64.

Hartford, Margaret E. (ed.) (1965). *Working Papers Toward a Frame of Reference for Social Group Work*. New York: NASW.

——— (1966). Changing Approaches in Practice Theory and Techniques. In *Trends in Social Work Practice and Knowledge*, 132–44. NASW 10th Anniversary Symposium. New York: NASW.

——— (1971). *Groups in Social Work*. New York: Columbia University Press.

Hartup, W. (1983). Poor Relations. In *Handbook of Child Psychology*, vol 4: *Socialization, Personality and Social Development*, ed. E. M. Hetherington, 103–196. New York: Wiley.

——— (1989). Social Relationships and Their Developmental Significance. *American Psychologist* 44: 120–26.

Haslett, Diana C. (2005). *Group Activities in Generalist Practice*. Belmont, Cal.: Thompson Brooks/Cole.

Haviland, Jeannette M., and Arlene S. Walker-Androus (1992). Emotional Socialization: A View from Development and Ethology. In *Handbook of Social Development: A Lifespan Perspective*, ed. V. B. Van Hasselt and M. Herson, 29–50. New York: Plenum.

Heap, Ken (1979). *Process and Action in Work with Groups: The Pre-conditions for Treatment and Growth*. Oxford: Pergamon Press.

Hinde, R. A. (1976). On Describing Relationships. *Journal of Child Psychology and Psychiatry* 17: 1–19.

——— (1992). Human Social development: An Ethological/Relationship Perspective. In *Childhood Social Development: Contemporary Perspectives*, ed. H. McGurk. Hillsdale, N.J.: Erlbaum.

Hollis, Florence, and Mary E. Woods (1981). *Casework: A Psychosocial Therapy*. 3rd ed. New York: Random House.

Howard, V. A,. and J. H. Barton (1986). *Thinking on Paper*. New York: Morrow.

Howes, C. (1987). Social Competence with Peers in Young Children: Developmental Sequences. *Developmental Review* 71: 252–72.

Hutchby, Ian, and Jo Moran-Ellis (eds.) (1998). *Children and Social Competence: Arenas of Action*. London: Falmer Press.

Inkeles, A. (1969). Social Structure and Socialization. In *Handbook of Socialization Theory and Research*, ed. D. A. Goslin, 615–32. Chicago: Rand McNally.

Jablin, F. M., and P. M. Scott (2001). Communication Competence. In *The New Handbook of Organizational Communication: Advances in Theory, Research and Methods*, ed. F. M. Jablin and L. L. Putnam. Thousand Oaks, Cal.: Sage.

Jacobs, Joseph (1964). Social Action as Therapy in a Mental Hospital. *Social Work* 9, no. 1: 54–61.

Jennings, H. H. (1950). *Leadership and Isolation*. New York: Longmans, Green.

Junn-Krebs, Uni (2003). Group Work with Seniors Who Have Alzheimer's or Dementia in a Social Adult Day Program. *Social Work with Groups* 28, no. 2: 51–64.

Katz, A. H., and E. I. Bender (1976). *The Strength in Us: Self-Help Groups in The Modern World*. New York: New Viewpoints.

Kelly, T. B., and T. Berman-Rossi (1999). Advancing Stages of Group Development Theory: The Case of Institutionalized Older Persons. *Social Work with Groups* 22, no. 2/3: 119–38.

Kelsey, Anne. (2004). Healing Through Companionship. *Social Work with Groups* 27, no. 3/4: 23–33.

Klein, Alan F. (1953). *Society, Democracy and the Group*. New York: Woman's Press and Morrow.

——— (1970). *Social Work Through Group Process*. Albany: State University of New York Press.

——— (1972). *Effective Group Work*. New York: Association Press.

Klemp, George O. (1979). Identifying, Measuring and Integrating Competences. In *Defining and Measuring Competences*, ed. Pabel S. Pottinger et al., 41–52. San Francisco: Jossey-Bass.

Konopka, Gisela (1949). *Therapeutic Group Work with Children*. Minneapolis: University of Minnesota Press.

——— (1963). *Social Group Work: A Helping Process*. Englewood Cliffs, N.J.: Prentice-Hall.

Krech, D., R. S. Crutchfield, and E. L. Ballachy (1962). *Individual in Society*. New York: McGraw-Hill.

Kropotkin, P. (1914). *Mutual Aid*. Boston: Extending Horizon Books.

Kuhn, Thomas S. (1970). *The Structure of Scientific Revolutions*. 2nd ed. *Foundations of the Unity of Science* 11, no. 2. Chicago: University of Chicago Press.

Kurland, Roselle (1978). Planning: The Neglected Component of Group Development. *Social Work with Groups* 1, no. 2: 173–78.

———. (1982). *Group Formation: A Guide to the Development of Successful Groups*. Albany: Continuing Education Program, School of Social Welfare, State University of New York, and United Neighborhood Centers of America.

Lang, Norma C. (1963). "The Funday Group." Unpublished group record of social work with emotionally disturbed children.

——— (1967). "The Nature of the Social Work Group." Unpublished paper, Dora Wilensky Foundation for Advanced Study.

——— (1969). "The Small Professionalized Organizational Form: Its Nature and Rationalization." Unpublished paper, Case Western Reserve University.

——— (1972a). A Broad Range Model of Practice in the Social Work Group. *Social Service Review* 46, no. 1: 76–89.

——— (1972b). "Social Worker Actions in Response to Group Conditions. Representing Three Group Forms: A Test of Theory." Ph.D. dissertation, Case Western Reserve University.

———— (1979a). A Comparative Examination of Therapeutic Uses of Groups in Social Work and in Adjacent Human Services Professions: Part I—The Literature from 1955–1968. *Social Work with Groups* 2, no. 2: 101–15.

———— (1979b). A Comparative Examination of Therapeutic Uses of Groups in Social Work and in Adjacent Human Services Professions: Part II—The Literature from 1969–1978. *Social Work with Groups* 2, no. 3: 197–220.

———— (1981). Some Defining Characteristics of the Social Work Group: Unique Social Form. In *Proceedings, 1st Symposium of the Committee for the Advancement of Social Work with Groups*, ed. Sonia Leib Abels and Paul Abels, 18–50. Hebron, Conn.: Practitioners Press.

———— (1986). Social Work Practice in Small Social Forms: Identifying Collectivity. *Social Work with Groups* 9, no. 4.

———— (1987). Social Work Practice in Small Social Forms: Identifying Collectivity. In *Collectivity in Social Group Work: Concept and Practice*, ed. N. C. Lang and J. Sulman, 7–32. New York: Haworth Press.

———— (1996). "Group Work Practice with Socially Disabled Populations: Requirements for a Special Practice Methodology." Paper presented at the 18th Symposium of the Association for the Advancement of Social Work with Groups, Ann Arbor, Mich.

———— (2000). "An Emergent Model of Social Work Practice with Groups Composed of Socially Disabled Populations." Paper presented at the 22nd Symposium of the Association for the Advancement of Social Work with Groups, Toronto.

———— (2001). "A Typology of Forms of Non-Competent Social Interaction Requiring Special Adaptations to Social Work Practice with Groups: The Means of Growth and Development for Persons Who Cannot Form Group Unaided." Paper presented at the 23rd Symposium of the Association for the Advancement of Social Work with Groups, Akron, Ohio.

———— (2002). "An Adapted Methodology for Use with Socially Non-Competent Populations in Social Work Practice with Groups." Paper presented at the 24th Symposium of the Association for the Advancement of Social Work with Groups, New York.

———— (2003). "From Pre-Social to Social: Creating Simulations of Groupness with Populations Which Lack the Social Competence to Generate Group—Prelude to Group Formation." Paper presented at the 25th Symposium of the Association for the Advancement of Social Work with Groups, Boston.

———— (2004a). Concurrent Interventions in Multiple Domains: The Essence of Social Work with Groups. *Social Work with Groups* 27, no. 1: 35–51.

———— (2004b). "Specifics of Intervention in the Pre-Group Period with Socially Non-Competent Populations: Adaptations to the Technology of Social Work with Groups." Paper presented at 26th symposium of the Association for the Advancement of Social Work with Groups, Detroit.

Leaky, Daphne (2004). How and Why Movement Works: A Movement Workshop for Adults with Schizophrenic Disorders. *Social Work with Groups* 27, no. 2/3: 113–27.

Lee, Judith A. B. (1982). The Group: A Chance at Human Connection for the Mentally Impaired Older Person. *Social Work with Groups* 5, no. 2: 43–56.

—— (1986). No Place To Go: Homeless Women. In *Mutual Aid Groups and the Life Cycle*, ed. Alex Gitterman and Laurence Shulman, 245–62. Itasca, Ill.: F. E. Peacock.

—— (1994). *The Empowerment Approach to Social Work Practice.* New York: Association Press.

Leiberman, Florence (1979). *Social Work with Children.* New York: Human Sciences Press.

Lerner, Howard D., and Joshua Ehrlich. (1992). *Psychodynamic Models.* In *Handbook of Social Development: A Lifespan Perspective*, ed. V. B. Van Hasselt and M. Hersen, 51–80. New York: Plenum.

Levey, Gregory (2009). Lament for the i Generation. *Toronto Life* (October): 33–40.

Levine, B. (1979). *Group Psychotherapy.* Englewood Cliffs, N.J.: Prentice Hall.

Lewis, Elizabeth (1983). Social Group Work in Community Life: Group Characteristics and Worker Role. *Social Work with Groups* 6, no. 2: 3–18.

Li, Ming-hui (2008). A Model Parents' Group for Enhancing Aggressive Children's Social Competence. *Social Work with Groups* 31, no. 1: 71–87.

Liberman, R. P., W. J. De Risi, and K. T. Mueser. (1989). *Social Skills Training for Psychiatric Patients.* New York: Pergamon Press.

Lidz, Theodore (1968). *The Person: His Development Through the Life Cycle.* New York: Basic Books.

Lindeman, E.C. (1939). Group Work and Democracy—A Philosophical Note. In *New Trends in Group Work*, ed. J. Lieberman, 47–53. New York: Association Press.

Lindsay, Trevor, and Sue Orton (2008). *Groupwork Practice in Social Work.* Exeter, U.K.: Learning Matters.

Loeb, Martin B. (1960). The Backdrop for Social Research: Theory-making and Model-building. In *Social Science Theory and Social Work Research*, ed. Leonard S. Kogan, 3–15. New York: NASW.

Lowy, Louis (1983). Social Group Work with Vulnerable Older Persons: A Theoretical Perspective. *Social Work with Groups* 5, no. 2: 21–32.

Lutz, Werner (1968). "Emerging Models of Social Casework Practice." Unpublished paper, School of Social Work, University of Connecticut.

Lynn, Maxine (1989). An Action-Oriented Group Work Approach with the Chronically Mentally Ill. In *Proceedings. 11th Symposium of the Association for the Advancement of Social Work with Groups*, vol. 1: 979–87. Montreal.

Macgowan, Mark J. (2008). *A Guide to Evidence-Based Group Work.* New York: Oxford University Press.

Maier, H. W. (1965). The Social Group Work Method and Residential Treatment. In *Group Work as Part of Residential Treatment*, ed. H. W. Maier, 26–44. New York: NASW.

Malekoff, Andrew (2004). Strengths-Based Group Work with Children and Adolescents. In *Handbook of Social Work with Groups*, ed. Charles D. Garvin, Lorraine M. Gutierrez, and Maeda J. Galinsky, 227–244. New York: Guilford Press.

Maluccio, Anthony N. (ed.) (1981). *Promoting Competence in Clients*. New York: Free Press.

Manor, Oded (2000). *Choosing a Groupwork Approach. An Inclusive Stance*. London: Jessica Kingsley.

Mayo, Elton (1945). *Social Problems of an Industrial Civilization*. Cambridge: Harvard University Press.

McBroom, Elizabeth (1965). Helping AFDC Families: A Comparative Study. *Social Service Review* 39: 390–98.

McMillen, J. Curtis, Lisa Morris, and Michael Sherraden (2004). Ending Social Work's Grudge Match: Problems vs. Strengths. *Families in Society* 85, no. 3.

Middleman, Ruth R. (1968). *The Non-Verbal Method in Working with Groups*. New York: Association Press.

—— (1981). The Pursuit of Competence Through Involvement in Structured Groups. In *Promoting Competence in Clients*, ed. Anthony N. Maluccio, 185–210. New York: Free Press.

—— (ed.) (1983). Activities and Action in Group Work. *Social Work with Groups* 6, no. 1.

—— (1986). "The Issues of Group Work: Groupness." Paper presented at NASW National Conference on Clinical Social Work, San Francisco.

—— (1987). "'Seeing' the Group in Group Work: Skills for Dealing with the Groupness of Groups." Paper presented at 9th Symposium of the Committee for the Advancement of Social Work with Groups, Boston.

—— (2005). The Use of Program: Review and Update. *Social Work with Groups* 28, no. 3/4: 29–48.

Middleman, Ruth R., and Gail Goldberg Wood (1990). *Skills for Direct Practice in Social Work*. New York: Columbia University Press.

Miller, Rachel (2002). Will the Real Healer Please Take a Bow. *Social Work with Groups* 25, no. 1/2: 65–72.

Mills, Theodore M. (1967). *The Sociology of Small Groups*. Englewood Cliffs, N.J.: Prentice-Hall.

Moos, Rudolph H. (ed.) (1976). *Human Adaptation*. Lexington, Mass.: D. C. Heath.

Murphy, Marjorie (1959). *The Social Group Work Method in Social Work Education*, vol. 11: *Curriculum Study*. New York: Council on Social Work Education.

Murray, Donald M. (1982). *Learning by Teaching: Selected Articles on Writing and Teaching*. Portsmouth, N.H.: Boynton/Cook.

Muskat, Barbara (2005). Enhancing Social and Emotional Well-Being in Children with Asperger Syndrome. In *Children, Youth and Adults with Asperger Syndrome*, ed. Kevin P. Stoddard, 60–71. London: Jessica Kingsley.

Nakanishi, Manuel, and Phyllis Pastore (1999). Group Work: Empowering Adults with Developmental Disabilities. In *Rebuilding Communities: Challenges for Group Work*, ed. H. Bertcher, L. Kurtz, and A. Lamont, 189–199. New York: Haworth Press.

Newman, Barbara M. (1976). The Development of Social Interaction from Infancy Through Adolescence. *Small Group Behaviour* 7, no. 1: 19–32.

Newstetter, Wilber I. (1930). *Wawokiye Camp: A Research Project in Group Work*. Cleveland: Western Reserve University, School of Applied Social Sciences.

Newstetter, Wilber I., Marc J. Feldstein, and Theodore M. Newcomb (1938). Group Adjustment: *A Study in Experimental Sociology*. Cleveland: Western Reserve University, School of Applied Social Sciences.

Northen, Helen (1969). *Social Work with Groups*. New York: Columbia University Press.

––––––– (1988). *Social Work with Groups*. 2nd ed. New York: Columbia University Press.

Northen, Helen, and Roselle Kurland (2001). *Social Work with Groups*. 3rd ed. New York: Columbia University Press.

Papell, Catherine P., and Beulah Rothman (1966). Social Group Work Models: Possession and Heritage. *Journal on Education for Social Work* 2, no. 2: 66–77.

––––––– (1980a). Relating the Mainstream Model of Social Work with Groups to Group Psychotherapy and the Structured Group Approach. *Social Work with Groups* 3, no. 2, 5–23.

––––––– (1980b). Social Group Work Models: Possession and Heritage. In *Perspectives on Social Group Work Practice*, ed. A. Alissi, 116–32. New York: Free Press.

Park, M. R. (1994). Communication Competence and the Quest for Interpersonal Competence. In *Handbook of Interpersonal Communication*, ed. M. L. Knapp and G. R. Miller, 589–618. Thousand Oaks, Calif.: Sage.

Perlman, Helen H. (1957). *Social Casework: A Problem-Solving Process*. Chicago: University of Chicago Press.

––––––– (1965). Social Work Method: A Review of the First Decade. *Social Work* 10: 166–78.

––––––– (1967). " . . . And Gladly teach." *Journal on Education for Social Work* 3, no. 1: 41–50.

Pettit, Gregory S. (1992). Developmental Theories. In *Handbook of Social Development: A Lifespan Perspective*, ed. V. B. Van Hasselt and M. Hersen, 3–28. New York: Plenum.

Phillips, G. M. (1984). A Competent View of "Competence." *Communication Education* 32: 25–26.

Phillips, Helen U. (1957). *Essentials of Social Group Work Skill*. New York: Association Press.

Poertner, John, and John Ronnau (1992). A Strengths Approach to Children with Emotional Disabilities. In *The Strengths Perspective in Social Work Practice*, ed. Dennis Saleeby, 111–21. White Plains, N.Y.: Longman.

Pomerantz, Eva, and Karen D. Rudolph (2003). What Ensues from Emotional Distress? Implications for Competence Estimation. *Child Development* 74, no. 2: 329–45.

Prince, G. M. (1970). *The Practice of Creativity: A Manual for Dynamic Group Problem Solving*. New York: Collier.

Rappaport, Julian, Thomas M. Reischl, and Marc A. Zimmerman (1992). Mutual Help Mechanisms in the Empowerment of Former Mental Patients. In *The Strengths Perspective in Social Work Practice*, ed. Dennis Saleeby, 84–97. White Plains, N.Y.: Longman.

Rathborn-McCuen, Eloise (1992). Aged Adult Protective Services Clients: People of Unrecognized Potential. In *The Strengths Perspective in Social Work Practice*, ed. Dennis Saleeby, 98–110. White Plains, N.Y.: Longman.

Roberts, Robert W., and Robert H. Nee (eds.) (1970). *Theories of Social Casework*. Chicago: University of Chicago Press.

Roberts, R. W., and H. Northen (eds.) (1976). *Theories of Social Work with Groups*. New York: Columbia University Press.

Rose-Krasnor, Linda (1997). The Nature of Social Competence: A Theoretical Review. *Social Development* 6, no. 1: 111–35.

Rosenthal, William (1970). "A Theory of Beginnings in Social Group Work Processes." D.S.W. dissertation, University of Pennsylvania. Available through University Microfilms, No. 70–25, 763. Ann Arbor, Michigan.

——— (1973). Social Group Work Theory. *Social Work* 18, no. 5: 60–66.

Ross, H., and S. Lollis (1989a). Communication Within Infant Social Games. *Developmental Psychology* 23: 241–48.

——— (1989b). A Social Relations Analysis of Toddler Peer Relationships. *Child Development* 60: 1082–91.

Rothman, Jack (1968). Models of Community Organization Practice. In *Social Work Practice*, 15–47. New York: National Conference on Social Welfare.

Rothman, Beulah, and Catherine P. Papell (1988). Social Group Work as a Clinical Paradigm. In *Paradigms of Clinical Social Work*, ed. Rachelle A. Dorfman, 149–78. New York: Brunner/Mazel.

Rotter, Julian B. (1982). *The Development and Application of Social Learning Theory*. New York: Praeger.

Rubin, K., W. Bukowski, and J. G. Packer (1993). Peer Interactions: Relationships and Groups. In *Handbook of Child Psychology*, vol. 3: *Social, Emotional and Personality Development*, ed. N. Eisenberg, 619–700. New York: Wiley.

Rubin, K., and L. Rose-Krasnor (1992). Interpersonal Problem Solving and Social competence in Children. In *Handbook of Social Development: A Lifespan Perspective*, ed. V. B. Van Hasselt and M. Herson, 283–323. New York: Plenum.

Rubin, K., and H. S. Ross (eds.) (1982). *Peer Relationships and Social Skills in Childhood*. New York: Springer-Verlag.

—— (1988). Towards The Study of Social Competence, Social Status, and Social Relations. *Monographs of the Society for Research in Child Development* 53, no. 1, serial no. 217: 79–87.

Saami, C. (1990). Emotional Competence. In *Nebraska Symposium: Socio-emotional Development*, ed. R. Thompson, 115–61. Lincoln: University of Nebraska Press.

Saint-Arnaud, Y. (1978). *Les Petits Groups: Participation et Communication*. Montreal: Les Presses de l'Université de Montreal.

Saleebey, Dennis (1992). *The Strengths Perspective in Social Work Practice*. White Plains, N.Y.: Longman.

—— (1996). The Strengths Perspective in Social Work Practice: Extensions and Cautions. *Social Work* 41, no. 3, 296–305.

—— (ed.) (2009). *The Strength Perspective in Social Work Practice*. 5th ed. Boston: Allyn and Bacon.

Sarri, R. C., and M. J. Galinsky (1964). A Conceptual Framework for Teaching Group Development in Social Group Work. In *A Conceptual Framework for the Teaching of the Social Group Work Method in the Classroom*, 20–36. New York: CSWE.

—— (1974). A Conceptual Framework for Group Development. In *Individual Change Through Small Groups*, ed. P. Glasser, R. Sarri, and R. Vinter, 71–85. New York: Free Press.

—— (1985). A Conceptual Framework for Group Development. In *Individual Change Through Small Groups*, ed. M. Sundet, P. Glasser, R. Sarri, and R. Vinter, 70–86. New York: Free Press.

Schaffer, H. Rudolph (1996). *Social Development*. Oxford: Blackwell.

Schiller, Linda Yael. (1997). Rethinking Steps of Development in Women's Groups: Implications for Practice. *Social Work with Groups* 20, no. 3: 3–19.

—— (2002). Process of an Idea: How the Relational Model of Group Work Developed. *Social Work with Groups* 25, no. 1/2: 159–66.

—— (2007). Not for Women Only: Applying the Relational Model of Group Development with Vulnerable Populations. *Social Work with Groups* 30, no. 2: 11–26.

Schneider, Barry H., Grazin Attili, Jacquelina Nadel, and Roger D. Weissberg (eds.) (1988). *Social Competence in Developmental Perspective. Proceedings of the NATO Advanced Study Institute, Les Arcs, France*. Dardecht: Kluwer Academic Publishers.

Schnekenburger, Erica (1995). Waking the Heart Up: A Writing Group's Story. *Social Work with Groups* 18, no. 4: 19–37.

Schulze, Susanne (ed.) (1951). *Creative Group Living in a Children's Institution.* New York: Association Press.

Schwartz, William (1961a). The Social Worker in the Group. In *New Perspectives on Services to Groups: Theory, Organization, Practice.* Selected papers on group work, National Conference on Social Welfare, Minneapolis, Minn. New York: NASW.

——— (1961b). The Social Worker in the Group. In *The Social Welfare Forum. Proceedings of National Conference on Social Welfare.* New York: Columbia University Press.

——— (1962). Toward a Strategy of Group Work Practice. *Social Service Review* 36: 268–79.

——— (1971a). Social Group Work: The Interactionist Approach. In *Encyclopedia of Social Work* 16, vol. 2, ed. Robert Morris, 1252–62. New York: NASW.

——— (1971b). On the Use of Groups in Social Work Practice. In *The Practice of Group Work*, ed. W. Schwartz and S. Zalba, 3–24. New York: Columbia University Press.

——— (1977). Social Group Work: The Interactionist Approach. In *Encyclopedia of Social Work*, 17, vol. 2, ed. John B. Turner, 1328–37. Washington, D.C.: NASW.

——— (1994). The Social Worker in the Group. In *Social Work: The Collected Writings of William Schwartz*, ed. Toby Berman-Rossi, 257–276. Itasca, Ill.: F. E. Peacock.

Segrin, Chris, and Michella Givertz (2003). Methods of Social Skills Training and Development. In *Handbook of Communication and Social Interaction Skills*, ed. John O. Greene and Brant R. Burleson, 135–149. London: Erlbaum.

Seguin, M. M. (1972). "Opportunity for Peer Socialization to Old Age in a Retirement Community." D.S.W. dissertation, University of Southern California.

Shapiro, B. Z. (1977). Mutual Helping: A Neglected Theme in Social Work Practice Theory. *Canadian Journal of Social Work Education* 3, no. 1: 33–44.

Shulman, L. (1968). *A Casebook of Social Work with Groups: The Mediating Model.* New York: Council on Social Work Education.

——— (1971). Program in Group Work: Another Look. In *The Practice of Group Work*, ed. W. Schwartz and S. R. Zalba, 221–40. New York: Columbia University Press.

——— (1979). *The Skills of Helping Individuals and Groups.* Itasca, Ill.: F. E. Peacock.

Simon, Paul (ed.) (1971). *Play and Game Theory: A Collection of Papers by Neva Boyd.* Chicago: University of Illinois, Jane Addams School of Social Work.

Small, Sheila (1986). Learning to Get Along: Learning Disabled Adolescents. In *Mutual Aid and the Life Cycle*, ed. A. Gitterman and L. Shulman, 161–76. Itasca, Ill.: F. E. Peacock.

Somers, M. L. (1976). Problem-Solving in Small Groups. In *Theories of Social Work with Groups*, ed. R. Roberts and H. Northen, 331–67. New York: Columbia University Press.

Spitzberg, B. H. (1989). Issues in Developing a Theory of Interpersonal Competence in the Intercultural Context. *International Journal of Intercultural Relations* 13: 241–68.

—— (1993). The Dialectics of (In) Competence. *Journal of Social and Personal Relationships* 10: 137–58.

Spitzberg, B. H., and W. R. Cupach (1989). *Handbook of Interpersonal Competence Research*. New York: Springer-Verlag.

Steinberg, Dominique Moyse (1997). *The Mutual Aid Approach to Working with Groups*. North Vale, N.J.: Jason Aronson.

—— (2004). *The Mutual Aid Approach to Working with Groups: Helping People Help Each Other*. 2nd ed. New York: Haworth Press.

Sullivan, Nancy (1996). "A Qualitative Research Study of the Development, Nature and Significance of 'Family-Like' Features in a Social Work Group." Ph.D. dissertation, University of Toronto.

Sundberg, Norman D., Lonnie R. Snowdon, and William M. Reynolds (1978). Towards Assessment of Personal Competence and Incompetence in Life Situations. *Annual Review of Psychology* 29: 179–211.

Thelen, Herbert (1958), *Dynamics of Groups at Work*. Chicago: University of Chicago Press.

Theodorson, G.., and A. Theodorson (eds.) (1969). *A Modern Dictionary of Sociology*. New York: Crowell.

Trecker, Harleigh (1949, 1955, 1972). *Social Group Work*. New York: Association Press.

Tropp, Emanuel (1969). *A Humanistic Foundation for Group Work Practice*. New York: Selected Academic Readings.

—— (1971). Social Group Work: The Developmental Approach. In *Encyclopedia of Social Work*, 16, vol. 2, ed. Robert Morris, 1246–52. New York: NASW.

—— (1977). Social Group Work: The Developmental Approach. In *Encyclopedia of Social Work*, 17, vol. 2, ed. John B. Turner, 1321–28. Washington, D.C.: NASW.

Tuckman, Bruce (1964). Personality Structure, Group Composition, and Group Functioning. *Sociometry* 27: 469–87.

Turner, John B. (ed.) (1968). *Neighborhood Organization for Community Action*. New York: NASW.

Van Hasselt, V. B., and M. Herson (eds.) (1992). *Handbook of Social Development: A Lifespan Perspective*. New York: Plenum.

Verba, S. (1961). *Small Groups and Political Behavior: A Study of Leadership*. Princeton, N.J.: Princeton University Press.

Vinter, Robert (1960). Problems and Processes in Developing Group Work Practice Principles. In *Theory-building in Social Group Work*, 2–16. Workshop Report, Annual Program Meeting. New York: Council on Social Work Education.

———— (1965). Social Group Work. In *Encyclopedia of Social Work*, 15, ed. Harry L. Lurie, 715–23. New York: NASW.

———— (ed.) (1967). *Readings in Group Work Practice*. Ann Arbor, Mich.: Campus Publishers.

———— (1974). An Approach to Group Work Practice. In *Individual Change Through Small Groups*, ed. P. Glasser, R. Sarri, and R. Vinter, 3–8. New York: Free Press.

———— (1985a). Program Activities: An Analysis of Their Effects on Participant Behavior. In *Individual Change Through Small Groups*, ed. M. Sundel et al., 226–36. 2nd ed. New York: Free Press.

———— (1985b). The Essential Components of Social Group Work Practice. In *Individual Change Through Small Groups*, ed. M. Sundel et al., 11–34. 2nd ed. New York: Free Press.

Warren, Paula (1986). The Social Therapeutic Club: A Collectivity for Ex-Psychiatric Patients. In *Collectivity in Social Group Work: Concept and Practice*, ed. N. C. Lang and J. Sulman, 91–101. New York: Haworth.

Wayne, Julianne, and Alex Gitterman (2003). Offensive Behaviour in Groups: Challenges and Opportunities. *Social Work with Groups* 26, no. 2: 23–34.

Webster's New Collegiate Dictionary (1977). Springfield, Mass.: Merriam.

Webster's New International Dictionary (1957). 2nd ed., unabridged. Springfield, Mass.: Merriam.

Weick, Ann (1992). Building a Strengths Perspective for Social Work. In *The Strengths Perspective in Social Work Practice*, ed. D. Saleebey. White Plains, N.Y.: Longman.

Weick, A., C. Rapp, W. P. Sullivan, and S. Kisthardt. (1989). A Strengths Perspective for Social Work Practice. *Social Work* 34: 350–54.

Weinstein, E. A. (1969). The Development of Interpersonal Competence. In *Handbook of Socialization Theory and Research*, ed. D. Goslin, 753–75. Chicago: Rand McNally.

Weissberg, R. (1989). Challenges Inherent in Translating Theory and Basic Research into Effective Social Competence Promotion Programs. In *Social Competence in Developmental Perspective*, ed. B. Schneider et al. Dordecht: Kuwer Academic Publishers.

Weissman, Celia B., and Paula Schwartz (1989). Worker Expectations in Group Work with the Frail Elderly: Modifying the Models for a Better Fit. *Social Work with Groups* 13, no. 3: 47–55.

White, Robert W. (1959). Motivation Reconsidered: The Concept of Competence. *Psychological Review* 66: 297–333.

———— (1963a). *Ego and Reality in Psychoanalytic Theory. Psychological Issues*, 3, no. 3, monograph 11. New York: International Universities Press.

——— (1963b). A Way of Conceiving of Independent Ego Energies: Efficacy and Competence. *Ego and Reality in Psychoanalytic Theory. Psychological Issues* 3, no. 3, monograph 2: 24–43. New York: International Universities Press.

——— (1974). Strategies of Adaptation: An Attempt at Systemic Description. In *Coping and Adaptation*, ed. George Coelho, David A. Hamburg, and John E. Adams, 47–68. New York: Basic Books.

Whittaker, James (1970). Models of Group Development: Implications for Social Group Work Practice. *Social Service Review* 44, no. 3: 308–22.

———. (1985). Program Activities: Their Selection and Use in a Therapeutic Milieu. In *Individual Change Through Small Groups*, ed. M. Sundel et al., 237–50. 2nd ed. New York: Free Press.

Wilson, Gertrude, and Gladys Ryland (1949). *Social Group Work Practice*. Cambridge, Mass.: Riverside Press, Houghton Mifflin.

Wilson, Steven R., and Christina M. Sabee (2003). Explicating Communicative Competence as a Theoretical Term. In *Handbook of Communication and Social Interaction Skills*, ed. John G. Green and Brant R. Burleson, 3–50. Mahwah, N.J.: Erlbaum.

Wiseman, J. M., and J. J. Bradoc (1989). Meta Theoretical Issues in the Study of Communicative Competence: Structural and Functional Approaches. In *Progress in Communication Sciences*, vol. 9, ed. B. Dervin and M. J. Veight, 261–84. Norwood, N.J.: Ablex.

Wolff, Kurt H. (ed.) (1950). *The Sociology of George Simmel*. New York: Free Press.

Wright, Whitney (2005). The Use of Purpose in On-Going Activity Groups: A Framework for Maximizing the Therapeutic Impact. *Social Work with Groups* 28, no. 3/4: 205–28.

Index